Dot Markers Act

Happy Hanukkah

Ages 2+

This book is made to be used with paint daubers or dot markers. Each page has a black background on the reverse to help with bleed-through. Also, you can cut out each page using the trim line or use a separate piece of paper between pages. Have fun!

This book belongs to:

_____

Let's practice with dot markers!

Let's practice with dot markers!

Amendment by Pub. L. 94–240 effective on expiration of one year after Mar. 23, 1976, see section 6 of Pub. L. 94–240, set out as an Effective Date note under section 1667 of this title.

Effective Date of 1974 Amendment

For effective date of amendment by Pub. L. 93–495, see section 308 of Pub. L. 93–495, set out as an Effective Date note under section 1666 of this title.

Effective Date

Pub. L. 90–321, title V, §504(a), May 29, 1968, 82 Stat. 167, provided that: "Except as otherwise specified, the provisions of this Act [see Short Title note set out below] take effect upon enactment [May 29, 1968]."

Short Title of 2018 Amendment

Pub. L. 115–174, §1(a), May 24, 2018, 132 Stat. 1296, provided that: "This Act [see Tables for classification] may be cited as the 'Economic Growth, Regulatory Relief, and Consumer Protection Act'."

Short Title of 2015 Amendment

Pub. L. 114–94, div. G, title LXXXIX, §89001, Dec. 4, 2015, 129 Stat. 1799, provided that: "This title [amending sections 1639c and 1639d of this title and enacting provisions set out as a note under section 5512 of Title 12, Banks and Banking] may be cited as the 'Helping Expand Lending Practices in Rural Communities Act of 2015' or the 'HELP Rural Communities Act of 2015'."

Short Title of 2010 Amendment

Pub. L. 111–319, §1, Dec. 18, 2010, 124 Stat. 3457, provided that: "This Act [amending section 1681m of this title and enacting provisions set out as a note under section 1681m of this title] may be cited as the 'Red Flag Program Clarification Act of 2010'."

Pub. L. 111–203, title XIV, §1400(a), July 21, 2010, 124 Stat. 2136, provided that: "This title [see Tables for classification] may be cited as the 'Mortgage Reform and Anti-Predatory Lending Act'."

Short Title of 2009 Amendment

Pub. L. 111–93, §1, Nov. 6, 2009, 123 Stat. 2998, provided that: "This Act [amending section 1666b of this title] may be cited as the 'Credit CARD Technical Corrections Act of 2009'."

Pub. L. 111–24, §1(a), May 22, 2009, 123 Stat. 1734, provided that: "This Act [enacting sections 1616, 1651, 1665c to 1665e, 1666i–1, 1666i–2, and 1693l–1 of this title and section 1a–7b of Title 16, Conservation, amending sections 1602, 1632, 1637, 1640, 1650, 1666b, 1666c, 1666j, 1681b, 1681j, and 1693m to 1693r of this title, enacting provisions set out as notes under sections 1602, 1637, 1638, 1666b, 1681j, and 1693l–1 of this title and section 5311 of Title 31, Money and Finance, and amending provisions set out as notes under sections 1638 and 1693 of this title] may be cited as the 'Credit Card Accountability Responsibility and Disclosure Act of 2009' or the 'Credit CARD Act of 2009'."

Short Title of 2008 Amendment

Pub. L. 110–315, title X, §1001, Aug. 14, 2008, 122 Stat. 3478, provided that: "This title [enacting section 1650 of this title and sections 1019d and 9709 of Title 20, Education, amending sections 1602, 1603, 1638, and 1640 of this title, section 2903 of Title 12, Banks and Banking, and section 1092 of Title 20, and enacting provisions set out as notes under sections 1638 and 1640 of this title, section 2903 of Title 12, and section 9709 of Title 20] may be cited as the 'Private Student Loan Transparency and Improvement Act of 2008'."

Pub. L. 110–289, div. B, title V, §2501, July 30, 2008, 122 Stat. 2855, provided that: "This title [amending sections 1638 and 1640 of this title and sections 24 and 338a of Title 12, Banks and Banking, and enacting provisions set out as a note under section 1638 of this title] may be cited as the 'Mortgage Disclosure Improvement Act of 2008'."

Pub. L. 110–241, §1, June 3, 2008, 122 Stat. 1565, provided that: "This Act [amending section 1681n of this title and enacting provisions set out as notes under section 1681n of this title] may be cited as the 'Credit and Debit Card Receipt Clarification Act of 2007'."

Short Title of 2003 Amendment

Pub. L. 108–159, §1(a), Dec. 4, 2003, 117 Stat. 1952, provided that: "This Act [enacting sections 1681c–1, 1681c–2, 1681s–3, 1681w, and 1681x of this title and sections 9701 to 9708 of Title 20, Education, amending sections 1681a, 1681b, 1681c, 1681g, 1681i, 1681j, 1681m, 1681o, 1681p, 1681s, 1681s–2, 1681t, 1681u, and 1681v of this title and section 5318 of Title 31, Money and Finance, enacting provisions set out as notes under this section, sections 1681, 1681a, 1681b, 1681c, 1681c–1, 1681i, 1681j, 1681m, 1681n, 1681s–2, 1681s–3 of this title, and section 9701 of Title 20, and amending provisions set out as a note under this section] may be cited as the 'Fair and Accurate Credit Transactions Act of 2003'."

SHORT TITLE OF 1999 AMENDMENT

Pub. L. 106–102, title VII, §701, Nov. 12, 1999, 113 Stat. 1463, provided that: "This subtitle [subtitle A (§§701–705) of title VII of Pub. L. 106–102, amending sections 1693b, 1693c, and 1693h of this title] may be cited as the 'ATM Fee Reform Act of 1999'."

SHORT TITLE OF 1998 AMENDMENT

Pub. L. 105–347, §1, Nov. 2, 1998, 112 Stat. 3208, provided that: "This Act [amending sections 1681a to 1681c, 1681g, 1681i, 1681k, and 1681s of this title and enacting provisions set out as a note under section 1681a of this title] may be cited as the 'Consumer Reporting Employment Clarification Act of 1998'."

SHORT TITLE OF 1996 AMENDMENT

Pub. L. 104–208, div. A, title II, §2401, Sept. 30, 1996, 110 Stat. 3009–426, provided that: "This chapter [chapter 1 (§§2401–2422) of subtitle D of title II of div. A of Pub. L. 104–208, enacting section 1681s–2 of this title, amending sections 1681a to 1681e, 1681g to 1681j, 1681m to 1681o, 1681q to 1681s, and 1681t of this title, and enacting provisions set out as notes under sections 1681a, 1681b, and 1681g of this title] may be cited as the 'Consumer Credit Reporting Reform Act of 1996'."

SHORT TITLE OF 1995 AMENDMENTS

Pub. L. 104–29, §1, Sept. 30, 1995, 109 Stat. 271, provided that: "This Act [enacting section 1649 of this title, amending sections 1605, 1631, 1635, 1640, and 1641 of this title, and enacting provisions set out as notes under section 1605 of this title] may be cited as the 'Truth in Lending Act Amendments of 1995'."

Pub. L. 104–12, §1, May 18, 1995, 109 Stat. 161, provided that: "This Act [amending section 1640 of this title] may be cited as the 'Truth in Lending Class Action Relief Act of 1995'."

SHORT TITLE OF 1994 AMENDMENT

Pub. L. 103–325, title I, §151, Sept. 23, 1994, 108 Stat. 2190, provided that: "This subtitle [subtitle B (§§151–158) of title I of Pub. L. 103–325, enacting sections 1639 and 1648 of this title, amending sections 1602, 1604, 1610, 1640, 1641, and 1647 of this title, and enacting provisions set out as notes under this section and section 1602 of this title] may be cited as the 'Home Ownership and Equity Protection Act of 1994'."

SHORT TITLE OF 1992 AMENDMENT

Pub. L. 102–537, §1, Oct. 27, 1992, 106 Stat. 3531, provided that: "This Act [enacting section 1681s–1 of this title, amending section 1681a of this title, and enacting provisions set out as a note under section 1681a of this title] may be cited as the 'Ted Weiss Child Support Enforcement Act of 1992'."

SHORT TITLE OF 1988 AMENDMENTS

Pub. L. 100–709, §1, Nov. 23, 1988, 102 Stat. 4725, provided that: "This Act [enacting sections 1637a, 1647, and 1665b of this title, amending sections 1632 and 1637 of this title, and enacting provisions set out as notes under section 1637a of this title] may be cited as the 'Home Equity Loan Consumer Protection Act of 1988'."

Pub. L. 100–583, §1, Nov. 3, 1988, 102 Stat. 2960, provided that: "This Act [amending sections 1610, 1632, 1637, 1640, and 1646 of this title and enacting provisions set out as a note under section 1637 of this title] may be cited as the 'Fair Credit and Charge Card Disclosure Act of 1988'."

SHORT TITLE OF 1981 AMENDMENT

Pub. L. 97–25, §1, July 27, 1981, 95 Stat. 144, provided: "That this Act [amending sections 1602 and 1666f of this title, section 29 of Title 12, Banks and Banking, and sections 205 and 212 of Title 42, The Public Health and Welfare; enacting provisions set out as notes under this section and sections 1602 and 1666f of this title; and amending provisions set out as notes under sections 1602 and 1666f of this title] may be cited as the 'Cash Discount Act'."

SHORT TITLE OF 1980 AMENDMENT

Pub. L. 96–221, title VI, §601, Mar. 31, 1980, 94 Stat. 168, provided that: "This title [enacting section 1646 of this title, amending sections 57a, 1602 to 1607, 1610, 1612, 1613, 1631, 1632, 1635, 1637, 1638, 1640, 1641, 1643, 1663, 1664, 1665a, 1666, 1666d, 1667d, and 1691f of this title, repealing sections 1614, 1636, and 1639 of this title, and enacting provisions set out as notes under sections 1602 and 1607 of this title] may be cited as the 'Truth in Lending Simplification and Reform Act'."

Short Title of 1976 Amendments

Pub. L. 94–240, §1, Mar. 23, 1976, 90 Stat. 257, provided that: "This Act [enacting sections 1667 to 1667e of this title, amending this section and section 1640 of this title, and enacting provisions set out as a note under section 1667 of this title] may be cited as the 'Consumer Leasing Act of 1976'."

Pub. L. 94–239, §1(a), Mar. 23, 1976, 90 Stat. 251, provided that: "This Act [enacting section 1691f of this title, amending this section and sections 1691b, 1691c, 1691d, 1691e of this title, repealing section 1609 of this title, enacting provisions set out as notes under this section, and repealing provision set out as a note under this section] may be cited as the 'Equal Credit Opportunity Act Amendments of 1976'."

Short Title of 1974 Amendment

Pub. L. 93–495, title III, §301, Oct. 28, 1974, 88 Stat. 1511, provided that: "This title [enacting sections 1666 to 1666j of this title, amending this section and sections 1602, 1610, 1631, 1632, and 1637 of this title, and enacting provision set out as a note under section 1666 of this title] may be cited as the 'Fair Credit Billing Act'."

Pub. L. 93–495, title V, §501, Oct. 28, 1974, 88 Stat. 1521, which provided that title V of Pub. L. 93–495 (enacting subchapter IV of this chapter and notes set out under section 1691 of this title) could be cited as the "Equal Credit Opportunity Act", was repealed by Pub. L. 94–239, §1(c), Mar. 23, 1976, 90 Stat. 251.

Short Title

Pub. L. 90–321, §1, May 29, 1968, 82 Stat. 146, provided that: "This Act [enacting this chapter, sections 891 to 896 of Title 18, Crimes and Criminal Procedure, and provisions set out as notes under this section, sections 1631 and 1671 of this title, and section 891 of Title 18] may be cited as the 'Consumer Credit Protection Act'."

Pub. L. 90–321, title I, §101, May 29, 1968, 82 Stat. 146, provided that: "This title [enacting this subchapter] may be cited as the 'Truth in Lending Act'."

Pub. L. 90–321, title IV, §401, as added by Pub. L. 104–208, div. A, title II, §2451, Sept. 30, 1996, 110 Stat. 3009–454, provided that: "This title [enacting subchapter II–A of this chapter] may be cited as the 'Credit Repair Organizations Act'."

Pub. L. 90–321, title VI, §601, as added by Pub. L. 91–508, title VI, §601, Oct. 26, 1970, 84 Stat. 1128, as amended by Pub. L. 108–159, title VIII, §811(a), Dec. 4, 2003, 117 Stat. 2011, provided that: "This title [enacting subchapter III of this chapter] may be cited as the 'Fair Credit Reporting Act'."

Pub. L. 90–321, title VII, §709, as added by Pub. L. 94–239, §1(b), Mar. 23, 1976, 90 Stat. 251, provided that: "This title [enacting subchapter IV of this chapter and notes set out under section 1691 of this title] may be cited as the 'Equal Credit Opportunity Act'."

Pub. L. 90–321, title VIII, §801, as added by Pub. L. 95–109, Sept. 20, 1977, 91 Stat. 874, provided that: "This title [enacting subchapter V of this chapter] may be cited as the 'Fair Debt Collection Practices Act'."

Pub. L. 90–321, title IX, §901, as added by Pub. L. 95–630, title XX, §2001, Nov. 10, 1978, 92 Stat. 3728, provided that: "This title [enacting subchapter VI of this chapter] may be cited as the 'Electronic Fund Transfer Act'."

Severability

Pub. L. 90–321, title V, §501, May 29, 1968, 82 Stat. 167, provided that: "If a provision enacted by this Act [see Short Title note above], is held invalid, all valid provisions that are severable from the invalid provision remain in effect. If a provision enacted by this Act is held invalid in one or more of its applications, the provision remains in effect in all valid applications that are severable from the invalid application or applications."

Exemption or Modification of Mortgage Disclosure Requirements

Pub. L. 111–203, title XIV, §1405(b), July 21, 2010, 124 Stat. 2142, provided that: "Notwithstanding any other provision of this title [see Tables for classification], in order to improve consumer awareness and understanding of transactions involving residential mortgage loans through the use of disclosures, the Board may, by rule, exempt from or modify disclosure requirements, in whole or in part, for any class of residential mortgage loans if the Board determines that such exemption or modification is in the interest of consumers and in the public interest."

Analysis of Further Restrictions on Offers of Credit or Insurance

Pub. L. 108–159, title II, §213(e), Dec. 4, 2003, 117 Stat. 1979, provided that:

"(1) In general.—The Board shall conduct a study of—

"(A) the ability of consumers to avoid receiving written offers of credit or insurance in connection with transactions not initiated by the consumer; and

"(B) the potential impact that any further restrictions on providing consumers with such written offers of credit or insurance would have on consumers.

"(2) REPORT.—The Board shall submit a report summarizing the results of the study required under paragraph (1) to the Congress not later than 12 months after the date of enactment of this Act [Dec. 4, 2003], together with such recommendations for legislative or administrative action as the Board may determine to be appropriate.

"(3) CONTENT OF REPORT.—The report described in paragraph (2) shall address the following issues:

"(A) The current statutory or voluntary mechanisms that are available to a consumer to notify lenders and insurance providers that the consumer does not wish to receive written offers of credit or insurance.

"(B) The extent to which consumers are currently utilizing existing statutory and voluntary mechanisms to avoid receiving offers of credit or insurance.

"(C) The benefits provided to consumers as a result of receiving written offers of credit or insurance.

"(D) Whether consumers incur significant costs or are otherwise adversely affected by the receipt of written offers of credit or insurance.

"(E) Whether further restricting the ability of lenders and insurers to provide written offers of credit or insurance to consumers would affect—

"(i) the cost consumers pay to obtain credit or insurance;

"(ii) the availability of credit or insurance;

"(iii) consumers' knowledge about new or alternative products and services;

"(iv) the ability of lenders or insurers to compete with one another; and

"(v) the ability to offer credit or insurance products to consumers who have been traditionally underserved."

[For definitions of terms used in section 213(e) of Pub. L. 108–159, set out above, see section 2 of Pub. L. 108–159, set out as a Definitions note under section 1681 of this title.]

FEDERAL RESERVE STUDY OF HOME EQUITY LENDING AND APPROPRIATE INTEREST RATE INDEX

Pub. L. 103–325, title I, §157, Sept. 23, 1994, 108 Stat. 2197, provided that during the period beginning 180 days after Sept. 23, 1994, and ending 2 years after that date, the Board of Governors of the Federal Reserve System was to conduct a study and submit to the Congress a report, including recommendations for any appropriate legislation, regarding whether consumers engaging in open end credit transactions as defined in section 1602 of this title secured by principal dwellings have adequate Federal protection and whether a more appropriate interest rate index existed for purposes of section 1602(bb)(1)(A) of this title than the yield on Treasury securities.

HEARINGS ON HOME EQUITY LENDING

Pub. L. 103–325, title I, §158, Sept. 23, 1994, 108 Stat. 2197, as amended by Pub. L. 111–203, title X, §1096, July 21, 2010, 124 Stat. 2102, provided that:

"(a) HEARINGS.—Not less than once during the 3-year period beginning on the date of enactment of this Act [Sept. 23, 1994], and regularly thereafter, the Bureau, in consultation with the Advisory Board to the Bureau, shall conduct a public hearing to examine the home equity loan market and the adequacy of existing regulatory and legislative provisions and the provisions of this subtitle [see Short Title of 1994 Amendment note above] in protecting the interests of consumers, and low-income consumers in particular.

"(b) PARTICIPATION.—In conducting hearings required by subsection (a), the Bureau shall solicit participation from consumers, representatives of consumers, lenders, and other interested parties."

STUDY BY FEDERAL RESERVE BOARD OF GOVERNORS COVERING EFFECT OF CHARGE CARD TRANSACTIONS UPON CARD ISSUERS, MERCHANTS, AND CONSUMERS

Pub. L. 97–25, title II, §202, July 27, 1981, 95 Stat. 145, directed Board of Governors of Federal Reserve System, not later than 2 years after July 27, 1981, to prepare a study and submit its findings to Congress on the effect of charge card transactions upon card issuers, merchants, and consumers.

INFERENCE OF LEGISLATIVE INTENT IN SECTION CAPTIONS AND CATCHLINES

Pub. L. 90–321, title V, §502, May 29, 1968, 82 Stat. 167, provided that: "Captions and catchlines are intended solely as aids to convenient reference, and no inference as to the legislative intent with respect to any provision enacted by this Act [enacting this chapter, section 891 to 896 of Title 18, Crimes and

Criminal Procedure, and provisions set out as notes under this section, sections 1631 and 1671 of this title, and section 891 of Title 18] may be drawn from them."

GRAMMATICAL USAGES

Pub. L. 90–321, title V, §503, May 30, 1968, 82 Stat. 167, provided that: "In this Act [enacting this chapter, sections 891 to 896 of Title 18, Crimes and Criminal Procedure, and provisions set out as notes under this section, sections 1631 and 1671 of this title, and section 891 of Title 18]:

"(1) The word 'may' is used to indicate that an action either is authorized or is permitted.

"(2) The word 'shall' is used to indicate that an action is both authorized and required.

"(3) The phrase 'may not' is used to indicate that an action is both unauthorized and forbidden.

"(4) Rules of law are stated in the indicative mood."

DEFINITION

Pub. L. 111–203, title XIV, §1495, July 21, 2010, 124 Stat. 2207, provided that: "For purposes of this title [see Tables for classification], the term 'designated transfer date' means the date established under section 1062 of this Act [12 U.S.C. 5582]."

§1602. Definitions and rules of construction

(a) The definitions and rules of construction set forth in this section are applicable for the purposes of this subchapter.

(b) BUREAU.—The term "Bureau" means the Bureau of Consumer Financial Protection.

(c) The term "Board" refers to the Board of Governors of the Federal Reserve System.

(d) The term "organization" means a corporation, government or governmental subdivision or agency, trust, estate, partnership, cooperative, or association.

(e) The term "person" means a natural person or an organization.

(f) The term "credit" means the right granted by a creditor to a debtor to defer payment of debt or to incur debt and defer its payment.

(g) The term "creditor" refers only to a person who both (1) regularly extends, whether in connection with loans, sales of property or services, or otherwise, consumer credit which is payable by agreement in more than four installments or for which the payment of a finance charge is or may be required, and (2) is the person to whom the debt arising from the consumer credit transaction is initially payable on the face of the evidence of indebtedness or, if there is no such evidence of indebtedness, by agreement. Notwithstanding the preceding sentence, in the case of an open-end credit plan involving a credit card, the card issuer and any person who honors the credit card and offers a discount which is a finance charge are creditors. For the purpose of the requirements imposed under part D of this subchapter and sections 1637(a)(5), 1637(a)(6), 1637(a)(7), 1637(b)(1), 1637(b)(2), 1637(b)(3), 1637(b)(8), and 1637(b)(10) of this title, the term "creditor" shall also include card issuers whether or not the amount due is payable by agreement in more than four installments or the payment of a finance charge is or may be required, and the Bureau shall, by regulation, apply these requirements to such card issuers, to the extent appropriate, even though the requirements are by their terms applicable only to creditors offering open-end credit plans. Any person who originates 2 or more mortgages referred to in subsection (aa) in any 12-month period or any person who originates 1 or more such mortgages through a mortgage broker shall be considered to be a creditor for purposes of this subchapter. The term "creditor" includes a private educational lender (as that term is defined in section 1650 of this title) for purposes of this subchapter.

(h) The term "credit sale" refers to any sale in which the seller is a creditor. The term includes any contract in the form of a bailment or lease if the bailee or lessee contracts to pay as compensation for use a sum substantially equivalent to or in excess of the aggregate value of the property and services involved and it is agreed that the bailee or lessee will become, or for no other or a nominal consideration has the option to become, the owner of the property upon full compliance with his obligations under the contract.

(i) The adjective "consumer", used with reference to a credit transaction, characterizes the transaction as one in which the party to whom credit is offered or extended is a natural person, and the money, property, or services which are the subject of the transaction are primarily for personal, family, or household purposes.

(j) The terms "open end credit plan" and "open end consumer credit plan" mean a plan under which the creditor reasonably contemplates repeated transactions, which prescribes the terms of such transactions, and which provides for a finance charge which may be computed from time to time on the outstanding unpaid balance. A credit plan or open end consumer credit plan which is an open end credit plan or open end consumer credit plan within the meaning of the preceding sentence is an open end credit plan or open end consumer credit plan even if credit information is verified from time to time.

(k) The term "adequate notice," as used in section 1643 of this title, means a printed notice to a cardholder which sets forth the pertinent facts clearly and conspicuously so that a person against whom it is to operate could reasonably be expected to have noticed it and understood its meaning. Such notice may be given to a cardholder by printing the notice on any credit card, or on each periodic statement of account, issued to the cardholder, or by any other means reasonably assuring the receipt thereof by the cardholder.

(l) The term "credit card" means any card, plate, coupon book or other credit device existing for the purpose of obtaining money, property, labor, or services on credit.

(m) The term "accepted credit card" means any credit card which the cardholder has requested and received or has signed or has used, or authorized another to use, for the purpose of obtaining money, property, labor, or services on credit.

(n) The term "cardholder" means any person to whom a credit card is issued or any person who has agreed with the card issuer to pay obligations arising from the issuance of a credit card to another person.

(o) The term "card issuer" means any person who issues a credit card, or the agent of such person with respect to such card.

(p) The term "unauthorized use," as used in section 1643 of this title, means a use of a credit card by a person other than the cardholder who does not have actual, implied, or apparent authority for such use and from which the cardholder receives no benefit.

(q) The term "discount" as used in section 1666f of this title means a reduction made from the regular price. The term "discount" as used in section 1666f of this title shall not mean a surcharge.

(r) The term "surcharge" as used in this section and section 1666f of this title means any means of increasing the regular price to a cardholder which is not imposed upon customers paying by cash, check, or similar means."

(s) The term "State" refers to any State, the Commonwealth of Puerto Rico, the District of Columbia, and any territory or possession of the United States.

(t) The term "agricultural purposes" includes the production, harvest, exhibition, marketing, transportation, processing, or manufacture of agricultural products by a natural person who cultivates, plants, propagates, or nurtures those agricultural products, including but not limited to the acquisition of farmland, real property with a farm residence, and personal property and services used primarily in farming.

(u) The term "agricultural products" includes agricultural, horticultural, viticultural, and dairy products, livestock, wildlife, poultry, bees, forest products, fish and shellfish, and any products thereof, including processed and manufactured products, and any and all products raised or produced on farms and any processed or manufactured products thereof.

(v) The term "material disclosures" means the disclosure, as required by this subchapter, of the annual percentage rate, the method of determining the finance charge and the balance upon which a finance charge will be imposed, the amount of the finance charge, the amount to be financed, the total of payments, the number and amount of payments, the due dates or periods of payments scheduled to repay the indebtedness, and the disclosures required by section 1639(a) of this title.

(w) The term "dwelling" means a residential structure or mobile home which contains one to four family housing units, or individual units of condominiums or cooperatives.

(x) The term "residential mortgage transaction" means a transaction in which a mortgage, deed of trust, purchase money security interest arising under an installment sales contract, or equivalent consensual security interest is created or retained against the consumer's dwelling to finance the acquisition or initial construction of such dwelling.

(y) As used in this section and section 1666f of this title, the term "regular price" means the tag or posted price charged for the property or service if a single price is tagged or posted, or the price charged for the property or service when payment is made by use of an open-end credit plan or a credit card if either (1) no price is tagged or posted, or (2) two prices are tagged or posted, one of which is charged when payment is made by use of an open-end credit plan or a credit card and the other when payment is made by use of cash, check, or similar means. For purposes of this definition, payment by check, draft, or other negotiable instrument which may result in the debiting of an open-end credit plan or a credit cardholder's open-end account shall not be considered payment made by use of the plan or the account.

(z) Any reference to any requirement imposed under this subchapter or any provision thereof includes reference to the regulations of the Bureau under this subchapter or the provision thereof in question.

(aa) The disclosure of an amount or percentage which is greater than the amount or percentage required to be disclosed under this subchapter does not in itself constitute a violation of this subchapter.

(bb) HIGH-COST MORTGAGE.—

(1) DEFINITION.—

(A) IN GENERAL.—The term "high-cost mortgage", and a mortgage referred to in this subsection, means a consumer credit transaction that is secured by the consumer's principal dwelling, other than a reverse mortgage transaction, if—

(i) in the case of a credit transaction secured—

(I) by a first mortgage on the consumer's principal dwelling, the annual percentage rate at consummation of the transaction will exceed by more than 6.5 percentage points (8.5 percentage points, if the dwelling is personal property and the transaction is for less than $50,000) the average prime offer rate, as defined in section 1639c(b)(2)(B) of this title, for a comparable transaction; or

(II) by a subordinate or junior mortgage on the consumer's principal dwelling, the annual percentage rate at consummation of the transaction will exceed by more than 8.5 percentage points the average prime offer rate, as defined in section 1639c(b)(2)(B) of this title, for a comparable transaction;

(ii) the total points and fees payable in connection with the transaction, other than bona fide third party charges not retained by the mortgage originator, creditor, or an affiliate of the creditor or mortgage originator, exceed—

(I) in the case of a transaction for $20,000 or more, 5 percent of the total transaction amount; or

(II) in the case of a transaction for less than $20,000, the lesser of 8 percent of the total transaction amount or $1,000 (or such other dollar amount as the Board shall prescribe by regulation); or

(iii) the credit transaction documents permit the creditor to charge or collect prepayment fees or penalties more than 36 months after the transaction closing or such fees or penalties exceed, in the aggregate, more than 2 percent of the amount prepaid.

(B) INTRODUCTORY RATES TAKEN INTO ACCOUNT.—For purposes of subparagraph (A)(i), the annual percentage rate of interest shall be determined based on the following interest rate:

(i) In the case of a fixed-rate transaction in which the annual percentage rate will not vary during the term of the loan, the interest rate in effect on the date of consummation of the transaction.

(ii) In the case of a transaction in which the rate of interest varies solely in accordance with an index, the interest rate determined by adding the index rate in effect on the date of consummation of the transaction to the maximum margin permitted at any time during the loan agreement.

(iii) In the case of any other transaction in which the rate may vary at any time during the term of the loan for any reason, the interest charged on the transaction at the maximum rate that may be charged during the term of the loan.

(C) MORTGAGE INSURANCE.—For the purposes of computing the total points and fees under paragraph (4), the total points and fees shall exclude—

(i) any premium provided by an agency of the Federal Government or an agency of a State;

(ii) any amount that is not in excess of the amount payable under policies in effect at the time of origination under section 203(c)(2)(A) of the National Housing Act (12 U.S.C. 1709(c)(2)(A)), provided that the premium, charge, or fee is required to be refundable on a pro-rated basis and the refund is automatically issued upon notification of the satisfaction of the underlying mortgage loan; and

(iii) any premium paid by the consumer after closing.

(2)(A) After the 2-year period beginning on the effective date of the regulations promulgated under section 155 of the Riegle Community Development and Regulatory Improvement Act of 1994, and no more frequently than biennially after the first increase or decrease under this subparagraph, the Bureau may by regulation increase or decrease the number of percentage points specified in paragraph (1)(A), if the Bureau determines that the increase or decrease is—

(i) consistent with the consumer protections against abusive lending provided by the amendments made by subtitle B of title I of the Riegle Community Development and Regulatory Improvement Act of 1994; and

(ii) warranted by the need for credit.

(B) An increase or decrease under subparagraph (A)—

(i) may not result in the number of percentage points referred to in paragraph (1)(A)(i)(I) being less than 6 percentage points or greater than 10 percentage points; and

(ii) may not result in the number of percentage points referred to in paragraph (1)(A)(i)(II) being less than 8 percentage points or greater than 12 percentage points.

(C) In determining whether to increase or decrease the number of percentage points referred to in subparagraph (A), the Bureau shall consult with representatives of consumers, including low-income consumers, and lenders.

(3) The amount specified in paragraph (1)(B)(ii) shall be adjusted annually on January 1 by the annual percentage change in the Consumer Price Index, as reported on June 1 of the year preceding such adjustment.

(4) For purposes of paragraph (1)(B), points and fees shall include—

(A) all items included in the finance charge, except interest or the time-price differential;

(B) all compensation paid directly or indirectly by a consumer or creditor to a mortgage originator from any source, including a mortgage originator that is also the creditor in a table-funded transaction;

(C) each of the charges listed in section 1605(e) of this title (except an escrow for future payment of taxes), unless—

(i) the charge is reasonable;

(ii) the creditor receives no direct or indirect compensation; and

(iii) the charge is paid to a third party unaffiliated with the creditor; and

(D) premiums or other charges payable at or before closing for any credit life, credit disability, credit unemployment, or credit property insurance, or any other accident, loss-of-income, life or health insurance, or any payments directly or indirectly for any debt cancellation or suspension agreement or contract, except that insurance premiums or debt cancellation or suspension fees calculated and paid in full on a monthly basis shall not be considered financed by the creditor;

(E) the maximum prepayment fees and penalties which may be charged or collected under the terms of the credit transaction;

(F) all prepayment fees or penalties that are incurred by the consumer if the loan refinances a previous loan made or currently held by the same creditor or an affiliate of the creditor; and

(G) such other charges as the Bureau determines to be appropriate.

(5) CALCULATION OF POINTS AND FEES FOR OPEN-END CONSUMER CREDIT PLANS.—In the case of open-end consumer credit plans, points and fees shall be calculated, for purposes of this section and section 1639 of this title, by adding the total points and fees known at or before closing, including the maximum prepayment penalties which may be charged or collected under the terms of the credit transaction, plus the minimum additional fees the consumer would be required to pay to draw down an amount equal to the total credit line.

(6) This subsection shall not be construed to limit the rate of interest or the finance charge that a person may charge a consumer for any extension of credit.

(cc) The term "reverse mortgage transaction" means a nonrecourse transaction in which a mortgage, deed of trust, or equivalent consensual security interest is created against the consumer's principal dwelling—

(1) securing one or more advances; and

(2) with respect to which the payment of any principal, interest, and shared appreciation or equity is due and payable (other than in the case of default) only after—

(A) the transfer of the dwelling;

(B) the consumer ceases to occupy the dwelling as a principal dwelling; or

(C) the death of the consumer.

(dd) DEFINITIONS RELATING TO MORTGAGE ORIGINATION AND RESIDENTIAL MORTGAGE LOANS.—

(1) COMMISSION.—Unless otherwise specified, the term "Commission" means the Federal Trade Commission.

(2) MORTGAGE ORIGINATOR.—The term "mortgage originator"—

(A) means any person who, for direct or indirect compensation or gain, or in the expectation of direct or indirect compensation or gain—

(i) takes a residential mortgage loan application;

(ii) assists a consumer in obtaining or applying to obtain a residential mortgage loan; or

(iii) offers or negotiates terms of a residential mortgage loan;

(B) includes any person who represents to the public, through advertising or other means of communicating or providing information (including the use of business cards, stationery, brochures, signs, rate lists, or other promotional items), that such person can or will provide any of the services or perform any of the activities described in subparagraph (A);

(C) does not include any person who is—

(i) not otherwise described in subparagraph (A) or (B) and who performs purely administrative or clerical tasks on behalf of a person who is described in any such subparagraph; or

(ii) a retailer of manufactured or modular homes or an employee of the retailer if the retailer or employee, as applicable—

(I) does not receive compensation or gain for engaging in activities described in subparagraph (A) that is in excess of any compensation or gain received in a comparable cash transaction;

(II) discloses to the consumer—

(aa) in writing any corporate affiliation with any creditor; and

(bb) if the retailer has a corporate affiliation with any creditor, at least 1 unaffiliated creditor; and

(III) does not directly negotiate with the consumer or lender on loan terms (including rates, fees, and other costs).

(D) does not include a person or entity that only performs real estate brokerage activities and is licensed or registered in accordance with applicable State law, unless such person or entity is compensated by a lender, a mortgage broker, or other mortgage originator or by any agent of such lender, mortgage broker, or other mortgage originator;

(E) does not include, with respect to a residential mortgage loan, a person, estate, or trust that provides mortgage financing for the sale of 3 properties in any 12-month period to purchasers of such properties, each of which is owned by such person, estate, or trust and serves as security for the loan, provided that such loan—

(i) is not made by a person, estate, or trust that has constructed, or acted as a contractor for the construction of, a residence on the property in the ordinary course of business of such person, estate, or trust;

(ii) is fully amortizing;

(iii) is with respect to a sale for which the seller determines in good faith and documents that the buyer has a reasonable ability to repay the loan;

(iv) has a fixed rate or an adjustable rate that is adjustable after 5 or more years, subject to reasonable annual and lifetime limitations on interest rate increases; and

(v) meets any other criteria the Board may prescribe;

(F) does not include the creditor (except the creditor in a table-funded transaction) under paragraph (1), (2), or (4) of section 1639b(c) of this title; and

(G) does not include a servicer or servicer employees, agents and contractors, including but not limited to those who offer or negotiate terms of a residential mortgage loan for purposes of renegotiating, modifying, replacing and subordinating principal of existing mortgages where borrowers are behind in their payments, in default or have a reasonable likelihood of being in default or falling behind.

(3) NATIONWIDE MORTGAGE LICENSING SYSTEM AND REGISTRY.—The term "Nationwide Mortgage Licensing System and Registry" has the same meaning as in the Secure and Fair Enforcement for Mortgage Licensing Act of 2008 [12 U.S.C. 5101 et seq.].

(4) OTHER DEFINITIONS RELATING TO MORTGAGE ORIGINATOR.—For purposes of this subsection, a person "assists a consumer in obtaining or applying to obtain a residential mortgage loan" by, among other things, advising on residential mortgage loan terms (including rates, fees, and other costs), preparing residential mortgage loan packages, or collecting information on behalf of the consumer with regard to a residential mortgage loan.

(5) RESIDENTIAL MORTGAGE LOAN.—The term "residential mortgage loan" means any consumer credit transaction that is secured by a mortgage, deed of trust, or other equivalent consensual security interest on a dwelling or on residential real property that includes a dwelling, other than a consumer credit transaction under an open end credit plan or, for purposes of sections 1639b and 1639c of this title and section 1638(a) (16), (17), (18), and (19) of this title, and sections 1638(f) and 1640(k) of this title, and any regulations promulgated thereunder, an extension of credit relating to a plan described in section 101(53D) of title 11.

(6) SECRETARY.—The term "Secretary", when used in connection with any transaction or person involved with a residential mortgage loan, means the Secretary of Housing and Urban Development.

(7) SERVICER.—The term "servicer" has the same meaning as in section 2605(i)(2) of title 12.

(ee) BONA FIDE DISCOUNT POINTS AND PREPAYMENT PENALTIES.—For the purposes of determining the amount of points and fees for purposes of subsection (aa), either the amounts described in paragraph (1) or (2) of the following paragraphs, but not both, shall be excluded:

(1) Up to and including 2 bona fide discount points payable by the consumer in connection with the mortgage, but only if the interest rate from which the mortgage's interest rate will be discounted does not exceed by more than 1 percentage point—

(A) the average prime offer rate, as defined in section 1639c of this title; or

(B) if secured by a personal property loan, the average rate on a loan in connection with which insurance is provided under title I of the National Housing Act (12 U.S.C. 1702 et seq.).

(2) Unless 2 bona fide discount points have been excluded under paragraph (1), up to and including 1 bona fide discount point payable by the consumer in connection with the mortgage, but only if the interest rate from which the mortgage's interest rate will be discounted does not exceed by more than 2 percentage points—

(A) the average prime offer rate, as defined in section 1639c of this title; or

(B) if secured by a personal property loan, the average rate on a loan in connection with which insurance is provided under title I of the National Housing Act (12 U.S.C. 1702 et seq.).

(3) For purposes of paragraph (1), the term "bona fide discount points" means loan discount points which are knowingly paid by the consumer for the purpose of reducing, and which in fact result in a bona fide reduction of, the interest rate or time-price differential applicable to the mortgage.

(4) Paragraphs (1) and (2) shall not apply to discount points used to purchase an interest rate reduction unless the amount of the interest rate reduction purchased is reasonably consistent with established industry norms and practices for secondary mortgage market transactions.

(Pub. L. 90–321, title I, §103, May 29, 1968, 82 Stat. 147; Pub. L. 91–508, title V, §501, Oct. 26, 1970, 84 Stat. 1126; Pub. L. 93–495, title III, §303, Oct. 28, 1974, 88 Stat. 1511; Pub. L. 94–222, §3(a), Feb. 27, 1976, 90 Stat. 197; Pub. L. 96–221, title VI, §§602, 603(a), (b), 604, 612(a)(2), (b), Mar. 31, 1980, 94 Stat. 168, 169, 175, 176; Pub. L. 97–25, title I, §102, July 27, 1981, 95 Stat. 144; Pub. L. 97–320, title VII, §702(a), Oct. 15, 1982, 96 Stat. 1538; Pub. L. 103–325, title I, §§152(a)–(c), 154(a), Sept. 23, 1994, 108 Stat. 2190, 2191, 2196; Pub. L. 110–315, title X, §1011(b), Aug. 14, 2008, 122 Stat. 3481; Pub. L. 111–24, title I, §108, May 22, 2009, 123 Stat. 1743; Pub. L. 111–203, title X, §1100A(1), (2), title XIV, §§1401, 1431, July 21, 2010, 124 Stat. 2107, 2137, 2157; Pub. L. 115–174, title I, §107, May 24, 2018, 132 Stat. 1304.)

EDITORIAL NOTES

REFERENCES IN TEXT

The Riegle Community Development and Regulatory Improvement Act of 1994, referred to in subsec. (bb)(2)(A)(i), is Pub. L. 103–325, Sept. 23, 1994, 108 Stat. 2160. Section 155 of the Act is set out below. For classification of subtitle B of title I of the Act, known as the "Home Ownership and Equity Protection Act of

1994", see Short Title of 1994 Amendment note set out under section 1601 of this title. For complete classification of this Act to the Code, see Short Title note set out under section 4701 of Title 12, Banks and Banking, and Tables.

The Secure and Fair Enforcement for Mortgage Licensing Act of 2008, referred to in subsec. (dd)(3), is title V of div. A of Pub. L. 110–289, July 30, 2008, 122 Stat. 2810, also known as the S.A.F.E. Mortgage Licensing Act of 2008, which is classified generally to chapter 51 (§5101 et seq.) of Title 12, Banks and Banking. For complete classification of this Act to the Code, see Short Title note set out under section 5101 of Title 12 and Tables.

The National Housing Act, referred to in subsec. (ee)(1)(B), (2)(B), is act June 27, 1934, ch. 847, 48 Stat. 1246. Title I of the Act is classified generally to subchapter II (§1702 et seq.) of chapter 13 of Title 12, Banks and Banking. For complete classification of this Act to the Code, see section 1701 of Title 12 and Tables.

AMENDMENTS

2018—Subsecs. (cc), (dd). Pub. L. 115–174, §107(1), redesignated subsec. (cc), relating to definitions relating to mortgage origination and residential mortgage loans, as (dd). Former subsec. (dd) redesignated (ee).

Subsec. (dd)(2)(C). Pub. L. 115–174, §107(2), added subpar. (C) and struck out former subpar. (C) which read as follows: "does not include any person who is (i) not otherwise described in subparagraph (A) or (B) and who performs purely administrative or clerical tasks on behalf of a person who is described in any such subparagraph, or (ii) an employee of a retailer of manufactured homes who is not described in clause (i) or (iii) of subparagraph (A) and who does not advise a consumer on loan terms (including rates, fees, and other costs);".

Subsec. (ee). Pub. L. 115–174, §107(1), redesignated subsec. (dd) as (ee).

2010—Pub. L. 111–203, §1100A(2), which directed substitution of "Bureau" for "Board" wherever appearing, was executed by making the substitution wherever appearing in subsecs. (g), (z), and (bb)(2) (A), (C), (4)(D), but not in subsec. (c), to reflect the probable intent of Congress.

Subsecs. (b) to (z). Pub. L. 111–203, §1100(A)(1), added subsec. (b) and redesignated former subsecs. (b) to (z) as (c) to (aa), respectively.

Subsec. (bb). Pub. L. 111–203, §1431(a), which directed amendment of subsec. (aa) by inserting subsec. heading, adding par. (1), and striking out former par. (1), was executed by making the amendment to subsec. (bb) to reflect the probable intent of Congress and the redesignation of subsec. (aa) as (bb) by Pub. L. 111–203, §1100(A)(1). See below. Text of former par. (1) read as follows: "A mortgage referred to in this subsection means a consumer credit transaction that is secured by the consumer's principal dwelling, other than a residential mortgage transaction, a reverse mortgage transaction, or a transaction under an open end credit plan, if—

"(A) the annual percentage rate at consummation of the transaction will exceed by more than 10 percentage points the yield on Treasury securities having comparable periods of maturity on the fifteenth day of the month immediately preceding the month in which the application for the extension of credit is received by the creditor; or

"(B) the total points and fees payable by the consumer at or before closing will exceed the greater of—

"(i) 8 percent of the total loan amount; or
"(ii) $400."

Pub. L. 111–203, §1100(A)(1), redesignated subsec. (aa) as (bb). Former subsec. (bb) redesignated (cc).

Subsec. (bb)(2)(B). Pub. L. 111–203, §1431(b), which directed amendment of subsec. (aa)(2) by adding subpar. (B) and striking out former subpar. (B), was executed by making the amendment to subsec. (bb) (2) to reflect the probable intent of Congress and the redesignation of subsec. (aa) as (bb) by Pub. L. 111–203, §1100(A)(1). See above. Text of former subpar. (B) read as follows: "An increase or decrease under subparagraph (A) may not result in the number of percentage points referred to in subparagraph (A) being—

"(i) less that 8 percentage points; or
"(ii) greater than 12 percentage points."

Subsec. (bb)(4)(B). Pub. L. 111–203, §1431(c)(1)(A), which directed amendment of subsec. (aa)(4) by adding subpar. (B) and struck out former subpar. (B), was executed by making the amendment to subsec. (bb)(4) to reflect the probable intent of Congress and the redesignation of subsec. (aa) as (bb) by Pub. L. 111–203, §1100(A)(1). See above. Text of former subpar. (B) read as follows: "all compensation paid to mortgage brokers;".

Subsec. (bb)(4)(D) to (G). Pub. L. 111–203, §1431(c)(1)(B), (C), which directed amendment of subsec. (aa)(4) by adding subpars. (D) to (F) and redesignating former subpar. (D) as (G), was executed by making the amendment to subsec. (bb)(4) to reflect the probable intent of Congress and the redesignation of subsec. (aa) as (bb) by Pub. L. 111–203, §1100(A)(1). See above.

Subsec. (bb)(5), (6). Pub. L. 111–203, §1431(c)(2), which directed amendment of subsec. (aa) by adding par. (5) and redesignating former par. (5) as (6), was executed by making the amendment to subsec. (bb) to reflect the probable intent of Congress and the redesignation of subsec. (aa) as (bb) by Pub. L. 111–203, §1100(A)(1). See above.

Subsec. (cc). Pub. L. 111–203, §1401, added subsec. (cc) relating to definitions relating to mortgage origination and residential mortgage loans.

Pub. L. 111–203, §1100(A)(1), redesignated subsec. (bb) as (cc) defining the term "reverse mortgage transaction".

Subsec. (dd). Pub. L. 111–203, §1431(d), added subsec. (dd).

2009—Subsec. (i). Pub. L. 111–24 substituted "terms 'open end credit plan' and 'open end consumer credit plan' mean" for "term 'open end credit plan' means" in first sentence and inserted "or open end consumer credit plan" after "credit plan" wherever appearing in second sentence.

2008—Subsec. (f). Pub. L. 110–315 inserted at end "The term 'creditor' includes a private educational lender (as that term is defined in section 1650 of this title) for purposes of this subchapter."

1994—Subsec. (f). Pub. L. 103–325, §152(c), inserted at end "Any person who originates 2 or more mortgages referred to in subsection (aa) in any 12-month period or any person who originates 1 or more such mortgages through a mortgage broker shall be considered to be a creditor for purposes of this subchapter."

Subsec. (u). Pub. L. 103–325, §152(b), substituted "the due dates" for "and the due dates" and inserted before period at end ", and the disclosures required by section 1639(a) of this title".

Subsec. (aa). Pub. L. 103–325, §152(a), added subsec. (aa).

Subsec. (bb). Pub. L. 103–325, §154(a), added subsec. (bb).

1982—Subsec. (f). Pub. L. 97–320 struck out provision that a person who regularly arranged for the extension of consumer credit payable in more than four installments or for which the payment of a finance charge was or might have been required from persons not creditors was a creditor, and provision that this subchapter applied to any creditor, irrespective of his or its status as a natural person or any type of organization, who was a card issuer.

1981—Subsecs. (x) to (z). Pub. L. 97–25 added subsec. (z) and, effective Apr. 10, 1982, redesignated subsecs. (x), (y), and (z) as (y), (z), and (x), respectively.

1980—Subsec. (f). Pub. L. 96–221, §602(a), substituted provisions defining term "creditor" as referring only to a person who both regularly extends consumer credit, subject to specified conditions, and is the person to whom the debt arising is initially payable on the face of the indebtedness or by agreement, and notwithstanding such provisions, also refers to a person regularly arranging for the extension of consumer credit, and a card issuer and any person honoring the credit card, subject to specified conditions, for provisions defining term "creditor" as referring only to creditors who regularly extend, or arrange for the extension of credit payable in more than four installments or where a finance charge is or may be required, and substituted "(a)(5)" for "(a)(6)", "(a)(6)" for "(a)(7)", "(a)(7)" for "(a)(8)", "(b)(8)" for "(b)(9)", and "(b)(10)" for "(b)(11)".

Subsec. (g). Pub. L. 96–221, §602(b), substituted "in which the seller is a creditor" for "with respect to which credit is extended or arranged by the seller".

Subsec. (h). Pub. L. 96–221, §603(a), struck out applicability to agricultural purposes.

Subsec. (i). Pub. L. 96–221, §604, inserted provisions respecting the reasonable contemplations of the creditor, and verification of credit information from time to time.

Subsecs. (s), (t). Pub. L. 96–221, §603(b), added subsecs. (s) and (t). Former subsecs. (s) and (t) redesignated (x) and (y), respectively.

Subsec. (u). Pub. L. 96–221, §612(a)(2), added subsec. (u).

Subsecs. (v), (w). Pub. L. 96–221, §612(b), added subsecs. (v) and (w).

Subsecs. (x), (y). Pub. L. 96–221, §603(b), redesignated former subsecs. (s) and (t) as (x) and (y), respectively.

1976—Subsecs. (p) to (t). Pub. L. 94–222 added subsecs. (p) and (q) and redesignated former subsecs. (p) to (r) as (r) to (t), respectively.

1974—Subsec. (f). Pub. L. 93–495 inserted provision requiring the credit to be payable by agreement in more than four installments and defining term "creditor" for the purposes of the requirements imposed under the enumerated sections of this chapter.

1970—Subsecs. (j) to (r). Pub. L. 91–508 added subsecs. (j) to (o) and redesignated former subsecs. (j) to (l) as (p) to (r), respectively.

STATUTORY NOTES AND RELATED SUBSIDIARIES

Effective Date of 2010 Amendment

Amendment by section 1100A(1), (2) of Pub. L. 111–203 effective on the designated transfer date, see section 1100H of Pub. L. 111–203, set out as a note under section 552a of Title 5, Government Organization and Employees.

Amendment by sections 1401 and 1431 of Pub. L. 111–203 effective on the date on which final regulations implementing that amendment take effect, or on the date that is 18 months after the designated transfer date if such regulations have not been issued by that date, see section 1400(c) of Pub. L. 111–203, set out as a note under section 1601 of this title.

Effective Date of 2009 Amendment

Pub. L. 111–24, §3, May 22, 2009, 123 Stat. 1735, provided that: "This Act [enacting sections 1616, 1651, 1665c to 1665e, 1666i–1, 1666i–2, and 1693l–1 of this title and section 1a–7b of Title 16, Conservation, amending this section and sections 1632, 1637, 1640, 1650, 1666b, 1666c, 1666j, 1681b, 1681j, and 1693m to 1693r of this title, enacting provisions set out as notes under this section and sections 1637, 1638, 1666b, 1681j, and 1693l–1 of this title and section 5311 of Title 31, Money and Finance, and amending provisions set out as notes under sections 1638 and 1693 of this title] and the amendments made by this Act shall become effective 9 months after the date of enactment of this Act [May 22, 2009], except as otherwise specifically provided in this Act."

Effective Date of 1982 Amendment

Pub. L. 97–320, title VII, §702(b), Oct. 15, 1982, 96 Stat. 1538, provided that: "The amendment made by subsection (a) [amending this section] shall take effect on the effective date of title VI of the Depository Institutions Deregulation and Monetary Control Act of 1980 [two years and six months after Mar. 31, 1980, see Effective Date of 1980 Amendment note below]."

Effective Date of 1981 Amendment

Section 102(b) of Pub. L. 97–25 provided that the amendment made by that section is effective Apr. 10, 1982.

Effective Date of 1980 Amendment

Pub. L. 96–221, title VI, §625, Mar. 31, 1980, 94 Stat. 185, as amended by Pub. L. 97–25, title III, §301, July 27, 1981, 95 Stat. 145; Pub. L. 97–110, title III, §301, Dec. 26, 1981, 95 Stat. 1515, provided that:

"(a) Except as provided in section 608(b) [set out as an Effective Date of 1980 Amendment note under section 1607 of this title], the amendments made by this title [enacting section 1646 of this title, amending sections 57a, 1602 to 1606, 1610, 1612, 1613, 1631, 1632, 1635, 1637, 1638, 1640, 1641, 1643, 1663, 1664, 1665a, 1666, 1666d, 1667d, and 1691f of this title, repealing sections 1614, 1636, and 1639 of this title, and enacting provisions set out as a note under section 1601 of this title] shall take effect upon the expiration of two years and six months after the date of enactment of this title [Mar. 31, 1980].

"(b) All regulations, forms, and clauses required to be prescribed under the amendments made by this title shall be promulgated at least one year prior to such effective date.

"(c) Notwithstanding subsections (a) and (b), any creditor may comply with the amendments made by this title, in accordance with the regulations, forms, and clauses prescribed by the Board, prior to such effective date. Any creditor who elects to comply with such amendments and any assignee of such a creditor shall be subject to the provisions of sections 130 and 131 of the Truth in Lending Act, as amended by sections 615 and 616, respectively, of this title [sections 1640 and 1641 of this title]."

Effective Date of 1974 Amendment

For effective date of amendment by Pub. L. 93–495, see section 308 of Pub. L. 93–495, set out as an Effective Date note under section 1666 of this title.

Regulations

Pub. L. 111–24, §2, May 22, 2009, 123 Stat. 1735, provided that: "The Board of Governors of the Federal Reserve System (in this Act [see Short Title of 2009 Amendment note set out under section 1601 of this title] referred to as the 'Board') may issue such rules and publish such model forms as it considers necessary to carry out this Act and the amendments made by this Act."

Pub. L. 103–325, title I, §155, Sept. 23, 1994, 108 Stat. 2197, provided that: "Not later than 180 days after the date of enactment of this Act [Sept. 23, 1994], the Board of Governors of the Federal Reserve System shall issue such regulations as may be necessary to carry out this subtitle [subtitle B (§§151–158) of title I of Pub. L. 103–325, see Short Title of 1994 Amendment note set out under section 1601 of this title], and such regulations shall become effective on the date on which disclosure regulations are required to become effective under section 105(d) of the Truth in Lending Act [15 U.S.C. §1604(d)]."

APPLICABILITY OF 1994 AMENDMENTS AND REGULATIONS TO SUBSECTION (AA) MORTGAGES

Pub. L. 103–325, title I, §156, Sept. 23, 1994, 108 Stat. 2197, provided that: "This subtitle [subtitle B (§§151–158) of title I of Pub. L. 103–325, see Short Title of 1994 Amendment note set out under section 1601 of this title], and the amendments made by this subtitle, shall apply to every mortgage referred to in section 103(aa) of the Truth in Lending Act [now 15 U.S.C. 1602(bb)] (as added by section 152(a) of this Act) consummated on or after the date on which regulations issued under section 155 [set out above] become effective."

§1603. Exempted transactions

This subchapter does not apply to the following:

(1) Credit transactions involving extensions of credit primarily for business, commercial, or agricultural purposes, or to government or governmental agencies or instrumentalities, or to organizations.

(2) Transactions in securities or commodities accounts by a broker-dealer registered with the Securities and Exchange Commission.

(3) Credit transactions, other than those in which a security interest is or will be acquired in real property, or in personal property used or expected to be used as the principal dwelling of the consumer and other than private education loans (as that term is defined in section 1650(a) of this title), in which the total amount financed exceeds $50,000.[1]

(4) Transactions under public utility tariffs, if the Bureau determines that a State regulatory body regulates the charges for the public utility services involved, the charges for delayed payment, and any discount allowed for early payment.

(5) Transactions for which the Bureau, by rule, determines that coverage under this subchapter is not necessary to carry out the purposes of this subchapter.

(6) Repealed. Pub. L. 96–221, title VI, §603(c)(3), Mar. 31, 1980, 94 Stat. 169.

(7) Loans made, insured, or guaranteed pursuant to a program authorized by title IV of the Higher Education Act of 1965 [20 U.S.C. 1070 et seq.].

(Pub. L. 90–321, title I, §104, May 29, 1968, 82 Stat. 147; Pub. L. 93–495, title IV, §402, Oct. 28, 1974, 88 Stat. 1517; Pub. L. 96–221, title VI, §603(c), Mar. 31, 1980, 94 Stat. 169; Pub. L. 97–320, title VII, §701(a), Oct. 15, 1982, 96 Stat. 1538; Pub. L. 104–208, div. A, title II, §2102(a), Sept. 30, 1996, 110 Stat. 3009–398; Pub. L. 110–315, title X, §1022, Aug. 14, 2008, 122 Stat. 3488; Pub. L. 111–203, title X, §§1100A(2), 1100E(a)(1), July 21, 2010, 124 Stat. 2107, 2111.)

EDITORIAL NOTES

REFERENCES IN TEXT

The Higher Education Act of 1965, referred to in par. (7), is Pub. L. 89–329, Nov. 8, 1965, 79 Stat. 1219. Title IV of the Act is classified generally to subchapter IV (§1070 et seq.) of chapter 28 of Title 20, Education. For complete classification of this Act to the Code, see Short Title note set out under section 1001 of Title 20 and Tables.

AMENDMENTS

2010—Par. (3). Pub. L. 111–203, §1100E(a)(1), substituted "$50,000" for "$25,000".

Pars. (4), (5). Pub. L. 111–203, §1100A(2), substituted "Bureau" for "Board".

2008—Par. (3). Pub. L. 110–315 inserted "and other than private education loans (as that term is defined in section 1650(a) of this title)" after "consumer".

1996—Pars. (5) to (7). Pub. L. 104–208 added par. (5) and redesignated former pars. (5) and (6) as (6) and (7), respectively.

1982—Par. (6). Pub. L. 97–320 added par. (6).

1980—Par. (1). Pub. L. 96–221, §603(c)(1), inserted provision relating to applicability to agricultural purposes.

Par. (3). Pub. L. 96–221, §603(c)(2), substituted provision excepting security interest in real property, or in personal property used as the consumer's principal dwelling, for provisions excepting real property transactions.

Par. (5). Pub. L. 96–221, §603(c)(3), struck out par. (5) which related to credit transactions primarily for agricultural purposes where the amount financed exceeds $25,000.

1974—Par. (5). Pub. L. 93–495 added par. (5).

STATUTORY NOTES AND RELATED SUBSIDIARIES

EFFECTIVE DATE OF 2010 AMENDMENT

Amendment by Pub. L. 111–203 effective on the designated transfer date, see section 1100H of Pub. L. 111–203, set out as a note under section 552a of Title 5, Government Organization and Employees.

EFFECTIVE DATE OF 1982 AMENDMENT

Section 701(c) of Pub. L. 97–320, as amended by Pub. L. 97–457, §31, Jan. 12, 1983, 96 Stat. 2511, provided that: "The amendment made by subsection (a) [amending this section] and subsection (b) [enacting section 1099 of Title 20, Education] shall be effective with respect to loans made prior to, on, and after the date of the enactment of this Act [Oct. 15, 1982]."

EFFECTIVE DATE OF 1980 AMENDMENT

Amendment by Pub. L. 96–221 effective on expiration of two years and six months after Mar. 31, 1980, with all regulations, forms, and clauses required to be prescribed to be promulgated at least one year prior to such effective date, and allowing any creditor to comply with any amendments, in accordance with the regulations, forms, and clauses prescribed by the Board prior to such effective date, see section 625 of Pub. L. 96–221, set out as a note under section 1602 of this title.

EFFECTIVE DATE OF 1974 AMENDMENT

Amendment by Pub. L. 93–495 effective Oct. 28, 1974, see section 416 of Pub. L. 93–495, set out as an Effective Date note under section 1665a of this title.

EXCEPTIONS IN AREAS WHERE MAJOR DISASTER EXISTS

Board of Governors of Federal Reserve System authorized to make exceptions to requirements of this subchapter for transactions within an area in which the President has determined that a major disaster exists, if Board determines that exception can reasonably be expected to alleviate hardships to the public that outweigh possible adverse effects, see section 50002 of Pub. L. 105–18, set out as a note under section 4008 of Title 12, Banks and Banking, and similar provisions listed thereunder.

ADJUSTMENTS FOR INFLATION

Pub. L. 111–203, title X, §1100E(b), July 21, 2010, 124 Stat. 2111, provided that: "On and after December 31, 2011, the Bureau [of Consumer Financial Protection] shall adjust annually the dollar amounts described in sections 104(3) and 181(1) of the Truth in Lending Act [15 U.S.C. 1603(3), 1667(1)] (as amended by this section), by the annual percentage increase in the Consumer Price Index for Urban Wage Earners and Clerical Workers, as published by the Bureau of Labor Statistics, rounded to the nearest multiple of $100, or $1,000, as applicable." Threshold amounts in effect during particular periods of time can be found in Code of Federal Regulations, Title 12, Supplement I to Part 1013, under Section 1013.2—Definitions, under 2(e)—Consumer Lease, paragraph 11.

[1] See Adjustments for Inflation note below.

§1604. Disclosure guidelines

(a) Promulgation, contents, etc., of regulations

The Bureau shall prescribe regulations to carry out the purposes of this subchapter. Except with respect to the provisions of section 1639 of this title that apply to a mortgage referred to in section 1602(aa) [1] of this title, such regulations may contain such additional requirements, classifications, differentiations, or other provisions, and may provide for such adjustments and exceptions for all or any class of transactions, as in the judgment of the Bureau are necessary or proper to effectuate the purposes of this subchapter, to prevent circumvention or evasion thereof, or to facilitate compliance therewith.

(b) Model disclosure forms and clauses; publication, criteria, compliance, etc.

The Bureau shall publish a single, integrated disclosure for mortgage loan transactions (including real estate settlement cost statements) which includes the disclosure requirements of this subchapter in conjunction with the disclosure requirements of the Real Estate Settlement Procedures Act of 1974 [12 U.S.C. 2601 et seq.] that, taken together, may apply to a transaction that is subject to both or either provisions of law. The purpose of such model disclosure shall be to facilitate compliance with the disclosure requirements of this subchapter and the Real Estate Settlement Procedures Act of 1974, and to aid the borrower or lessee in understanding the transaction by utilizing readily understandable language to simplify the technical nature of the disclosures. In devising such forms, the Bureau shall consider the use by creditors or lessors of data processing or similar automated equipment. Nothing in this subchapter may be construed to require a creditor or lessor to use any such model form or clause prescribed by the Bureau under this section. A creditor or lessor shall be deemed to be in compliance with the disclosure provisions of this subchapter with respect to other than numerical disclosures if the creditor or lessor (1) uses any appropriate model form or clause as published by the Bureau, or (2) uses any such model form or clause and changes it by (A) deleting any information which is not required by this subchapter, or (B) rearranging the format, if in making such deletion or rearranging the format, the creditor or lessor does not affect the substance, clarity, or meaningful sequence of the disclosure.

(c) Procedures applicable for adoption of model forms and clauses

Model disclosure forms and clauses shall be adopted by the Bureau after notice duly given in the Federal Register and an opportunity for public comment in accordance with section 553 of title 5.

(d) Effective dates of regulations containing new disclosure requirements

Any regulation of the Bureau, or any amendment or interpretation thereof, requiring any disclosure which differs from the disclosures previously required by this part, part D, or part E or by any regulation of the Bureau promulgated thereunder shall have an effective date of that October 1 which follows by at least six months the date of promulgation, except that the Bureau may at its discretion take interim action by regulation, amendment, or interpretation to lengthen the period of time permitted for creditors or lessors to adjust their forms to accommodate new requirements or shorten the length of time for creditors or lessors to make such adjustments when it makes a specific finding that such action is necessary to comply with the findings of a court or to prevent unfair or deceptive disclosure practices. Notwithstanding the previous sentence, any creditor or lessor may comply with any such newly promulgated disclosure requirements prior to the effective date of the requirements.

(e) Disclosure for charitable mortgage loan transactions

With respect to a mortgage loan transaction involving a residential mortgage loan offered at 0 percent interest with only bonafide and reasonable fees and that is primarily for charitable purposes by an organization described in section 501(c)(3) of title 26 and exempt from taxation under section 501(a) of such title, forms HUD–1 and GFE (as defined under section 1024.2(b) of title 12, Code of Federal Regulations) together with a disclosure substantially in the form of the Loan Model Form H–2 (as depicted in Appendix H to part 1026 of title 12, Code of Federal Regulations) shall, collectively, be an appropriate model form for purposes of subsection (b) of this section.

(f) Exemption authority

(1) In general

The Bureau may exempt, by regulation, from all or part of this subchapter all or any class of transactions, other than transactions involving any mortgage described in section 1602(aa) [1] of this title, for which, in the determination of the Bureau, coverage under all or part of this subchapter does not provide a meaningful benefit to consumers in the form of useful information or protection.

(2) Factors for consideration

In determining which classes of transactions to exempt in whole or in part under paragraph (1), the Bureau shall consider the following factors and publish its rationale at the time a proposed exemption is published for comment:
(A) The amount of the loan and whether the disclosures, right of rescission, and other provisions provide a benefit to the consumers who are parties to such transactions, as determined by the Bureau.
(B) The extent to which the requirements of this subchapter complicate, hinder, or make more expensive the credit process for the class of transactions.
(C) The status of the borrower, including—
(i) any related financial arrangements of the borrower, as determined by the Bureau;
(ii) the financial sophistication of the borrower relative to the type of transaction; and
(iii) the importance to the borrower of the credit, related supporting property, and coverage under this subchapter, as determined by the Bureau;

(D) whether the loan is secured by the principal residence of the consumer; and
(E) whether the goal of consumer protection would be undermined by such an exemption.

(g) Waiver for certain borrowers

(1) In general

The Bureau, by regulation, may exempt from the requirements of this subchapter certain credit transactions if—
(A) the transaction involves a consumer—
(i) with an annual earned income of more than $200,000; or
(ii) having net assets in excess of $1,000,000 at the time of the transaction; and

(B) a waiver that is handwritten, signed, and dated by the consumer is first obtained from the consumer.

(2) Adjustments by the Bureau

The Bureau, at its discretion, may adjust the annual earned income and net asset requirements of paragraph (1) for inflation.

(h) Deference

Notwithstanding any power granted to any Federal agency under this subchapter, the deference that a court affords to the Bureau with respect to a determination made by the Bureau relating to the meaning or interpretation of any provision of this subchapter, other than section 1639e or 1639h of this title, shall be applied as if the Bureau were the only agency authorized to apply, enforce, interpret, or administer the provisions of this subchapter.

(i) Authority of the Board to prescribe rules

Notwithstanding subsection (a), the Board shall have authority to prescribe rules under this subchapter with respect to a person described in section 5519(a) of title 12. Regulations prescribed under this subsection may contain such classifications, differentiations, or other provisions, as in the judgment of the Board are necessary or proper to effectuate the purposes of this subchapter, to prevent circumvention or evasion thereof, or to facilitate compliance therewith.

(Pub. L. 90–321, title I, §105, May 29, 1968, 82 Stat. 148; Pub. L. 96–221, title VI, §605, Mar. 31, 1980, 94 Stat. 170; Pub. L. 103–325, title I, §152(e)(2)(A), Sept. 23, 1994, 108 Stat. 2194; Pub. L. 104–208, div. A, title II, §§2102(b), 2104, Sept. 30, 1996, 110 Stat. 3009–399, 3009–401; Pub. L. 111–203, title X, §1100A(2), (4)–(7), title XIV, §1472(c), July 21, 2010, 124 Stat. 2107, 2108, 2190; Pub. L. 116–342, §2(a), Jan. 13, 2021, 134 Stat. 5134.)

Editorial Notes

References in Text

Section 1602(aa) of this title, referred to in subsecs. (a) and (f)(1), was redesignated section 1602(bb) of this title by Pub. L. 111–203, title X, §1100A(1)(A), July 21, 2010, 124 Stat. 2107.

The Real Estate Settlement Procedures Act of 1974, referred to in subsec. (b), is Pub. L. 93–533, Dec. 22, 1974, 88 Stat. 1724, which is classified principally to chapter 27 (§2601 et seq.) of Title 12, Banks and Banking. For complete classification of this Act to the Code, see Short Title note set out under section 2601 of Title 12 and Tables.

Amendments

2021—Subsec. (e). Pub. L. 116–342 added subsec. (e).

2010—Subsec. (a). Pub. L. 111–203, §1100A(2), (4), substituted "Bureau" for "Board" in two places, substituted "Except with respect to the provisions of section 1639 of this title that apply to a mortgage referred to in section 1602(aa) of this title, such regulations may contain such additional requirements,"for "Except in the case of a mortgage referred to in section 1602(aa) of this title, these regulations may contain such", and inserted "all or" after "exceptions for".

Subsec. (b). Pub. L. 111–203, §1100A(2), (5), substituted "Bureau" for "Board" wherever appearing in last three sentences and substituted first two sentences for former first sentence which read as follows: "The Board shall publish model disclosure forms and clauses for common transactions to facilitate compliance with the disclosure requirements of this subchapter and to aid the borrower or lessee in understanding the transaction by utilizing readily understandable language to simplify the technical nature of the disclosures."

Subsecs. (c), (d). Pub. L. 111–203, §1100A(2), substituted "Bureau" for "Board" wherever appearing.

Subsec. (f). Pub. L. 111–203, §1100A(2), (6), substituted "Bureau" for "Board" wherever appearing and inserted "all or" after "from all or part of this subchapter" in par. (1).

Subsec. (g). Pub. L. 111–203, §1100A(2), substituted "Bureau" for "Board" in pars. (1) and (2).

Subsec. (h). Pub. L. 111–203, §1472(c), which directed addition of subsec. (h) at end of section, was executed by adding subsec. (h) before subsec. (i), to reflect the probable intent of Congress and prior amendment by Pub. L. 111–203, §1100A(7). See below.

Subsec. (i). Pub. L. 111–203, §1100A(7), added subsec. (i).

1996—Subsec. (f). Pub. L. 104–208, §2102(b), added subsec. (f).

Subsec. (g). Pub. L. 104–208, §2104, added subsec. (g).

1994—Subsec. (a). Pub. L. 103–325 substituted "Except in the case of a mortgage referred to in section 1602(aa) of this title, these" for "These" in second sentence.

1980—Pub. L. 96–221 designated existing provisions as subsec. (a) and added subsecs. (b) to (d).

Statutory Notes and Related Subsidiaries

Amendment by section 1100A(2), (4)–(7) of Pub. L. 111–203 effective on the designated transfer date, see section 1100H of Pub. L. 111–203, set out as a note under section 552a of Title 5, Government Organization and Employees.

Amendment by section 1472(c) of Pub. L. 111–203 effective on the date on which final regulations implementing that amendment take effect, or on the date that is 18 months after the designated transfer date if such regulations have not been issued by that date, see section 1400(c) of Pub. L. 111–203, set out as a note under section 1601 of this title.

EFFECTIVE DATE OF 1980 AMENDMENT

Amendment by Pub. L. 96–221 effective on expiration of two years and six months after Mar. 31, 1980, with all regulations, forms, and clauses required to be prescribed to be promulgated at least one year prior to such effective date, and allowing any creditor to comply with any amendments, in accordance with the regulations, forms, and clauses prescribed by the Board prior to such effective date, see section 625 of Pub. L. 96–221, set out as a note under section 1602 of this title.

[1] *See References in Text note below.*

§1605. Determination of finance charge

(a) "Finance charge" defined

Except as otherwise provided in this section, the amount of the finance charge in connection with any consumer credit transaction shall be determined as the sum of all charges, payable directly or indirectly by the person to whom the credit is extended, and imposed directly or indirectly by the creditor as an incident to the extension of credit. The finance charge does not include charges of a type payable in a comparable cash transaction. The finance charge shall not include fees and amounts imposed by third party closing agents (including settlement agents, attorneys, and escrow and title companies) if the creditor does not require the imposition of the charges or the services provided and does not retain the charges. Examples of charges which are included in the finance charge include any of the following types of charges which are applicable:

(1) Interest, time price differential, and any amount payable under a point, discount, or other system or additional charges.

(2) Service or carrying charge.

(3) Loan fee, finder's fee, or similar charge.

(4) Fee for an investigation or credit report.

(5) Premium or other charge for any guarantee or insurance protecting the creditor against the obligor's default or other credit loss.

(6) Borrower-paid mortgage broker fees, including fees paid directly to the broker or the lender (for delivery to the broker) whether such fees are paid in cash or financed.

(b) Life, accident, or health insurance premiums included in finance charge

Charges or premiums for credit life, accident, or health insurance written in connection with any consumer credit transaction shall be included in the finance charges unless

(1) the coverage of the debtor by the insurance is not a factor in the approval by the creditor of the extension of credit, and this fact is clearly disclosed in writing to the person applying for or obtaining the extension of credit; and

(2) in order to obtain the insurance in connection with the extension of credit, the person to whom the credit is extended must give specific affirmative written indication of his desire to do so after written disclosure to him of the cost thereof.

(c) Property damage and liability insurance premiums included in finance charge

Charges or premiums for insurance, written in connection with any consumer credit transaction, against loss of or damage to property or against liability arising out of the ownership or use of property, shall be included in the finance charge unless a clear and specific statement in writing is furnished by the creditor to the person to whom the credit is extended, setting forth the cost of the insurance if obtained from or through the creditor, and stating that the person to whom the credit is extended may choose the person through which the insurance is to be obtained.

(d) Items exempted from computation of finance charge in all credit transactions

If any of the following items is itemized and disclosed in accordance with the regulations of the Bureau in connection with any transaction, then the creditor need not include that item in the computation of the finance charge with respect to that transaction:

(1) Fees and charges prescribed by law which actually are or will be paid to public officials for determining the existence of or for perfecting or releasing or satisfying any security related to the credit transaction.

(2) The premium payable for any insurance in lieu of perfecting any security interest otherwise required by the creditor in connection with the transaction, if the premium does not exceed the fees and charges described in paragraph (1) which would otherwise be payable.

(3) Any tax levied on security instruments or on documents evidencing indebtedness if the payment of such taxes is a precondition for recording the instrument securing the evidence of indebtedness.

(e) Items exempted from computation of finance charge in extensions of credit secured by an interest in real property

The following items, when charged in connection with any extension of credit secured by an interest in real property, shall not be included in the computation of the finance charge with respect to that transaction:

(1) Fees or premiums for title examination, title insurance, or similar purposes.

(2) Fees for preparation of loan-related documents.

(3) Escrows for future payments of taxes and insurance.

(4) Fees for notarizing deeds and other documents.

(5) Appraisal fees, including fees related to any pest infestation or flood hazard inspections conducted prior to closing.

(6) Credit reports.

(f) Tolerances for accuracy

In connection with credit transactions not under an open end credit plan that are secured by real property or a dwelling, the disclosure of the finance charge and other disclosures affected by any finance charge—

(1) shall be treated as being accurate for purposes of this subchapter if the amount disclosed as the finance charge—

(A) does not vary from the actual finance charge by more than $100; or

(B) is greater than the amount required to be disclosed under this subchapter; and

(2) shall be treated as being accurate for purposes of section 1635 of this title if—

(A) except as provided in subparagraph (B), the amount disclosed as the finance charge does not vary from the actual finance charge by more than an amount equal to one-half of one percent of the total amount of credit extended; or

(B) in the case of a transaction, other than a mortgage referred to in section 1602(aa) [1] of this title, which—

(i) is a refinancing of the principal balance then due and any accrued and unpaid finance charges of a residential mortgage transaction as defined in section 1602(w) [1] of this title, or is any subsequent refinancing of such a transaction; and

(ii) does not provide any new consolidation or new advance;

if the amount disclosed as the finance charge does not vary from the actual finance charge by more than an amount equal to one percent of the total amount of credit extended.

(Pub. L. 90–321, title I, §106, May 29, 1968, 82 Stat. 148; Pub. L. 96–221, title VI §606, Mar. 31, 1980, 94 Stat. 170; Pub. L. 104–29, §§2(a), (b)(1), (c)–(e), 3(a), Sept. 30, 1995, 109 Stat. 271, 272; Pub. L. 111–203, title X, §1100A(2), July 21, 2010, 124 Stat. 2107.)

EDITORIAL NOTES

REFERENCES IN TEXT

Subsecs. (aa) and (w) of section 1602 of this title, referred to in subsec. (f)(2)(B), were redesignated subsecs. (bb) and (x), respectively, of section 1602 of this title by Pub. L. 111–203, title X, §1100A(1)(A), July 21, 2010, 124 Stat. 2107.

AMENDMENTS

2010—Subsec. (d). Pub. L. 111–203 substituted "Bureau" for "Board" in introductory provisions.

1995—Subsec. (a). Pub. L. 104–29, §2(a), in introductory provisions inserted after second sentence "The finance charge shall not include fees and amounts imposed by third party closing agents (including settlement agents, attorneys, and escrow and title companies) if the creditor does not require the imposition of the charges or the services provided and does not retain the charges."

Subsec. (a)(6). Pub. L. 104–29, §2(b)(1), added par. (6).

Subsec. (d)(3). Pub. L. 104–29, §2(c), added par. (3).

Subsec. (e)(2). Pub. L. 104–29, §2(d), amended par. (2) generally, substituting "loan-related" for "a deed, settlement statement, or other".

Subsec. (e)(5). Pub. L. 104–29, §2(e), inserted before period ", including fees related to any pest infestation or flood hazard inspections conducted prior to closing".

Subsec. (f). Pub. L. 104–29, §3(a), added subsec. (f).

1980—Subsec. (a). Pub. L. 96–221, §606(a), inserted provisions excluding charges of a type payable in comparable cash transactions and indicated that pars. (1) to (5) are examples of charges.

Subsec. (d). Pub. L. 96–221, §606(b), struck out pars. (3) and (4) setting forth applicability to taxes and any other type of charge, respectively.

STATUTORY NOTES AND RELATED SUBSIDIARIES

EFFECTIVE DATE OF 2010 AMENDMENT

Amendment by Pub. L. 111–203 effective on the designated transfer date, see section 1100H of Pub. L. 111–203, set out as a note under section 552a of Title 5, Government Organization and Employees.

EFFECTIVE DATE OF 1995 AMENDMENT

Pub. L. 104–29, §2(b)(2), Sept. 30, 1995, 109 Stat. 271, provided that: "The amendment made by paragraph (1) [amending this section] shall take effect on the earlier of—

"(A) 60 days after the date on which the Board of Governors of the Federal Reserve System issues final regulations under paragraph (3) [set out below]; or

"(B) the date that is 12 months after the date of the enactment of this Act [Sept. 30, 1995]."

EFFECTIVE DATE OF 1980 AMENDMENT

Amendment by Pub. L. 96–221 effective on expiration of two years and six months after Mar. 31, 1980, with all regulations, forms, and clauses required to be prescribed to be promulgated at least one year prior to such effective date, and allowing any creditor to comply with any amendments, in accordance with the regulations, forms, and clauses prescribed by the Board prior to such effective date, see section 625 of Pub. L. 96–221, set out as a note under section 1602 of this title.

REGULATIONS

Pub. L. 104–29, §2(b)(3), Sept. 30, 1995, 109 Stat. 271, provided that: "The Board of Governors of the Federal Reserve System shall promulgate regulations implementing the amendment made by paragraph (1) [amending this section] by no later than 6 months after the date of the enactment of this Act [Sept. 30, 1995]."

ENSURING THAT FINANCE CHARGES REFLECT COST OF CREDIT

Pub. L. 104–29, §2(f), Sept. 30, 1995, 109 Stat. 272, provided that:
"(1) REPORT.—
"(A) IN GENERAL.—Not later than 6 months after the date of the enactment of this Act [Sept. 30, 1995], the Board of Governors of the Federal Reserve System shall submit to the Congress a report containing recommendations on any regulatory or statutory changes necessary—
"(i) to ensure that finance charges imposed in connection with consumer credit transactions more accurately reflect the cost of providing credit; and
"(ii) to address abusive refinancing practices engaged in for the purpose of avoiding rescission.
"(B) REPORT REQUIREMENTS.—In preparing the report under this paragraph, the Board shall—
"(i) consider the extent to which it is feasible to include in finance charges all charges payable directly or indirectly by the consumer to whom credit is extended, and imposed directly or indirectly by the creditor as an incident to the extension of credit (especially those charges excluded from finance charges under section 106 of the Truth in Lending Act [15 U.S.C. 1605] as of the date of the enactment of this Act), excepting only those charges which are payable in a comparable cash transaction; and
"(ii) consult with and consider the views of affected industries and consumer groups.
"(2) REGULATIONS.—The Board of Governors of the Federal Reserve System shall prescribe any appropriate regulation in order to effect any change included in the report under paragraph (1), and shall publish the regulation in the Federal Register before the end of the 1-year period beginning on the date of enactment of this Act."

1 See References in Text note below.

§1606. Determination of annual percentage rate

(a) "Annual percentage rate" defined

The annual percentage rate applicable to any extension of consumer credit shall be determined, in accordance with the regulations of the Bureau,

(1) in the case of any extension of credit other than under an open end credit plan, as

(A) that nominal annual percentage rate which will yield a sum equal to the amount of the finance charge when it is applied to the unpaid balances of the amount financed, calculated according to the actuarial method of allocating payments made on a debt between the amount financed and the amount of the finance charge, pursuant to which a payment is applied first to the accumulated finance charge and the balance is applied to the unpaid amount financed; or

(B) the rate determined by any method prescribed by the Bureau as a method which materially simplifies computation while retaining reasonable accuracy as compared with the rate determined under subparagraph (A).[1]

(2) in the case of any extension of credit under an open end credit plan, as the quotient (expressed as a percentage) of the total finance charge for the period to which it relates divided by the amount upon which the finance charge for that period is based, multiplied by the number of such periods in a year.

(b) Computation of rate of finance charges for balances within a specified range

Where a creditor imposes the same finance charge for balances within a specified range, the annual percentage rate shall be computed on the median balance within the range, except that if the Bureau determines that a rate so computed would not be meaningful, or would be materially misleading, the annual percentage rate shall be computed on such other basis as the Bureau may be regulation require.

(c) Allowable tolerances for purposes of compliance with disclosure requirements

The disclosure of an annual percentage rate is accurate for the purpose of this subchapter if the rate disclosed is within a tolerance not greater than one-eighth of 1 per centum more or less than the actual rate or rounded to the nearest one-fourth of 1 per centum. The Bureau may allow a greater tolerance to simplify compliance where irregular payments are involved.

(d) Use of rate tables or charts having allowable variance from determined rates

The Bureau may authorize the use of rate tables or charts which may provide for the disclosure of annual percentage rates which vary from the rate determined in accordance with subsection (a)(1)(A) by not more than such tolerances as the Bureau may allow. The Bureau may not allow a tolerance greater than 8 per centum of that rate except to simplify compliance where irregular payments are involved.

(e) Authorization of tolerances in determining annual percentage rates

In the case of creditors determining the annual percentage rate in a manner other than as described in subsection (d), the Bureau may authorize other reasonable tolerances.

(Pub. L. 90–321, title I, §107, May 29, 1968, 82 Stat. 149; Pub. L. 96–221, title VI, §607, Mar. 31, 1980, 94 Stat. 170; Pub. L. 111–203, title X, §1100A(2), July 21, 2010, 124 Stat. 2107.)

EDITORIAL NOTES

AMENDMENTS

2010—Pub. L. 111–203 substituted "Bureau" for "Board" wherever appearing.

1980—Subsec. (c). Pub. L. 96–221, §607(a), substituted provisions relating to allowable tolerances for purposes of compliance with disclosure requirements, for provisions relating to rounding off of annual percentage rates which are converted from single add-on or other rates.

Subsec. (e). Pub. L. 96–221, §607(b), struck out reference to subsection (c) of this section.

Subsec. (f). Pub. L. 96–221, §607(c), struck out subsec. (f) setting forth requirements for form of expressing percentage rates prior to Jan. 1, 1971.

STATUTORY NOTES AND RELATED SUBSIDIARIES

EFFECTIVE DATE OF 2010 AMENDMENT

Amendment by Pub. L. 111–203 effective on the designated transfer date, see section 1100H of Pub. L. 111–203, set out as a note under section 552a of Title 5, Government Organization and Employees.

EFFECTIVE DATE OF 1980 AMENDMENT

Amendment by Pub. L. 96–221 effective on expiration of two years and six months after Mar. 31, 1980, with all regulations, forms, and clauses required to be prescribed to be promulgated at least one year prior to such effective date, and allowing any creditor to comply with any amendments, in accordance with the regulations, forms, and clauses prescribed by the Board prior to such effective date, see section 625 of Pub. L. 96–221, set out as a note under section 1602 of this title.

¹ So in original.

§1607. Administrative enforcement

(a) Enforcing agencies

Subject to subtitle B of the Consumer Financial Protection Act of 2010 [12 U.S.C. 5511 et seq.], compliance with the requirements imposed under this subchapter shall be enforced under—

(1) section 8 of the Federal Deposit Insurance Act [12 U.S.C. 1818], by the appropriate Federal banking agency, as defined in section 3(q) of the Federal Deposit Insurance Act (12 U.S.C. 1813(q)), with respect to—

(A) national banks, Federal savings associations, and Federal branches and Federal agencies of foreign banks;

(B) member banks of the Federal Reserve System (other than national banks), branches and agencies of foreign banks (other than Federal branches, Federal agencies, and insured State branches of foreign banks), commercial lending companies owned or controlled by foreign banks, and organizations operating under section 25 or 25A of the Federal Reserve Act [12 U.S.C. 601 et seq., 611 et seq.]; and

(C) banks and State savings associations insured by the Federal Deposit Insurance Corporation (other than members of the Federal Reserve System), and insured State branches of foreign banks;

(2) the Federal Credit Union Act [12 U.S.C. 1751 et seq.], by the Director of the National Credit Union Administration, with respect to any Federal credit union;

(3) part A of subtitle VII of title 49, by the Secretary of Transportation, with respect to any air carrier or foreign air carrier subject to that part;

(4) the Packers and Stockyards Act, 1921 [7 U.S.C. 181 et seq.] (except as provided in section 406 of that Act [7 U.S.C. 226, 227]), by the Secretary of Agriculture, with respect to any activities subject to that Act;

(5) the Farm Credit Act of 1971 [12 U.S.C. 2001 et seq.], by the Farm Credit Administration with respect to any Federal land bank, Federal land bank association, Federal intermediate credit bank, or production credit association; and

(6) subtitle E of the Consumer Financial Protection Act of 2010 [12 U.S.C. 5561 et seq.], by the Bureau, with respect to any person subject to this subchapter.

(7) sections 21B and 21C of the Securities Exchange Act of 1934 [15 U.S.C. 78u–2, 78u–3], in the case of a broker or dealer, other than a depository institution, by the Securities and Exchange Commission.

(b) Violations of this subchapter deemed violations of pre-existing statutory requirements; additional agency powers

For the purpose of the exercise by any agency referred to in subsection (a) of its powers under any Act referred to in that subsection, a violation of any requirement imposed under this subchapter shall be deemed to be a violation of a requirement imposed under that Act. In addition to its powers under any provision of law specifically referred to in subsection (a), each of the agencies referred to in that subsection may exercise, for the purpose of enforcing compliance with any requirement imposed under this subchapter, any other authority conferred on it by law.

(c) Overall enforcement authority of the Federal Trade Commission

Except to the extent that enforcement of the requirements imposed under this subchapter is specifically committed to some other Government agency under any of paragraphs (1) through (5) of subsection (a), and subject to subtitle B of the Consumer Financial Protection Act of 2010 [12 U.S.C. 5511 et seq.], the Federal Trade Commission shall be authorized to enforce such requirements. For the purpose of the exercise by the Federal Trade Commission of its functions and powers under the Federal Trade Commission Act [15 U.S.C. 41 et seq.], a violation of any requirement imposed under this subchapter shall be deemed a violation of a requirement imposed under that Act. All of the functions and powers of the Federal Trade Commission under the Federal Trade Commission Act are available to the Federal Trade Commission to enforce compliance by any person with the requirements under this subchapter, irrespective of whether that person is engaged in commerce or meets any other jurisdictional tests under the Federal Trade Commission Act.

(d) Rules and regulations

The authority of the Bureau to issue regulations under this subchapter does not impair the authority of any other agency designated in this section to make rules respecting its own procedures in enforcing compliance with requirements imposed under this subchapter.

(e) Adjustment of finance charges; procedures applicable, coverage, criteria, etc.

(1) In carrying out its enforcement activities under this section, each agency referred to in subsection (a) or (c), in cases where an annual percentage rate or finance charge was inaccurately disclosed, shall notify the creditor of such disclosure error and is authorized in accordance with the provisions of this subsection to require the creditor to make an adjustment to the account of the person to whom credit was extended, to assure that such person will not be

required to pay a finance charge in excess of the finance charge actually disclosed or the dollar equivalent of the annual percentage rate actually disclosed, whichever is lower. For the purposes of this subsection, except where such disclosure error resulted from a willful violation which was intended to mislead the person to whom credit was extended, in determining whether a disclosure error has occurred and in calculating any adjustment, (A) each agency shall apply (i) with respect to the annual percentage rate, a tolerance of one-quarter of 1 percent more or less than the actual rate, determined without regard to section 1606(c) of this title, and (ii) with respect to the finance charge, a corresponding numerical tolerance as generated by the tolerance provided under this subsection for the annual percentage rate; except that (B) with respect to transactions consummated after two years following March 31, 1980, each agency shall apply (i) for transactions that have a scheduled amortization of ten years or less, with respect to the annual percentage rate, a tolerance not to exceed one-quarter of 1 percent more or less than the actual rate, determined without regard to section 1606(c) of this title, but in no event a tolerance of less than the tolerances allowed under section 1606(c) of this title, (ii) for transactions that have a scheduled amortization of more than ten years, with respect to the annual percentage rate, only such tolerances as are allowed under section 1606(c) of this title, and (iii) for all transactions, with respect to the finance charge, a corresponding numerical tolerance as generated by the tolerances provided under this subsection for the annual percentage rate.

(2) Each agency shall require such an adjustment when it determines that such disclosure error resulted from (A) a clear and consistent pattern or practice of violations, (B) gross negligence, or (C) a willful violation which was intended to mislead the person to whom the credit was extended. Notwithstanding the preceding sentence, except where such disclosure error resulted from a willful violation which was intended to mislead the person to whom credit was extended, an agency need not require such an adjustment if it determines that such disclosure error—

(A) resulted from an error involving the disclosure of a fee or charge that would otherwise be excludable in computing the finance charge, including but not limited to violations involving the disclosures described in sections 1605(b), (c) and (d) of this title, in which event the agency may require such remedial action as it determines to be equitable, except that for transactions consummated after two years after March 31, 1980, such an adjustment shall be ordered for violations of section 1605(b) of this title;

(B) involved a disclosed amount which was 10 per centum or less of the amount that should have been disclosed and (i) in cases where the error involved a disclosed finance charge, the annual percentage rate was disclosed correctly, and (ii) in cases where the error involved a disclosed annual percentage rate, the finance charge was disclosed correctly; in which event the agency may require such adjustment as it determines to be equitable;

(C) involved a total failure to disclose either the annual percentage rate or the finance charge, in which event the agency may require such adjustment as it determines to be equitable; or

(D) resulted from any other unique circumstance involving clearly technical and nonsubstantive disclosure violations that do not adversely affect information provided to the consumer and that have not misled or otherwise deceived the consumer.

In the case of other such disclosure errors, each agency may require such an adjustment.
(3) Notwithstanding paragraph (2), no adjustment shall be ordered—

(A) if it would have a significantly adverse impact upon the safety or soundness of the creditor, but in any such case, the agency may—

(i) require a partial adjustment in an amount which does not have such an impact; or

(ii) require the full adjustment, but permit the creditor to make the required adjustment in partial payments over an extended period of time which the agency considers to be reasonable, if (in the case of an agency referred to in paragraph (1), (2), or (3) of subsection (a)), the agency determines that a partial adjustment or making partial payments over an extended period is necessary to avoid causing the creditor to become undercapitalized pursuant to section 38 of the Federal Deposit Insurance Act [12 U.S.C. 1831o];

(B) the [1] amount of the adjustment would be less than $1, except that if more than one year has elapsed since the date of the violation, the agency may require that such amount be paid into the Treasury of the United States, or

(C) except where such disclosure error resulted from a willful violation which was intended to mislead the person to whom credit was extended, in the case of an open-end credit plan, more than two years after the violation, or in the case of any other extension of credit, as follows:

(i) with respect to creditors that are subject to examination by the agencies referred to in paragraphs (1) through (3) of subsection (a) of this section, except in connection with violations arising from practices identified in the current examination and only in connection with transactions that are consummated after the date of the immediately preceding examination, except that where practices giving rise to violations identified in earlier examinations have not been corrected, adjustments for those violations shall be required in connection with transactions consummated after the date of examination in which such practices were first identified;

(ii) with respect to creditors that are not subject to examination by such agencies, except in connection with transactions that are consummated after May 10, 1978; and

(iii) in no event after the later of (I) the expiration of the life of the credit extension, or (II) two years after the agreement to extend credit was consummated.

(4)(A) Notwithstanding any other provision of this section, an adjustment under this subsection may be required by an agency referred to in subsection (a) or (c) only by an order issued in accordance with cease and desist procedures provided by the provision of law referred to in such subsections.

(B) In case of an agency which is not authorized to conduct cease and desist proceedings, such an order may be issued after an agency hearing on the record conducted at least thirty but not more than sixty days after notice of the alleged violation is served on the creditor. Such a hearing shall be deemed to be a hearing which is subject to the provisions of section 8(h) of the Federal Deposit Insurance Act [12 U.S.C. 1818(h)] and shall be subject to judicial review as provided therein.

(5) Except as otherwise specifically provided in this subsection and notwithstanding any provision of law referred to in subsection (a) or (c), no agency referred to in subsection (a) or (c) may require a creditor to make dollar adjustments for errors in any requirements under this subchapter, except with regard to the requirements of section 1666d of this title.

(6) A creditor shall not be subject to an order to make an adjustment, if within sixty days after discovering a disclosure error, whether pursuant to a final written examination report or through the creditor's own procedures, the creditor notifies the person concerned of the error and adjusts the account so as to assure that such person will not be required to pay a finance charge in excess of the finance charge actually disclosed or the dollar equivalent of the annual percentage rate actually disclosed, whichever is lower.

(7) Notwithstanding the second sentence of subsection (e)(1), subsection (e)(3)(C)(i), and subsection (e)(3)(C)(ii), each agency referred to in subsection (a) or (c) shall require an adjustment for an annual percentage rate disclosure error that exceeds a tolerance of one quarter of one percent less than the actual rate, determined without regard to section 1606(c) of this title, with respect to any transaction consummated between January 1, 1977, and March 31, 1980.

(Pub. L. 90–321, title I, §108, May 29, 1968, 82 Stat. 150; Pub. L. 91–206, §3, Mar. 10, 1970, 84 Stat. 49; Pub. L. 93–495, title IV, §403, Oct. 28, 1974, 88 Stat. 1517; Pub. L. 95–630, title V, §501, Nov. 10, 1978, 92 Stat. 3680; Pub. L. 96–221, title VI, §608(a), (c), Mar. 21, 1980, 94 Stat. 171, 173; Pub. L. 98–443, §9(n), Oct. 4, 1984, 98 Stat. 1708; Pub. L. 101–73, title VII, §744(k), Aug. 9, 1989, 103 Stat. 439; Pub. L. 102–242, title II, §212(b), Dec. 19, 1991, 105 Stat. 2299; Pub. L. 102–550, title XVI, §1604(a)(5), Oct. 28, 1992, 106 Stat. 4082; Pub. L. 104–208, div. A, title II, §2106, Sept. 30, 1996, 110 Stat. 3009–402; Pub. L. 111–203, title X, §1100A(2), (8), title XIV, §1414(b), July 21, 2010, 124 Stat. 2107, 2108, 2152.)

EDITORIAL NOTES

REFERENCES IN TEXT

The Consumer Financial Protection Act of 2010, referred to in subsecs. (a) and (c), is title X of Pub. L. 111–203, July 21, 2010, 124 Stat. 1955. Subtitles B (§§1021–1029A) and E (§§1051–1058) of the Act are classified generally to parts B (§5511 et seq.) and E (§5561 et seq.), respectively, of subchapter V of chapter 53 of Title 12, Banks and Banking. For complete classification of this Act to the Code, see Short Title note set out under section 5301 of Title 12 and Tables.

Sections 25 and 25A of the Federal Reserve Act, referred to in subsec. (a)(1)(B), are classified to subchapters I (§601 et seq.) and II (§611 et seq.), respectively, of chapter 6 of Title 12, Banks and Banking.

The Federal Credit Union Act, referred to in subsec. (a)(2), is act June 26, 1934, ch. 750, 48 Stat. 1216, which is classified generally to chapter 14 (§1751 et seq.) of Title 12. For complete classification of this Act to the Code, see section 1751 of Title 12 and Tables.

The Packers and Stockyards Act, 1921, referred to in subsec. (a)(4), is act Aug. 15, 1921, ch. 64, 42 Stat. 159, which is classified generally to chapter 9 (§181 et seq.) of Title 7, Agriculture. For complete classification of this Act to the Code, see section 181 of Title 7 and Tables.

The Farm Credit Act of 1971, referred to in subsec. (a)(5), is Pub. L. 92–181, Dec. 10, 1971, 85 Stat. 583, which is classified generally to chapter 23 (§2001 et seq.) of Title 12, Banks and Banking. For complete classification of this Act to the Code, see Short Title note set out under section 2001 of Title 12 and Tables.

The Federal Trade Commission Act, referred to in subsec. (c), is act Sept. 26, 1914, ch. 311, 38 Stat. 717, which is classified generally to subchapter I (§41 et seq.) of chapter 2 of this title. For complete classification of this Act to the Code, see section 58 of this title and Tables.

CODIFICATION

In subsec. (a)(3), "part A of subtitle VII of title 49" substituted for "the Federal Aviation Act of 1958" and "that part" substituted for "that Act" on authority of Pub. L. 103–272, §6(b), July 5, 1994, 108 Stat. 1378, the first section of which enacted subtitles II, III, and V to X of Title 49, Transportation.

AMENDMENTS

2010—Subsec. (a). Pub. L. 111–203, §1100A(8)(A), added subsec. (a) and struck out former subsec. (a) which listed agencies under which compliance with subchapter requirements would be enforced.

Subsec. (a)(7). Pub. L. 111–203, §1414(b), added par. (7).

Subsec. (c). Pub. L. 111–203, §1100A(8)(B), added subsec. (c) and struck out former subsec. (c). Prior to amendment, text read as follows: "Except to the extent that enforcement of the requirements imposed under this subchapter is specifically committed to some other Government agency under subsection (a) of this section, the Federal Trade Commission shall enforce such requirements. For the purpose of the exercise by the Federal Trade Commission of its functions and powers under the Federal Trade Commission Act, a violation of any requirement imposed under this subchapter shall be deemed a violation of a requirement imposed under that Act. All of the functions and powers of the Federal Trade Commission under the Federal Trade Commission Act are available to the Commission to enforce compliance by any person with the requirements imposed under this subchapter, irrespective of whether that person is engaged in commerce or meets any other jurisdictional tests in the Federal Trade Commission Act."

Subsec. (d). Pub. L. 111–203, §1100A(2), substituted "Bureau" for "Board".

1996—Subsec. (e)(3). Pub. L. 104–208 struck out "ordered (A) if" and inserted "ordered—
    "(A) if";
struck out "may require a partial" and inserted "may—
    "(i) require a partial";
struck out ", except that with respect to any transaction consumated after March 31, 1980, the agency shall require" and inserted "; or
    "(ii) require";
directed the substitution of "reasonable, if (in the case of an agency referred to in paragraph (1), (2), or (3) of subsection (a)), the agency determines that a partial adjustment or making partial payments over an extended period is necessary to avoid causing the creditor to become undercapitalized pursuant to section 38 of the Federal Deposit Insurance Act;
    "(B) the";
for "reasonable, (B) the", which was executed by making the substitution for "reasonable, (B) if the"; and struck out "(C) except" and inserted
    "(C) except".

1992—Subsec. (a)(1)(C). Pub. L. 102–550 substituted semicolon for period at end.

1991—Subsec. (a). Pub. L. 102–242, §212(b)(2), inserted at end "The terms used in paragraph (1) that are not defined in this subchapter or otherwise defined in section 3(s) of the Federal Deposit Insurance Act (12 U.S.C. 1813(s)) shall have the meaning given to them in section 1(b) of the International Banking Act of 1978 (12 U.S.C. 3101)."

Pub. L. 102–242, §212(b)(1), added par. (1) and struck out former par. (1) which read as follows: "section 8 of the Federal Deposit Insurance Act, in the case of
    "(A) national banks, by the Comptroller of the Currency.
    "(B) member banks of the Federal Reserve System (other than national banks), by the Board.
    "(C) banks insured by the Federal Deposit Insurance Corporation (other than members of the Federal Reserve System), by the Board of Directors of the Federal Deposit Insurance Corporation."

1989—Subsec. (a)(2). Pub. L. 101–73 amended par. (2) generally. Prior to amendment, par. (2) read as follows: "section 5(d) of the Home Owner's Loan Act of 1933, section 407 of the National Housing Act, and sections 6(i) and 17 of the Federal Home Loan Bank Act, by the Federal Home Loan Bank Board (acting directly or through the Federal Savings and Loan Insurance Corporation), in the case of any institution subject to any of those provisions."

1984—Subsec. (a)(4). Pub. L. 98–443 substituted "Secretary of Transportation" for "Civil Aeronautics Board".

1980—Subsec. (e). Pub. L. 96–221, §608(a), added subsec. (e).

Pub. L. 96–221, §608(c), struck out in pars. (1)(A)(i) and (7) ", except in the case of an irregular mortgage lending transaction" after "section 1606(c) of this title". See Effective Date of 1980 Amendment note below.

1974—Subsec. (a)(4) to (6). Pub. L. 93–495 redesignated pars. (5) and (6) as (4) and (5), respectively. Former par. (4), which related to enforcement by the Interstate Commerce Commission, was struck out.

STATUTORY NOTES AND RELATED SUBSIDIARIES

EFFECTIVE DATE OF 2010 AMENDMENT

Amendment by section 1100A(2), (8) of Pub. L. 111–203 effective on the designated transfer date, see section 1100H of Pub. L. 111–203, set out as a note under section 552a of Title 5, Government Organization and Employees.

Amendment by section 1414(b) of Pub. L. 111–203 effective on the date on which final regulations implementing that amendment take effect, or on the date that is 18 months after the designated transfer date if such regulations have not been issued by that date, see section 1400(c) of Pub. L. 111–203, set out as a note under section 1601 of this title.

Effective Date of 1992 Amendment

Amendment by Pub. L. 102–550 effective as if included in the Federal Deposit Insurance Corporation Improvement Act of 1991, Pub. L. 102–242, as of Dec. 19, 1991, see section 1609(a) of Pub. L. 102–550, set out as a note under section 191 of Title 12, Banks and Banking.

Effective Date of 1984 Amendment

Amendment by Pub. L. 98–443 effective Jan. 1, 1985, see section 9(v) of Pub. L. 98–443, set out as a note under section 5314 of Title 5, Government Organization and Employees.

Effective Date of 1980 Amendment

Pub. L. 96–221, title VI, §608(b), Mar. 31, 1980, 94 Stat. 173, provided that: "This section [amending this section] shall take effect on the date of enactment of the Truth in Lending Simplification and Reform Act [Mar. 31, 1980]."

Pub. L. 96–221, title VI, §608(c), Mar. 31, 1980, 94 Stat. 173, provided that the amendment made by that section is effective one year after Mar. 31, 1980.

Effective Date of 1974 Amendment

Amendment by Pub. L. 93–495 effective Oct. 28, 1974, see section 416 of Pub. L. 93–495, set out as an Effective Date note under section 1665a of this title.

Transfer of Functions

"National Credit Union Administration Board" substituted for "Director of the Bureau of Federal Credit Unions" in subsec. (a)(3) pursuant to section 3 of Pub. L. 91–206 and section 501 of Pub. L. 95–630 [12 U.S.C. 1752a] which transferred functions of Bureau of Federal Credit Unions, and Director thereof, to National Credit Union Administration and vested authority for management of Administration in National Credit Union Administration Board.

[1] *So in original. Probably should be preceded by "if".*

§1608. Views of other agencies

In the exercise of its functions under this subchapter, the Bureau may obtain upon requests the views of any other Federal agency which, in the judgment of the Bureau, exercises regulatory or supervisory functions with respect to any class of creditors subject to this subchapter.

(Pub. L. 90–321, title I, §109, May 29, 1968, 82 Stat. 150; Pub. L. 111–203, title X, §1100A(2), July 21, 2010, 124 Stat. 2107.)

Editorial Notes

Amendments

2010—Pub. L. 111–203 substituted "Bureau" for "Board" in two places.

Statutory Notes and Related Subsidiaries

Effective Date of 2010 Amendment

Amendment by Pub. L. 111–203 effective on the designated transfer date, see section 1100H of Pub. L. 111–203, set out as a note under section 552a of Title 5, Government Organization and Employees.

§1609. Repealed. Pub. L. 94–239, §3(b)(1), Mar. 23, 1976, 90 Stat. 253

Section, Pub. L. 90–321, title I, §110, May 29, 1968, 82 Stat. 151, provided for establishment of an advisory committee authorized to seek to achieve a fair representation of interests of sellers of merchandise on credit, lenders, and the public.

EFFECTIVE DATE OF REPEAL

Repeal effective Mar. 23, 1976, see section 708 of Pub. L. 90–321, set out as an Effective Date note under section 1691 of this title.

§1610. Effect on other laws

(a) Inconsistent provisions; procedures applicable for determination

(1) Except as provided in subsection (e), this part and parts B and C, do not annul, alter, or affect the laws of any State relating to the disclosure of information in connection with credit transactions, except to the extent that those laws are inconsistent with the provisions of this subchapter, and then only to the extent of the inconsistency. Upon its own motion or upon the request of any creditor, State, or other interested party which is submitted in accordance with procedures prescribed in regulations of the Bureau, the Bureau shall determine whether any such inconsistency exists. If the Bureau determines that a State-required disclosure is inconsistent, creditors located in that State may not make disclosures using the inconsistent term or form, and shall incur no liability under the law of that State for failure to use such term or form, notwithstanding that such determination is subsequently amended, rescinded, or determined by judicial or other authority to be invalid for any reason.

(2) Upon its own motion or upon the request of any creditor, State, or other interested party which is submitted in accordance with procedures prescribed in regulations of the Bureau, the Bureau shall determine whether any disclosure required under the law of any State is substantially the same in meaning as a disclosure required under this subchapter. If the Bureau determines that a State-required disclosure is substantially the same in meaning as a disclosure required by this subchapter, then creditors located in that State may make such disclosure in compliance with such State law in lieu of the disclosure required by this subchapter, except that the annual percentage rate and finance charge shall be disclosed as required by section 1632 of this title, and such State-required disclosure may not be made in lieu of the disclosures applicable to certain mortgages under section 1639 of this title.

(b) State credit charge statutes

Except as provided in section 1639 of this title, this subchapter does not otherwise annul, alter or affect in any manner the meaning, scope or applicability of the laws of any State, including, but not limited to, laws relating to the types, amounts or rates of charges, or any element or elements of charges, permissible under such laws in connection with the extension or use of credit, nor does this subchapter extend the applicability of those laws to any class of persons or transactions to which they would not otherwise apply. The provisions of section 1639 of this title do not annul, alter, or affect the applicability of the laws of any State or exempt any person subject to the provisions of section 1639 of this title from complying with the laws of any State, with respect to the requirements for mortgages referred to in section 1602(aa) [1] of this title, except to the extent that those State laws are inconsistent with any provisions of section 1639 of this title, and then only to the extent of the inconsistency.

(c) Disclosure as evidence

In any action or proceeding in any court involving a consumer credit sale, the disclosure of the annual percentage rate as required under this subchapter in connection with that sale may not be received as evidence that the sale was a loan or any type of transaction other than a credit sale.

(d) Contract or other obligations under State or Federal law

Except as specified in sections 1635, 1640, and 1666e of this title, this subchapter and the regulations issued thereunder do not affect the validity or enforceability of any contract or obligation under State or Federal law.

(e) Certain credit and charge card application and solicitation disclosure provisions

The provisions of subsection (c) of section 1632 of this title and subsections (c), (d), (e), and (f) of section 1637 of this title shall supersede any provision of the law of any State relating to the disclosure of information in any credit or charge card application or solicitation which is subject to the requirements of section 1637(c) of this title or any renewal notice which is subject to the requirements of section 1637(d) of this title, except that any State may employ or establish State laws for the purpose of enforcing the requirements of such sections.

(Pub. L. 90–321, title I, §111, May 29, 1968, 82 Stat. 151; Pub. L. 93–495, title III, §307(b), Oct. 28, 1974, 88 Stat. 1516; Pub. L. 96–221, title VI, §609, Mar. 31, 1980, 94 Stat. 173; Pub. L. 100–583, §4, Nov. 3, 1988, 102 Stat. 2967; Pub. L. 103–325, title I, §152(e)(2)(B), (C), Sept. 23, 1994, 108 Stat. 2194; Pub. L. 111–203, title X, §1100A(2), July 21, 2010, 124 Stat. 2107.)

EDITORIAL NOTES

REFERENCES IN TEXT

Section 1602(aa) of this title, referred to in subsec. (b), was redesignated section 1602(bb) of this title by Pub. L. 111–203, title X, §1100A(1)(A), July 21, 2010, 124 Stat. 2107.

AMENDMENTS

2010—Subsec. (a). Pub. L. 111–203 substituted "Bureau" for "Board" wherever appearing.

1994—Subsec. (a)(2). Pub. L. 103–325, §152(e)(2)(B), which directed the amendment of par. (2) by inserting ", and such State-required disclosure may not be made in lieu of the disclosures applicable to certain mortgages under section 1639 of this title" before period, was executed by making the insertion before period at end of par. (2), to reflect the probable intent of Congress.

Subsec. (b). Pub. L. 103–325, §152(e)(2)(C), substituted "Except as provided in section 1639 of this title, this subchapter" for "This subchapter" and inserted at end "The provisions of section 1639 of this title do not annul, alter, or affect the applicability of the laws of any State or exempt any person subject to the provisions of section 1639 of this title from complying with the laws of any State, with respect to the requirements for mortgages referred to in section 1602(aa) of this title, except to the extent that those State laws are inconsistent with any provisions of section 1639 of this title, and then only to the extent of the inconsistency."

1988—Subsec. (a)(1). Pub. L. 100–583, §4(1), substituted "Except as provided in subsection (e), this part" for "This part".

Subsec. (e). Pub. L. 100–583, §4(2), added subsec. (e).

1980—Subsec. (a). Pub. L. 96–221 designated existing provisions as par. (1), substituted provisions respecting the effect of this part and parts B and C of this subchapter, and procedures applicable for determination, for provisions respecting the effect of this subchapter, and added par. (2).

1974—Subsec. (d). Pub. L. 93–495 inserted reference to section 1666e of this title.

STATUTORY NOTES AND RELATED SUBSIDIARIES

EFFECTIVE DATE OF 2010 AMENDMENT

Amendment by Pub. L. 111–203 effective on the designated transfer date, see section 1100H of Pub. L. 111–203, set out as a note under section 552a of Title 5, Government Organization and Employees.

EFFECTIVE DATE OF 1980 AMENDMENT

Amendment by Pub. L. 96–221 effective on expiration of two years and six months after Mar. 31, 1980, with all regulations, forms, and clauses required to be prescribed to be promulgated at least one year prior to such effective date, and allowing any creditor to comply with any amendments, in accordance with the regulations, forms, and clauses prescribed by the Board prior to such effective date, see section 625 of Pub. L. 96–221, set out as a note under section 1602 of this title.

EFFECTIVE DATE OF 1974 AMENDMENT

For effective date of amendment by Pub. L. 93–495, see section 308 of Pub. L. 93–495, set out as an Effective Date note under section 1666 of this title.

[1] See References in Text note below.

§1611. Criminal liability for willful and knowing violation

Whoever willfully and knowingly

(1) gives false or inaccurate information or fails to provide information which he is required to disclose under the provisions of this subchapter or any regulation issued thereunder,

(2) uses any chart or table authorized by the Bureau under section 1606 of this title in such a manner as to consistently understate the annual percentage rate determined under section 1606(a)(1)(A) of this title, or

(3) otherwise fails to comply with any requirement imposed under this subchapter,

shall be fined not more than $5,000 or imprisoned not more than one year, or both.

(Pub. L. 90–321, title I, §112, May 29, 1968, 82 Stat. 151; Pub. L. 111–203, title X, §1100A(2), July 21, 2010, 124 Stat. 2107.)

EDITORIAL NOTES

AMENDMENTS

2010—Par. (2). Pub. L. 111–203 substituted "Bureau" for "Board".

STATUTORY NOTES AND RELATED SUBSIDIARIES

EFFECTIVE DATE OF 2010 AMENDMENT

Amendment by Pub. L. 111–203 effective on the designated transfer date, see section 1100H of Pub. L. 111–203, set out as a note under section 552a of Title 5, Government Organization and Employees.

§1612. Effect on government agencies

(a) Consultation requirements respecting compliance of credit instruments issued to participating creditor

Any department or agency of the United States which administers a credit program in which it extends, insures, or guarantees consumer credit and in which it provides instruments to a creditor which contain any disclosures required by this subchapter shall, prior to the issuance or continued use of such instruments, consult with the Bureau to assure that such instruments comply with this subchapter.

(b) Inapplicability of Federal civil or criminal penalties to Federal, State, and local agencies

No civil or criminal penalty provided under this subchapter for any violation thereof may be imposed upon the United States or any department or agency thereof, or upon any State or political subdivision thereof, or any agency of any State or political subdivision.

(c) Inapplicability of Federal civil or criminal penalties to participating creditor where violating instrument issued by United States

A creditor participating in a credit program administered, insured, or guaranteed by any department or agency or the United States shall not be held liable for a civil or criminal penalty under this subchapter in any case in which the violation results from the use of an instrument required by any such department or agency.

(d) Applicability of State penalties to violations by participating creditor

A creditor participating in a credit program administered, insured, or guaranteed by any department or agency of the United States shall not be held liable for a civil or criminal penalty under the laws of any State (other than laws determined under section 1610 of this title to be inconsistent with this subchapter) for any technical or procedural failure, such as a failure to use a specific form, to make information available at a specific place on an instrument, or to use a specific typeface, as required by State law, which is caused by the use of an instrument required to be used by such department or agency.

(Pub. L. 90–321, title I, §113, May 29, 1968, 82 Stat. 151; Pub. L. 96–221, title VI, §622(a), Mar. 31, 1980, 94 Stat. 184; Pub. L. 111–203, title X, §1100A(2), July 21, 2010, 124 Stat. 2107.)

EDITORIAL NOTES

AMENDMENTS

2010—Subsec. (a). Pub. L. 111–203 substituted "Bureau" for "Board".
1980—Pub. L. 96–221 amended section generally, designating existing provisions as subsec. (b) and adding subsecs. (a), (c), and (d).

STATUTORY NOTES AND RELATED SUBSIDIARIES

EFFECTIVE DATE OF 2010 AMENDMENT

Amendment by Pub. L. 111–203 effective on the designated transfer date, see section 1100H of Pub. L. 111–203, set out as a note under section 552a of Title 5, Government Organization and Employees.

EFFECTIVE DATE OF 1980 AMENDMENT

Amendment by Pub. L. 96–221 effective on expiration of two years and six months after Mar. 31, 1980, with all regulations, forms, and clauses required to be prescribed to be promulgated at least one year prior to such effective date, and allowing any creditor to comply with any amendments, in accordance with the regulations, forms, and clauses prescribed by the Board prior to such effective date, see section 625 of Pub. L. 96–221, set out as a note under section 1602 of this title.

§1613. Annual reports to Congress by Bureau

Each year the Bureau shall make a report to the Congress concerning the administration of its functions under this subchapter, including such recommendations as the Bureau deems necessary or appropriate. In addition, each report of the Bureau shall include its assessment of the extent to which compliance with the requirements imposed under this subchapter is being achieved.

(Pub. L. 90–321, title I, §114, May 29, 1968, 82 Stat. 151; Pub. L. 96–221, title VI, §610(a), Mar. 31, 1980, 94 Stat. 174; Pub. L. 97–375, title II, §209(b), Dec. 21, 1982, 96 Stat. 1825; Pub. L. 111–203, title X, §1100A(2), July 21, 2010, 124 Stat. 2107.)

§1614. Repealed. Pub. L. 96–221, title VI, §616(b), Mar. 31, 1980, 94 Stat. 182

Section, Pub. L. 90–321, title I, §115, as added Pub. L. 93–495, title IV, §413(a), Oct. 28, 1974, 88 Stat. 1520, related to liability of assignees. See section 1641 of this title.

§1615. Prohibition on use of "Rule of 78's" in connection with mortgage refinancings and other consumer loans

(a) Prompt refund of unearned interest required

(1) In general

If a consumer prepays in full the financed amount under any consumer credit transaction, the creditor shall promptly refund any unearned portion of the interest charge to the consumer.

(2) Exception for refund of de minimus [1] amount

No refund shall be required under paragraph (1) with respect to the prepayment of any consumer credit transaction if the total amount of the refund would be less than $1.

(3) Applicability to refinanced transactions and acceleration by the creditor

This subsection shall apply with respect to any prepayment of a consumer credit transaction described in paragraph (1) without regard to the manner or the reason for the prepayment, including—

(A) any prepayment made in connection with the refinancing, consolidation, or restructuring of the transaction; and

(B) any prepayment made as a result of the acceleration of the obligation to repay the amount due with respect to the transaction.

(b) Use of "Rule of 78's" prohibited

For the purpose of calculating any refund of interest required under subsection (a) for any precomputed consumer credit transaction of a term exceeding 61 months which is consummated after September 30, 1993, the creditor shall compute the refund based on a method which is at least as favorable to the consumer as the actuarial method.

(c) Statement of prepayment amount

(1) In general

Before the end of the 5-day period beginning on the date an oral or written request is received by a creditor from a consumer for the disclosure of the amount due on any precomputed consumer credit account, the creditor or assignee shall provide the consumer with a statement of—

(A) the amount necessary to prepay the account in full; and

(B) if the amount disclosed pursuant to subparagraph (A) includes an amount which is required to be refunded under this section with respect to such prepayment, the amount of such refund.

(2) Written statement required if request is in writing

If the customer's request is in writing, the statement under paragraph (1) shall be in writing.

(3) 1 free annual statement

A consumer shall be entitled to obtain 1 statement under paragraph (1) each year without charge.

(4) Additional statements subject to reasonable fees

Any creditor may impose a reasonable fee to cover the cost of providing any statement under paragraph (1) to any consumer in addition to the 1 free annual statement required under paragraph (3) if the amount of the charge for such additional statement is disclosed to the consumer before furnishing such statement.

(d) Definitions

For the purpose of this section—

(1) Actuarial method

The term "actuarial method" means the method of allocating payments made on a debt between the amount financed and the finance charge pursuant to which a payment is applied first to the accumulated finance charge and any remainder is subtracted from, or any deficiency is added to, the unpaid balance of the amount financed.

(2) Consumer, credit

The terms "consumer" and "creditor" have the meanings given to such terms in section 1602 of this title.

(3) Creditor

The term "creditor"—

(A) has the meaning given to such term in section 1602 of this title; and

(B) includes any assignee of any creditor with respect to credit extended in connection with any consumer credit transaction and any subsequent assignee with respect to such credit.

(Pub. L. 102–550, title IX, §933, Oct. 28, 1992, 106 Stat. 3891.)

EDITORIAL NOTES

CODIFICATION

Section was enacted as part of the Housing and Community Development Act of 1992, and not as part of the Consumer Credit Protection Act which comprises this chapter.

¹ *So in original. Probably should be "de minimis".*

§1616. Board review of consumer credit plans and regulations

(a) Required review

Not later than 2 years after the effective date of this Act and every 2 years thereafter, except as provided in subsection (c)(2), the Board shall conduct a review, within the limits of its existing resources available for reporting purposes, of the consumer credit card market, including—

(1) the terms of credit card agreements and the practices of credit card issuers;

(2) the effectiveness of disclosure of terms, fees, and other expenses of credit card plans;

(3) the adequacy of protections against unfair or deceptive acts or practices relating to credit card plans; and

(4) whether or not, and to what extent, the implementation of this Act and the amendments made by this Act has affected—

(A) cost and availability of credit, particularly with respect to non-prime borrowers;

(B) the safety and soundness of credit card issuers;

(C) the use of risk-based pricing; or

(D) credit card product innovation.

(b) Solicitation of public comment

In connection with conducting the review required by subsection (a), the Board shall solicit comment from consumers, credit card issuers, and other interested parties, such as through hearings or written comments.

(c) Regulations

(1) Notice

Following the review required by subsection (a), the Board shall publish a notice in the Federal Register that—

(A) summarizes the review, the comments received from the public solicitation, and other evidence gathered by the Board, such as through consumer testing or other research; and

(B) either—

(i) proposes new or revised regulations or interpretations to update or revise disclosures and protections for consumer credit cards, as appropriate; or

(ii) states the reason for the determination of the Board that new or revised regulations are not necessary.

(2) Revision of review period following material revision of regulations

In the event that the Board materially revises regulations on consumer credit card plans, a review need not be conducted until 2 years after the effective date of the revised regulations, which thereafter shall be treated as the new date for the biennial review required by subsection (a).

(d) Board report to the Congress

The Board shall report to Congress not less frequently than every 2 years, except as provided in subsection (c)(2), on the status of its most recent review, its efforts to address any issues identified from the review, and any recommendations for legislation.

(e) Additional reporting

The Federal banking agencies (as that term is defined in section 1813 of title 12) and the Federal Trade Commission shall provide annually to the Board, and the Board shall include in its annual report to Congress under section 247 of title 12, information about the supervisory and enforcement activities of the agencies with respect to compliance by credit card issuers with applicable Federal consumer protection statutes and regulations, including—

(1) this Act, the amendments made by this Act, and regulations prescribed under this Act and such amendments; and

(2) section 5 of the Federal Trade Commission Act [15 U.S.C. 45], and regulations prescribed under the Federal Trade Commission Act [15 U.S.C. 41 et seq.], including part 227 of title 12 of the Code of Federal Regulations, as prescribed by the Board (referred to as "Regulation AA").

(Pub. L. 111–24, title V, §502, May 22, 2009, 123 Stat. 1755.)

EDITORIAL NOTES

REFERENCES IN TEXT

The effective date of this Act, referred to in subsec. (a), is 9 months after May 22, 2009, except as otherwise specifically provided in Pub. L. 111–24, see section 3 of Pub. L. 111–24, set out as an Effective Date of 2009 Amendment note under section 1602 of this title.

This Act, referred to in subsecs. (a)(4) and (e)(1), is Pub. L. 111–24, May 22, 2009, 123 Stat. 1734, known as the Credit Card Accountability Responsibility and Disclosure Act of 2009, and also as the Credit CARD Act of 2009, which enacted this section and sections 1651, 1665c to 1665e, 1666i–1, 1666i–2, and 1693l–1 of this title and section 1a–7b of Title 16, Conservation, amended sections 1602, 1632, 1637, 1640, 1650, 1666b, 1666c, 1666j, 1681b, 1681j, and 1693m to 1693r of this title, enacted provisions set out as notes under sections 1602, 1637, 1638, 1666b, 1681j, and 1693l–1 of this title and section 5311 of Title 31, Money and Finance, and amended provisions set out as notes under sections 1638 and 1693 of this title. For complete classification of this Act to the Code, see Short Title of 2009 Amendment note set out under section 1601 of this title and Tables.

The Federal Trade Commission Act, referred to in subsec. (e)(2), is act Sept. 26, 1914, ch. 311, 38 Stat. 717, which is classified generally to subchapter I (§41 et seq.) of chapter 2 of this title. For complete classification of this Act to the Code, see section 58 of this title and Tables.

CODIFICATION

Section was enacted as part of the Credit Card Accountability Responsibility and Disclosure Act of 2009, also known as the Credit CARD Act of 2009, and not as part of the Consumer Credit Protection Act which comprises this chapter.

STATUTORY NOTES AND RELATED SUBSIDIARIES

EFFECTIVE DATE

Section effective 9 months after May 22, 2009, except as otherwise specifically provided, see section 3 of Pub. L. 111–24, set out as an Effective Date of 2009 Amendment note under section 1602 of this title.

DEFINITION

For definition of "Board", see section 2 of Pub. L. 111–24, set out as a Regulations note under section 1602 of this title.

PART B—CREDIT TRANSACTIONS

§1631. Disclosure requirements

(a) Duty of creditor or lessor respecting one or more than one obligor

Subject to subsection (b), a creditor or lessor shall disclose to the person who is obligated on a consumer lease or a consumer credit transaction the information required under this subchapter. In a transaction involving more than one obligor, a creditor or lessor, except in a transaction under section 1635 of this title, need not disclose to more than one of such obligors if the obligor given disclosure is a primary obligor.

(b) Creditor or lessor required to make disclosure

If a transaction involves one creditor as defined in section 1602(f) [1] of this title, or one lessor as defined in section 1667(3) of this title, such creditor or lessor shall make the disclosures. If a transaction involves more than one creditor or lessor, only one creditor or lessor shall by required to make the disclosures. The Bureau shall by regulation specify which creditor or lessor shall make the disclosures.

(c) Estimates as satisfying statutory requirements; basis of disclosure for per diem interest

The Bureau may provide by regulation that any portion of the information required to be disclosed by this subchapter may be given in the form of estimates where the provider of such information is not in a position to know exact information. In the case of any consumer credit transaction a portion of the interest on which is determined on a per diem basis and is to be collected upon the consummation of such transaction, any disclosure with respect to such portion of interest shall be deemed to be accurate for purposes of this subchapter if the disclosure is based on information actually known to the creditor at the time that the disclosure documents are being prepared for the consummation of the transaction.

(d) Tolerances for numerical disclosures

The Bureau shall determine whether tolerances for numerical disclosures other than the annual percentage rate are necessary to facilitate compliance with this subchapter, and if it determines that such tolerances are necessary to facilitate compliance, it shall by regulation permit disclosures within such tolerances. The Bureau shall exercise its authority to permit tolerances for numerical disclosures other than the annual percentage rate so that such tolerances are narrow enough to prevent such tolerances from resulting in misleading disclosures or disclosures that circumvent the purposes of this subchapter.

(Pub. L. 90–321, title I, §121, May 29, 1968, 82 Stat. 152; Pub. L. 93–495, title III, §307(c), (d), title IV, §409, Oct. 28, 1974, 88 Stat. 1516, 1519; Pub. L. 94–205, §11, Jan. 2, 1976, 89 Stat. 1159; Pub. L. 96–221, title VI, §611, Mar. 31, 1980, 94 Stat. 174; Pub. L. 104–29, §3(b), Sept. 30, 1995, 109 Stat. 273; Pub. L. 111–203, title X, §1100A(2), July 21, 2010, 124 Stat. 2107.)

REFERENCES IN TEXT

Section 1602(f) of this title, referred to in subsec. (b), was redesignated section 1602(g) of this title by Pub. L. 111–203, title X, §1100A(1)(A), July 21, 2010, 124 Stat. 2107.

AMENDMENTS

2010—Subsecs. (b) to (d). Pub. L. 111–203 substituted "Bureau" for "Board" wherever appearing.

1995—Subsec. (c). Pub. L. 104–29 inserted at end "In the case of any consumer credit transaction a portion of the interest on which is determined on a per diem basis and is to be collected upon the consummation of such transaction, any disclosure with respect to such portion of interest shall be deemed to be accurate for purposes of this subchapter if the disclosure is based on information actually known to the creditor at the time that the disclosure documents are being prepared for the consummation of the transaction."

1980—Subsec. (a). Pub. L. 96–221 substituted provisions respecting to which obligor duty of creditor or lessor, where one or more than one obligor is involved, is owed, for provisions setting forth clear and conspicuous disclosure requirements for creditors to persons extended consumer credit.

Subsec. (b). Pub. L. 96–221 substituted provisions relating to disclosure requirements of creditor or lessor, for provisions relating to statement of information where more than one obligor is involved.

Subsecs. (c), (d). Pub. L. 96–221 added subsecs. (c) and (d).

1976—Subsec. (c). Pub. L. 94–205 struck out subsec. (c) which related to disclosure including a full statement of closing costs incurred and permitted estimates of such information where the lender was not in a position to know exact information.

1974—Subsec. (a). Pub. L. 93–495, §307(c), inserted reference to part D of this subchapter and struck out "and upon whom a finance charge is or may be imposed" after "extended".

Subsec. (b). Pub. L. 93–495, §307(d), inserted reference to part D of this subchapter.

Subsec. (c). Pub. L. 93–495, §409, added subsec (c).

STATUTORY NOTES AND RELATED SUBSIDIARIES

EFFECTIVE DATE OF 2010 AMENDMENT

Amendment by Pub. L. 111–203 effective on the designated transfer date, see section 1100H of Pub. L. 111–203, set out as a note under section 552a of Title 5, Government Organization and Employees.

EFFECTIVE DATE OF 1980 AMENDMENT

Amendment by Pub. L. 96–221 effective on expiration of two years and six months after Mar. 31, 1980, with all regulations, forms, and clauses required to be prescribed to be promulgated at least one year prior to such effective date, and allowing any creditor to comply with any amendments, in accordance with the regulations, forms, and clauses prescribed by the Board prior to such effective date, see section 625 of Pub. L. 96–221, set out as a note under section 1602 of this title.

EFFECTIVE DATE OF 1976 AMENDMENT

Amendment by Pub. L. 94–205 effective Jan. 2, 1976, see section 12 of Pub. L. 94–205, set out as a note under section 2602 of Title 12, Banks and Banking.

EFFECTIVE DATE OF 1974 AMENDMENT

For effective date of amendment by section 307(c), (d) of Pub. L. 93–495, see section 308 of Pub. L. 93–495, set out as an Effective Date note under section 1666 of this title.

For effective date of amendment by section 409 of Pub. L. 93–495, see section 416 of Pub. L. 93–495, set out as an Effective Date note under section 1665a of this title.

EFFECTIVE DATE

Pub. L. 90–321, title V, §504(b), May 29, 1968, 82 Stat. 167, provided in part that chapter 2 of title I, which enacted sections 1631 to 1641 of this title, is effective July 1, 1969.

REAL ESTATE SETTLEMENT PROCEDURES

Provisions of Real Estate Settlement Procedures Act of 1974, as superseding provisions of subsec. (c) of this section insofar as applying to federally related mortgage loans, see section 2605 of Title 12, Banks and Banking.

§1632. Form of disclosure; additional information

(a) Information clearly and conspicuously disclosed; "annual percentage rate" and "finance charge"; order of disclosures and use of different terminology

Information required by this subchapter shall be disclosed clearly and conspicuously, in accordance with regulations of the Bureau. The terms "annual percentage rate" and "finance charge" shall be disclosed more conspicuously than other terms, data, or information provided in connection with a transaction, except information relating to the identify of the creditor. Except as provided in subsection (c), regulations of the Bureau need not require that disclosures pursuant to this subchapter be made in the order set forth in this subchapter and, except as otherwise provided, may permit the use of terminology different from that employed in this subchapter if it conveys substantially the same meaning.

(b) Optional information by creditor or lessor

Any creditor or lessor may supply additional information or explanation with any disclosures required under parts D and E and, except as provided in sections 1637a(b)(3) and 1638(b)(1) of this title, under this part.

(c) Tabular format required for certain disclosures under section 1637(c)

(1) In general

The information described in paragraphs (1)(A), (3)(B)(i)(I), (4)(A), and (4)(C)(i)(I) of section 1637(c) of this title shall be—

(A) disclosed in the form and manner which the Bureau shall prescribe by regulations; and

(B) placed in a conspicuous and prominent location on or with any written application, solicitation, or other document or paper with respect to which such disclosure is required.

(2) Tabular format

(A) Form of table to be prescribed

In the regulations prescribed under paragraph (1)(A) of this subsection, the Bureau shall require that the disclosure of such information shall, to the extent the Bureau determines to be practicable and appropriate, be in the form of a table which—

(i) contains clear and concise headings for each item of such information; and

(ii) provides a clear and concise form for stating each item of information required to be disclosed under each such heading.

(B) Bureau discretion in prescribing order and wording of table

In prescribing the form of the table under subparagraph (A), the Bureau may—

(i) list the items required to be included in the table in a different order than the order in which such items are set forth in paragraph (1)(A) or (4)(A) of section 1637(c) of this title; and

(ii) subject to subparagraph (C), employ terminology which is different than the terminology which is employed in section 1637(c) of this title if such terminology conveys substantially the same meaning.

(C) Grace period

Either the heading or the statement under the heading which relates to the time period referred to in section 1637(c)(1)(A)(iii) of this title shall contain the term "grace period".

(d) Additional electronic disclosures

(1) Posting agreements

Each creditor shall establish and maintain an Internet site on which the creditor shall post the written agreement between the creditor and the consumer for each credit card account under an open-end consumer credit plan.

(2) Creditor to provide contracts to the Bureau

Each creditor shall provide to the Bureau, in electronic format, the consumer credit card agreements that it publishes on its Internet site.

(3) Record repository

The Bureau shall establish and maintain on its publicly available Internet site a central repository of the consumer credit card agreements received from creditors pursuant to this subsection, and such agreements shall be easily accessible and retrievable by the public.

(4) Exception

This subsection shall not apply to individually negotiated changes to contractual terms, such as individually modified workouts or renegotiations of amounts owed by a consumer under an open end consumer credit plan.

(5) Regulations

The Bureau, in consultation with the other Federal banking agencies (as that term is defined in section 1681a of this title) and the Bureau,[1] may promulgate regulations to implement this subsection, including specifying the format for posting the agreements on the Internet sites of creditors and establishing exceptions to paragraphs (1) and (2), in any case in which the administrative burden outweighs the benefit of increased transparency, such as where a credit card plan has a de minimis number of consumer account holders.

(Pub. L. 90–321, title I, §122, May 29, 1968, 82 Stat. 152; Pub. L. 93–495, title III, §307(e), (f), Oct. 28, 1974, 88 Stat. 1516, 1517; Pub. L. 96–221, title VI, §611, Mar. 31, 1980, 94 Stat. 175; Pub. L. 100–583, §2(b), Nov. 3, 1988, 102 Stat. 2966; Pub. L. 100–709, §2(d), Nov. 23, 1988, 102 Stat. 4731; Pub. L. 111–24, title II, §204, May 22, 2009, 123 Stat. 1746; Pub. L. 111–203, title X, §1100A(2), (3), July 21, 2010, 124 Stat. 2107.)

EDITORIAL NOTES

AMENDMENTS

2010—Subsecs. (a), (c). Pub. L. 111–203, §1100A(2), substituted "Bureau" for "Board" wherever appearing.

Subsec. (d)(2), (3). Pub. L. 111–203, §1100A(2), substituted "Bureau" for "Board" wherever appearing.

Subsec. (d)(5). Pub. L. 111–203 substituted "The Bureau, in" for "The Board, in" and "and the Bureau, may" for "and the Federal Trade Commission, may".

2009—Subsec. (d). Pub. L. 111–24 added subsec. (d).

1988—Subsec. (a). Pub. L. 100–583, §2(b)(1), substituted "Except as provided in subsection (c), regulations" for "Regulations".

Subsec. (b). Pub. L. 100–709 substituted "sections 1637a(b)(3) and 1638(b)(1)" for "section 1638(b)(1)".

Subsec. (c). Pub. L. 100–583, §2(b)(2), added subsec. (c).

1980—Subsec. (a). Pub. L. 96–221 substituted provisions setting forth form of disclosure to meet requirements of this subchapter, for provisions setting forth form of disclosure authorized under this part or part D of this subchapter.

Subsec. (b). Pub. L. 96–221 substituted provisions setting forth disclosure requirements for additional information by creditors or lessors, for provisions setting forth disclosure requirements for additional information by creditors.

1974—Subsecs. (a), (b). Pub. L. 93–495 inserted references to part D of this subchapter.

STATUTORY NOTES AND RELATED SUBSIDIARIES

EFFECTIVE DATE OF 2010 AMENDMENT

Amendment by Pub. L. 111–203 effective on the designated transfer date, see section 1100H of Pub. L. 111–203, set out as a note under section 552a of Title 5, Government Organization and Employees.

EFFECTIVE DATE OF 2009 AMENDMENT

Amendment by Pub. L. 111–24 effective 9 months after May 22, 2009, except as otherwise specifically provided, see section 3 of Pub. L. 111–24, set out as a note under section 1602 of this title.

EFFECTIVE DATE OF 1988 AMENDMENT

For effective date of amendments by Pub. L. 100–709, see Regulations; Effective Date note below.

EFFECTIVE DATE OF 1980 AMENDMENT

Amendment by Pub. L. 96–221 effective on expiration of two years and six months after Mar. 31, 1980, with all regulations, forms, and clauses required to be prescribed to be promulgated at least one year prior to such effective date, and allowing any creditor to comply with any amendments, in accordance with the regulations, forms, and clauses prescribed by the Board prior to such effective date, see section 625 of Pub. L. 96–221, set out as a note under section 1602 of this title.

EFFECTIVE DATE OF 1974 AMENDMENT

For effective date of amendment by Pub. L. 93–495, see section 308 of Pub. L. 93–495, set out as an Effective Date note under section 1666 of this title.

REGULATIONS; EFFECTIVE DATE

For provisions relating to promulgation of regulations to implement amendment by Pub. L. 100–709, and effective date of such amendment in connection with those regulations, see section 7 of Pub. L. 100–709, set out as a note under section 1637a of this title.

For provisions relating to promulgation of regulations to implement amendment by Pub. L. 100–583, and effective date of such amendment in connection with those regulations, see section 7 of Pub. L. 100–583, set out as a note under section 1637 of this title.

---

¹ So in original.

[1] So in original.

§1633. Exemption for State-regulated transactions

The Bureau shall by regulation exempt from the requirements of this part any class of credit transactions within any State if it determines that under the law of that State that class of transactions is subject to requirements substantially similar to those imposed under this part, and that there is adequate provision for enforcement.

(Pub. L. 90–321, title I, §123, May 29, 1968, 82 Stat. 152; Pub. L. 111–203, title X, §1100A(2), July 21, 2010, 124 Stat. 2107.)

EDITORIAL NOTES

AMENDMENTS

2010—Pub. L. 111–203 substituted "Bureau" for "Board".

STATUTORY NOTES AND RELATED SUBSIDIARIES

EFFECTIVE DATE OF 2010 AMENDMENT

Amendment by Pub. L. 111–203 effective on the designated transfer date, see section 1100H of Pub. L. 111–203, set out as a note under section 552a of Title 5, Government Organization and Employees.

§1634. Effect of subsequent occurrence

If information disclosed in accordance with this part is subsequently rendered inaccurate as the result of any act, occurrence, or agreement subsequent to the delivery of the required disclosures, the inaccuracy resulting therefrom does not constitute a violation of this part.

(Pub. L. 90–321, title I, §124, May 29, 1968, 82 Stat. 152.)

§1635. Right of rescission as to certain transactions

(a) Disclosure of obligor's right to rescind

Except as otherwise provided in this section, in the case of any consumer credit transaction (including opening or increasing the credit limit for an open end credit plan) in which a security interest, including any such interest arising by operation of law, is or will be retained or acquired in any property which is used as the principal dwelling of the person to whom credit is extended, the obligor shall have the right to rescind the transaction until midnight of the third business day following the consummation of the transaction or the delivery of the information and rescission forms required under this section together with a statement containing the material disclosures required under this subchapter, whichever is later, by notifying the creditor, in accordance with regulations of the Bureau, of his intention to do so. The creditor shall clearly and conspicuously disclose, in accordance with regulations of the Bureau, to any obligor in a transaction subject to this section the rights of the obligor under this section. The creditor shall also provide, in accordance with regulations of the Bureau, appropriate forms for the obligor to exercise his right to rescind any transaction subject to this section.

(b) Return of money or property following rescission

When an obligor exercises his right to rescind under subsection (a), he is not liable for any finance or other charge, and any security interest given by the obligor, including any such interest arising by operation of law, becomes void upon such a rescission. Within 20 days after receipt of a notice of rescission, the creditor shall return to the obligor any money or property given as earnest money, downpayment, or otherwise, and shall take any action necessary or appropriate to reflect the termination of any security interest created under the transaction. If the creditor has delivered any property to the obligor, the obligor may retain possession of it. Upon the performance of the creditor's obligations under this section, the obligor shall tender the property to the creditor, except that if return of the property in kind would be impracticable or inequitable, the obligor shall tender its reasonable value. Tender shall be made at the location of the property or at the residence of the obligor, at the option of the obligor. If the creditor does not take possession of the property within 20 days after tender by the obligor, ownership of the property vests in the obligor without obligation on his part to pay for it. The procedures prescribed by this subsection shall apply except when otherwise ordered by a court.

(c) Rebuttable presumption of delivery of required disclosures

Notwithstanding any rule of evidence, written acknowledgment of receipt of any disclosures required under this subchapter by a person to whom information, forms, and a statement is required to be given pursuant to this section does no more than create a rebuttable presumption of delivery thereof.

(d) Modification and waiver of rights

The Bureau may, if it finds that such action is necessary in order to permit homeowners to meet bona fide personal financial emergencies, prescribe regulations authorizing the modification or waiver of any rights created under this section to the extent and under the circumstances set forth in those regulations.

(e) Exempted transactions; reapplication of provisions

This section does not apply to—

(1) a residential mortgage transaction as defined in section 1602(w) [1] of this title;

(2) a transaction which constitutes a refinancing or consolidation (with no new advances) of the principal balance then due and any accrued and unpaid finance charges of an existing extension of credit by the same creditor secured by an interest in the same property;

(3) a transaction in which an agency of a State is the creditor; or

(4) advances under a preexisting open end credit plan if a security interest has already been retained or acquired and such advances are in accordance with a previously established credit limit for such plan.

(f) Time limit for exercise of right

An obligor's right of rescission shall expire three years after the date of consummation of the transaction or upon the sale of the property, whichever occurs first, notwithstanding the fact that the information and forms required under this section or any other disclosures required under this part have not been delivered to the obligor, except that if (1) any agency empowered to enforce the provisions of this subchapter institutes a proceeding to enforce the provisions of this section within three years after the date of consummation of the transaction, (2) such agency finds a violation of this section, and (3) the obligor's right to rescind is based in whole or in part on any matter involved in such proceeding, then the obligor's right of rescission shall expire three years after the date of consummation of the transaction or upon the earlier sale of the property, or upon the expiration of one year following the conclusion of the proceeding, or any judicial review or period for judicial review thereof, whichever is later.

(g) Additional relief

In any action in which it is determined that a creditor has violated this section, in addition to rescission the court may award relief under section 1640 of this title for violations of this subchapter not relating to the right to rescind.

(h) Limitation on rescission

An obligor shall have no rescission rights arising solely from the form of written notice used by the creditor to inform the obligor of the rights of the obligor under this section, if the creditor provided the obligor the appropriate form of written notice published and adopted by the Bureau, or a comparable written notice of the rights of the obligor, that was properly completed by the creditor, and otherwise complied with all other requirements of this section regarding notice.

(i) Rescission rights in foreclosure

(1) In general

Notwithstanding section 1649 of this title, and subject to the time period provided in subsection (f), in addition to any other right of rescission available under this section for a transaction, after the initiation of any judicial or nonjudicial foreclosure process on the primary dwelling of an obligor securing an extension of credit, the obligor shall have a right to rescind the transaction equivalent to other rescission rights provided by this section, if—

(A) a mortgage broker fee is not included in the finance charge in accordance with the laws and regulations in effect at the time the consumer credit transaction was consummated; or

(B) the form of notice of rescission for the transaction is not the appropriate form of written notice published and adopted by the Bureau or a comparable written notice, and otherwise complied with all the requirements of this section regarding notice.

(2) Tolerance for disclosures

Notwithstanding section 1605(f) of this title, and subject to the time period provided in subsection (f), for the purposes of exercising any rescission rights after the initiation of any judicial or nonjudicial foreclosure process on the principal dwelling of the obligor securing an extension of credit, the disclosure of the finance charge and other disclosures affected by any finance charge shall be treated as being accurate for purposes of this section if the amount disclosed as the finance charge does not vary from the actual finance charge by more than $35 or is greater than the amount required to be disclosed under this subchapter.

(3) Right of recoupment under State law

Nothing in this subsection affects a consumer's right of rescission in recoupment under State law.

(4) Applicability

This subsection shall apply to all consumer credit transactions in existence or consummated on or after September 30, 1995.

(Pub. L. 90–321, title I, §125, May 29, 1968, 82 Stat. 153; Pub. L. 93–495, title IV, §§404, 405, 412, Oct. 28, 1974, 88 Stat. 1517, 1519; Pub. L. 96–221, title VI, §612(a)(1), (3)–(6), Mar. 31, 1980, 94 Stat. 175, 176; Pub. L. 98–479, title II, §205, Oct. 17, 1984, 98 Stat. 2234; Pub. L. 104–29, §§5, 8, Sept. 30, 1995, 109 Stat. 274, 275; Pub. L. 111–203, title X, §1100A(2), July 21, 2010, 124 Stat. 2107.)

EDITORIAL NOTES

REFERENCES IN TEXT

Section 1602(w) of this title, referred to in subsec. (e)(1), was redesignated section 1602(x) of this title by Pub. L. 111–203, title X, §1100A(1)(A), July 21, 2010, 124 Stat. 2107.

AMENDMENTS

2010—Subsecs. (a), (d), (h), (i)(1)(B). Pub. L. 111–203 substituted "Bureau" for "Board" wherever appearing.

1995—Subsec. (h). Pub. L. 104–29, §5, added subsec. (h).

Subsec. (i). Pub. L. 104–29, §8, added subsec. (i).

1984—Subsec. (e). Pub. L. 98–479 redesignated par. (1) as subsec. (e), redesignated subpars. (A), (B), (C), and (D) of par. (1) as pars. (1), (2), (3), and (4), respectively, and struck out par. (2) which read as follows: "The provisions of paragraph (1)(D) shall cease to be effective 3 years after the effective date of the Truth in Lending Simplification Reform Act."

1980—Subsec. (a). Pub. L. 96–221, §612(a)(1), substituted provisions relating to the right of rescission until midnight of the third business day following the consummation of the transaction or the delivery of the information and rescission forms required together with the statement containing the material disclosures required under this subchapter, whichever is later, for provisions relating to right of rescission until midnight of the third business day following the consummation of the transaction or the delivery of the required disclosures and all other material disclosures required under this part, whichever is later.

Subsec. (b). Pub. L. 96–221, §612(a)(3), (4), inserted provisions setting forth applicability of procedures prescribed by this subsection, and substituted "20" for "ten" in two places.

Subsec. (c). Pub. L. 96–221, §612(a)(5), inserted "information, forms, and" after "whom".

Subsec. (e). Pub. L. 96–221, §612(a)(6), substituted provisions relating to nonapplicability to residential mortgage transactions, refinancing or consolidation transactions, etc., for provisions relating to nonapplicability to creation or retention of first liens.

Subsec. (f). Pub. L. 96–221, §612(a)(6), substituted provisions setting forth duration of right of rescission where the required information and forms or other disclosures required under this part have not been delivered to the obligor, and exceptions to such term, for provisions setting forth duration of right of rescission where the required disclosures or any other material disclosures required under this part have not been delivered to the obligor.

Subsec. (g). Pub. L. 96–221, §612(a)(6), added subsec. (g).

1974—Subsecs. (a), (b). Pub. L. 93–495, §404, inserted provisions relating to security interest arising by operation of law.

Subsec. (e). Pub. L. 93–495, §412, inserted exemption for consumer credit transactions where a State agency is the creditor.

Subsec. (f). Pub. L. 93–495, §405, added subsec. (f).

STATUTORY NOTES AND RELATED SUBSIDIARIES

EFFECTIVE DATE OF 2010 AMENDMENT

Amendment by Pub. L. 111–203 effective on the designated transfer date, see section 1100H of Pub. L. 111–203, set out as a note under section 552a of Title 5, Government Organization and Employees.

EFFECTIVE DATE OF 1980 AMENDMENT

Amendment by Pub. L. 96–221 effective on expiration of two years and six months after Mar. 31, 1980, with all regulations, forms, and clauses required to be prescribed to be promulgated at least one year prior to such effective date, and allowing any creditor to comply with any amendments, in accordance with the regulations, forms, and clauses prescribed by the Board prior to such effective date, see section 625 of Pub. L. 96–221, set out as a note under section 1602 of this title.

Amendment by Pub. L. 93–495 effective Oct. 28, 1974, see section 416 of Pub. L. 93–495, set out as an Effective Date note under section 1665a of this title.

¹ *See References in Text note below.*

§1636. Repealed. Pub. L. 96–221, title VI, §614(e)(1), Mar. 31, 1980, 94 Stat. 180

Section, Pub. L. 90–321, title I, §126, May 29, 1968, 82 Stat. 153, related to contents of periodic statements.

STATUTORY NOTES AND RELATED SUBSIDIARIES

EFFECTIVE DATE OF REPEAL

Repeal effective on expiration of two years and six months after Mar. 31, 1980, with all regulations, forms, and clauses required to be prescribed to be promulgated at least one year prior to such effective date, and allowing any creditor to comply with any amendments, in accordance with the regulations, forms, and clauses prescribed by the Board prior to such effective date, see section 625 of Pub. L. 96–221, set out as an Effective Date of 1980 Amendment note under section 1602 of this title.

§1637. Open end consumer credit plans

(a) Required disclosures by creditor

Before opening any account under an open end consumer credit plan, the creditor shall disclose to the person to whom credit is to be extended each of the following items, to the extent applicable:

(1) The conditions under which a finance charge may be imposed, including the time period (if any) within which any credit extended may be repaid without incurring a finance charge, except that the creditor may, at his election and without disclosure, impose no such finance charge if payment is received after the termination of such time period. If no such time period is provided, the creditor shall disclose such fact.

(2) The method of determining the balance upon which a finance charge will be imposed.

(3) The method of determining the amount of the finance charge, including any minimum or fixed amount imposed as a finance charge.

(4) Where one or more periodic rates may be used to compute the finance charge, each such rate, the range of balances to which it is applicable, and the corresponding nominal annual percentage rate determined by multiplying the periodic rate by the number of periods in a year.

(5) Identification of other charges which may be imposed as part of the plan, and their method of computation, in accordance with regulations of the Bureau.

(6) In cases where the credit is or will be secured, a statement that a security interest has been or will be taken in (A) the property purchased as part of the credit transaction, or (B) property not purchased as part of the credit transaction identified by item or type.

(7) A statement, in a form prescribed by regulations of the Bureau of the protection provided by sections 1666 and 1666i of this title to an obligor and the creditor's responsibilities under sections 1666a and 1666i of this title. With respect to one billing cycle per calendar year, at intervals of not less than six months or more than eighteen months, the creditor shall transmit such statement to each obligor to whom the creditor is required to transmit a statement pursuant to subsection (b) for such billing cycle.

(8) In the case of any account under an open end consumer credit plan which provides for any extension of credit which is secured by the consumer's principal dwelling, any information which—

(A) is required to be disclosed under section 1637a(a) of this title; and

(B) the Bureau determines is not described in any other paragraph of this subsection.

(b) Statement required with each billing cycle

The creditor of any account under an open end consumer credit plan shall transmit to the obligor, for each billing cycle at the end of which there is an outstanding balance in that account or with respect to which a finance charge is imposed, a statement setting forth each of the following items to the extent applicable:

(1) The outstanding balance in the account at the beginning of the statement period.

(2) The amount and date of each extension of credit during the period, and a brief identification, on or accompanying the statement of each extension of credit in a form prescribed by the Bureau sufficient to enable the obligor either to identify the transaction or to relate it to copies of sales vouchers or similar instruments previously furnished, except that a creditor's failure to disclose such information in accordance with this paragraph shall not be deemed a failure to comply with this part or this subchapter if (A) the creditor maintains procedures reasonably

adapted to procure and provide such information, and (B) the creditor responds to and treats any inquiry for clarification or documentation as a billing error and an erroneously billed amount under section 1666 of this title. In lieu of complying with the requirements of the previous sentence, in the case of any transaction in which the creditor and seller are the same person, as defined by the Bureau, and such person's open end credit plan has fewer than 15,000 accounts, the creditor may elect to provide only the amount and date of each extension of credit during the period and the seller's name and location where the transaction took place if (A) a brief identification of the transaction has been previously furnished, and (B) the creditor responds to and treats any inquiry for clarification or documentation as a billing error and an erroneously billed amount under section 1666 of this title.

(3) The total amount credited to the account during the period.

(4) The amount of any finance charge added to the account during the period, itemized to show the amounts, if any, due to the application of percentage rates and the amount, if any, imposed as a minimum or fixed charge.

(5) Where one or more periodic rates may be used to compute the finance charge, each such rate, the range of balances to which it is applicable, and, unless the annual percentage rate (determined under section 1606(a)(2) of this title) is required to be disclosed pursuant to paragraph (6), the corresponding nominal annual percentage rate determined by multiplying the periodic rate by the number of periods in a year.

(6) Where the total finance charge exceeds 50 cents for a monthly or longer billing cycle, or the pro rata part of 50 cents for a billing cycle shorter than monthly, the total finance charge expressed as an annual percentage rate (determined under section 1606(a)(2) of this title), except that if the finance charge is the sum of two or more products of a rate times a portion of the balance, the creditor may, in lieu of disclosing a single rate for the total charge, disclose each such rate expressed as an annual percentage rate, and the part of the balance to which it is applicable.

(7) The balance on which the finance charge was computed and a statement of how the balance was determined. If the balance is determined without first deducting all credits during the period, that fact and the amount of such payments shall also be disclosed.

(8) The outstanding balance in the account at the end of the period.

(9) The date by which or the period (if any) within which, payment must be made to avoid additional finance charges, except that the creditor may, at his election and without disclosure, impose no such additional finance charge if payment is received after such date or the termination of such period.

(10) The address to be used by the creditor for the purpose of receiving billing inquiries from the obligor.

(11)(A) A written statement in the following form: "Minimum Payment Warning: Making only the minimum payment will increase the amount of interest you pay and the time it takes to repay your balance.", or such similar statement as is established by the Bureau pursuant to consumer testing.

(B) Repayment information that would apply to the outstanding balance of the consumer under the credit plan, including—

(i) the number of months (rounded to the nearest month) that it would take to pay the entire amount of that balance, if the consumer pays only the required minimum monthly payments and if no further advances are made;

(ii) the total cost to the consumer, including interest and principal payments, of paying that balance in full, if the consumer pays only the required minimum monthly payments and if no further advances are made;

(iii) the monthly payment amount that would be required for the consumer to eliminate the outstanding balance in 36 months, if no further advances are made, and the total cost to the consumer, including interest and principal payments, of paying that balance in full if the consumer pays the balance over 36 months; and

(iv) a toll-free telephone number at which the consumer may receive information about accessing credit counseling and debt management services.

(C)(i) Subject to clause (ii), in making the disclosures under subparagraph (B), the creditor shall apply the interest rate or rates in effect on the date on which the disclosure is made until the date on which the balance would be paid in full.

(ii) If the interest rate in effect on the date on which the disclosure is made is a temporary rate that will change under a contractual provision applying an index or formula for subsequent interest rate adjustment, the creditor shall apply the interest rate in effect on the date on which the disclosure is made for as long as that interest rate will apply under that contractual provision, and then apply an interest rate based on the index or formula in effect on the applicable billing date.

(D) All of the information described in subparagraph (B) shall—

(i) be disclosed in the form and manner which the Bureau shall prescribe, by regulation, and in a manner that avoids duplication; and

(ii) be placed in a conspicuous and prominent location on the billing statement.

(E) In the regulations prescribed under subparagraph (D), the Bureau shall require that the disclosure of such information shall be in the form of a table that—

(i) contains clear and concise headings for each item of such information; and

(ii) provides a clear and concise form stating each item of information required to be disclosed under each such heading.

(F) In prescribing the form of the table under subparagraph (E), the Bureau shall require that—

(i) all of the information in the table, and not just a reference to the table, be placed on the billing statement, as required by this paragraph; and

(ii) the items required to be included in the table shall be listed in the order in which such items are set forth in subparagraph (B).

(G) In prescribing the form of the table under subparagraph (D), the Bureau shall employ terminology which is different than the terminology which is employed in subparagraph (B), if such terminology is more easily understood and conveys substantially the same meaning.

(12) REQUIREMENTS RELATING TO LATE PAYMENT DEADLINES AND PENALTIES.—

(A) LATE PAYMENT DEADLINE REQUIRED TO BE DISCLOSED.—In the case of a credit card account under an open end consumer credit plan under which a late fee or charge may be imposed due to the failure of the obligor to make payment on or before the due date for such payment, the periodic statement required under subsection (b) with respect to the account shall include, in a conspicuous location on the billing statement, the date on which the payment is due or, if different, the date on which a late payment fee will be charged, together with the amount of the fee or charge to be imposed if payment is made after that date.

(B) DISCLOSURE OF INCREASE IN INTEREST RATES FOR LATE PAYMENTS.—If 1 or more late payments under an open end consumer credit plan may result in an increase in the annual percentage rate applicable to the account, the statement required under subsection (b) with respect to the account shall include conspicuous notice of such fact, together with the applicable penalty annual percentage rate, in close proximity to the disclosure required under subparagraph (A) of the date on which payment is due under the terms of the account.

(C) PAYMENTS AT LOCAL BRANCHES.—If the creditor, in the case of a credit card account referred to in subparagraph (A), is a financial institution which maintains branches or offices at which payments on any such account are accepted from the obligor in person, the date on which the obligor makes a payment on the account at such branch or office shall be considered to be the date on which the payment is made for purposes of determining whether a late fee or charge may be imposed due to the failure of the obligor to make payment on or before the due date for such payment.

(c) Disclosure in credit and charge card applications and solicitations

(1) Direct mail applications and solicitations

(A) Information in tabular format

Any application to open a credit card account for any person under an open end consumer credit plan, or a solicitation to open such an account without requiring an application, that is mailed to consumers shall disclose the following information, subject to subsection (e) and section 1632(c) of this title:

(i) Annual percentage rates

(I) Each annual percentage rate applicable to extensions of credit under such credit plan.

(II) Where an extension of credit is subject to a variable rate, the fact that the rate is variable, the annual percentage rate in effect at the time of the mailing, and how the rate is determined.

(III) Where more than one rate applies, the range of balances to which each rate applies.

(ii) Annual and other fees

(I) Any annual fee, other periodic fee, or membership fee imposed for the issuance or availability of a credit card, including any account maintenance fee or other charge imposed based on activity or inactivity for the account during the billing cycle.

(II) Any minimum finance charge imposed for each period during which any extension of credit which is subject to a finance charge is outstanding.

(III) Any transaction charge imposed in connection with use of the card to purchase goods or services.

(iii) Grace period

(I) The date by which or the period within which any credit extended under such credit plan for purchases of goods or services must be repaid to avoid incurring a finance charge, and, if no such period is offered, such fact shall be clearly stated.

(II) If the length of such "grace period" varies, the card issuer may disclose the range of days in the grace period, the minimum number of days in the grace period, or the average number of days in the grace period, if the disclosure is identified as such.

(iv) Balance calculation method

(I) The name of the balance calculation method used in determining the balance on which the finance charge is computed if the method used has been defined by the Bureau, or a detailed explanation of the balance calculation method used if the method has not been so defined.

(II) In prescribing regulations to carry out this clause, the Bureau shall define and name not more than the 5 balance calculation methods determined by the Bureau to be the most commonly used methods.

(B) Other information

In addition to the information required to be disclosed under subparagraph (A), each application or solicitation to which such subparagraph applies shall disclose clearly and conspicuously the following information, subject to subsections (e) and (f):

(i) Cash advance fee

Any fee imposed for an extension of credit in the form of cash.

(ii) Late fee

Any fee imposed for a late payment.

(iii) Over-the-limit fee

Any fee imposed in connection with an extension of credit in excess of the amount of credit authorized to be extended with respect to such account.

(2) Telephone solicitations

(A) In general

In any telephone solicitation to open a credit card account for any person under an open end consumer credit plan, the person making the solicitation shall orally disclose the information described in paragraph (1)(A).

(B) Exception

Subparagraph (A) shall not apply to any telephone solicitation if—
(i) the credit card issuer—
(I) does not impose any fee described in paragraph (1)(A)(ii)(I); or
(II) does not impose any fee in connection with telephone solicitations unless the consumer signifies acceptance by using the card;

(ii) the card issuer discloses clearly and conspicuously in writing the information described in paragraph (1) within 30 days after the consumer requests the card, but in no event later than the date of delivery of the card; and
(iii) the card issuer discloses clearly and conspicuously that the consumer is not obligated to accept the card or account and the consumer will not be obligated to pay any of the fees or charges disclosed unless the consumer elects to accept the card or account by using the card.

(3) Applications and solicitations by other means

(A) In general

Any application to open a credit card account for any person under an open end consumer credit plan, and any solicitation to open such an account without requiring an application, that is made available to the public or contained in catalogs, magazines, or other publications shall meet the disclosure requirements of subparagraph (B), (C), or (D).

(B) Specific information

An application or solicitation described in subparagraph (A) meets the requirement of this subparagraph if such application or solicitation contains—
(i) the information—
(I) described in paragraph (1)(A) in the form required under section 1632(c) of this title, subject to subsection (e), and
(II) described in paragraph (1)(B) in a clear and conspicuous form, subject to subsections (e) and (f);

(ii) a statement, in a conspicuous and prominent location on the application or solicitation, that—
(I) the information is accurate as of the date the application or solicitation was printed;
(II) the information contained in the application or solicitation is subject to change after such date; and
(III) the applicant should contact the creditor for information on any change in the information contained in the application or solicitation since it was printed;

(iii) a clear and conspicuous disclosure of the date the application or solicitation was printed; and
(iv) a disclosure, in a conspicuous and prominent location on the application or solicitation, of a toll free telephone number or a mailing address at which the applicant may contact the creditor to obtain any change in the information provided in the application or solicitation since it was printed.

(C) General information without any specific term

An application or solicitation described in subparagraph (A) meets the requirement of this subparagraph if such application or solicitation—
(i) contains a statement, in a conspicuous and prominent location on the application or solicitation, that—
(I) there are costs associated with the use of credit cards; and
(II) the applicant may contact the creditor to request disclosure of specific information of such costs by calling a toll free telephone number or by writing to an address, specified in the application;

(ii) contains a disclosure, in a conspicuous and prominent location on the application or solicitation, of a toll free telephone number and a mailing address at which the applicant may contact the creditor to obtain such information; and

(iii) does not contain any of the items described in paragraph (1).

(D) Applications or solicitations containing subsection (a) disclosures

An application or solicitation meets the requirement of this subparagraph if it contains, or is accompanied by—

(i) the disclosures required by paragraphs (1) through (6) of subsection (a);

(ii) the disclosures required by subparagraphs (A) and (B) of paragraph (1) of this subsection included clearly and conspiciously [1] (except that the provisions of section 1632(c) of this title shall not apply); and

(iii) a toll free telephone number or a mailing address at which the applicant may contact the creditor to obtain any change in the information provided.

(E) Prompt response to information requests

Upon receipt of a request for any of the information referred to in subparagraph (B), (C), or (D), the card issuer or the agent of such issuer shall promptly disclose all of the information described in paragraph (1).

(4) Charge card applications and solicitations

(A) In general

Any application or solicitation to open a charge card account shall disclose clearly and conspicuously the following information in the form required by section 1632(c) of this title, subject to subsection (e):

(i) Any annual fee, other periodic fee, or membership fee imposed for the issuance or availability of the charge card, including any account maintenance fee or other charge imposed based on activity or inactivity for the account during the billing cycle.

(ii) Any transaction charge imposed in connection with use of the card to purchase goods or services.

(iii) A statement that charges incurred by use of the charge card are due and payable upon receipt of a periodic statement rendered for such charge card account.

(B) Other information

In addition to the information required to be disclosed under subparagraph (A), each written application or solicitation to which such subparagraph applies shall disclose clearly and conspicuously the following information, subject to subsections (e) and (f):

(i) Cash advance fee

Any fee imposed for an extension of credit in the form of cash.

(ii) Late fee

Any fee imposed for a late payment.

(iii) Over-the-limit fee

Any fee imposed in connection with an extension of credit in excess of the amount of credit authorized to be extended with respect to such account.

(C) Applications and solicitations by other means

Any application to open a charge card account, and any solicitation to open such an account without requiring an application, that is made available to the public or contained in catalogs, magazines, or other publications shall contain—

(i) the information—

(I) described in subparagraph (A) in the form required under section 1632(c) of this title, subject to subsection (e), and

(II) described in subparagraph (B) in a clear and conspicuous form, subject to subsections (e) and (f);

(ii) a statement, in a conspicuous and prominent location on the application or solicitation, that—

(I) the information is accurate as of the date the application or solicitation was printed;

(II) the information contained in the application or solicitation is subject to change after such date; and

(III) the applicant should contact the creditor for information on any change in the information contained in the application or solicitation since it was printed;

(iii) a clear and conspicuous disclosure of the date the application or solicitation was printed; and

(iv) a disclosure, in a conspicuous and prominent location on the application or solicitation, of a toll free telephone number or a mailing address at which the applicant may contact the creditor to obtain any change in the information provided in the application or solicitation since it was printed.

(D) Issuers of charge cards which provide access to open end consumer credit plans

If a charge card permits the card holder to receive an extension of credit under an open end consumer credit plan, which is not maintained by the charge card issuer, the charge card issuer may provide the information described in subparagraphs (A) and (B) in the form required by such subparagraphs in lieu of the information required to be provided under paragraph (1), (2), or (3) with respect to any credit extended under such plan, if the charge card issuer discloses clearly and conspicuously to the consumer in the application or solicitation that—

    (i) the charge card issuer will make an independent decision as to whether to issue the card;

    (ii) the charge card may arrive before the decision is made with respect to an extension of credit under an open end consumer credit plan; and

    (iii) approval by the charge card issuer does not constitute approval by the issuer of the extension of credit.

The information required to be disclosed under paragraph (1) shall be provided to the charge card holder by the creditor which maintains such open end consumer credit plan before the first extension of credit under such plan.

(E) Charge card defined

For the purposes of this subsection, the term "charge card" means a card, plate, or other single credit device that may be used from time to time to obtain credit which is not subject to a finance charge.

(5) Regulatory authority of the Bureau

The Bureau may, by regulation, require the disclosure of information in addition to that otherwise required by this subsection or subsection (d), and modify any disclosure of information required by this subsection or subsection (d), in any application to open a credit card account for any person under an open end consumer credit plan or any application to open a charge card account for any person, or a solicitation to open any such account without requiring an application, if the Bureau determines that such action is necessary to carry out the purposes of, or prevent evasions of, any paragraph of this subsection.

(6) Additional notice concerning "introductory rates"

(A) In general

Except as provided in subparagraph (B), an application or solicitation to open a credit card account and all promotional materials accompanying such application or solicitation for which a disclosure is required under paragraph (1), and that offers a temporary annual percentage rate of interest, shall—

    (i) use the term "introductory" in immediate proximity to each listing of the temporary annual percentage rate applicable to such account, which term shall appear clearly and conspicuously;

    (ii) if the annual percentage rate of interest that will apply after the end of the temporary rate period will be a fixed rate, state in a clear and conspicuous manner in a prominent location closely proximate to the first listing of the temporary annual percentage rate (other than a listing of the temporary annual percentage rate in the tabular format described in section 1632(c) of this title), the time period in which the introductory period will end and the annual percentage rate that will apply after the end of the introductory period; and

    (iii) if the annual percentage rate that will apply after the end of the temporary rate period will vary in accordance with an index, state in a clear and conspicuous manner in a prominent location closely proximate to the first listing of the temporary annual percentage rate (other than a listing in the tabular format prescribed by section 1632(c) of this title), the time period in which the introductory period will end and the rate that will apply after that, based on an annual percentage rate that was in effect within 60 days before the date of mailing the application or solicitation.

(B) Exception

Clauses (ii) and (iii) of subparagraph (A) do not apply with respect to any listing of a temporary annual percentage rate on an envelope or other enclosure in which an application or solicitation to open a credit card account is mailed.

(C) Conditions for introductory rates

An application or solicitation to open a credit card account for which a disclosure is required under paragraph (1), and that offers a temporary annual percentage rate of interest shall, if that rate of interest is revocable under any circumstance or upon any event, clearly and conspicuously disclose, in a prominent manner on or with such application or solicitation—

    (i) a general description of the circumstances that may result in the revocation of the temporary annual percentage rate; and

    (ii) if the annual percentage rate that will apply upon the revocation of the temporary annual percentage rate—

        (I) will be a fixed rate, the annual percentage rate that will apply upon the revocation of the temporary annual percentage rate; or

        (II) will vary in accordance with an index, the rate that will apply after the temporary rate, based on an annual percentage rate that was in effect within 60 days before the date of mailing the application or solicitation.

(D) Definitions

In this paragraph—

    (i) the terms "temporary annual percentage rate of interest" and "temporary annual percentage rate" mean any rate of interest applicable to a credit card account for an introductory period of less than 1 year, if that rate is less than an annual percentage rate that was in effect within 60 days before the date of mailing the application or solicitation; and

(ii) the term "introductory period" means the maximum time period for which the temporary annual percentage rate may be applicable.

(E) Relation to other disclosure requirements

Nothing in this paragraph may be construed to supersede subsection (a) of section 1632 of this title, or any disclosure required by paragraph (1) or any other provision of this subsection.

(7) Internet-based solicitations

(A) In general

In any solicitation to open a credit card account for any person under an open end consumer credit plan using the Internet or other interactive computer service, the person making the solicitation shall clearly and conspicuously disclose—

(i) the information described in subparagraphs (A) and (B) of paragraph (1); and

(ii) the information described in paragraph (6).

(B) Form of disclosure

The disclosures required by subparagraph (A) shall be—

(i) readily accessible to consumers in close proximity to the solicitation to open a credit card account; and

(ii) updated regularly to reflect the current policies, terms, and fee amounts applicable to the credit card account.

(C) Definitions

For purposes of this paragraph—

(i) the term "Internet" means the international computer network of both Federal and non-Federal interoperable packet switched data networks; and

(ii) the term "interactive computer service" means any information service, system, or access software provider that provides or enables computer access by multiple users to a computer server, including specifically a service or system that provides access to the Internet and such systems operated or services offered by libraries or educational institutions.

(8) Applications from underage consumers

(A) Prohibition on issuance

No credit card may be issued to, or open end consumer credit plan established by or on behalf of, a consumer who has not attained the age of 21, unless the consumer has submitted a written application to the card issuer that meets the requirements of subparagraph (B).

(B) Application requirements

An application to open a credit card account by a consumer who has not attained the age of 21 as of the date of submission of the application shall require—

(i) the signature of a cosigner, including the parent, legal guardian, spouse, or any other individual who has attained the age of 21 having a means to repay debts incurred by the consumer in connection with the account, indicating joint liability for debts incurred by the consumer in connection with the account before the consumer has attained the age of 21; or

(ii) submission by the consumer of financial information, including through an application, indicating an independent means of repaying any obligation arising from the proposed extension of credit in connection with the account.

(C) Safe harbor

The Bureau shall promulgate regulations providing standards that, if met, would satisfy the requirements of subparagraph (B)(ii).

(d) Disclosure prior to renewal

(1) In general

A card issuer that has changed or amended any term of the account since the last renewal that has not been previously disclosed or that imposes any fee described in subsection (c)(1)(A)(ii)(I) or (c)(4)(A)(i) shall transmit to a consumer at least 30 days prior to the scheduled renewal date of the consumer's credit or charge card account a clear and conspicuous disclosure of—

(A) the date by which, the month by which, or the billing period at the close of which, the account will expire if not renewed;

(B) the information described in subsection (c)(1)(A) or (c)(4)(A) that would apply if the account were renewed, subject to subsection (e); and

(C) the method by which the consumer may terminate continued credit availability under the account.

(2) Short-term renewals

The Bureau may by regulation provide for fewer disclosures than are required by paragraph (1) in the case of an account which is renewable for a period of less than 6 months.

(e) Other rules for disclosures under subsections (c) and (d)

(1) Fees determined on the basis of a percentage

If the amount of any fee required to be disclosed under subsection (c) or (d) is determined on the basis of a percentage of another amount, the percentage used in making such determination and the identification of the amount against which such percentage is applied shall be disclosed in lieu of the amount of such fee.

(2) Disclosure only of fees actually imposed

If a credit or charge card issuer does not impose any fee required to be disclosed under any provision of subsection (c) or (d), such provision shall not apply with respect to such issuer.

(f) Disclosure of range of certain fees which vary by State allowed

If the amount of any fee required to be disclosed by a credit or charge card issuer under paragraph (1)(B), (3)(B)(i)(II), (4)(B), or (4)(C)(i)(II) of subsection (c) varies from State to State, the card issuer may disclose the range of such fees for purposes of subsection (c) in lieu of the amount for each applicable State, if such disclosure includes a statement that the amount of such fee varies from State to State.

(g) Insurance in connection with certain open end credit card plans

(1) Change in insurance carrier

Whenever a card issuer that offers any guarantee or insurance for repayment of all or part of the outstanding balance of an open end credit card plan proposes to change the person providing that guarantee or insurance, the card issuer shall send each insured consumer written notice of the proposed change not less than 30 days prior to the change, including notice of any increase in the rate or substantial decrease in coverage or service which will result from such change. Such notice may be included on or with the monthly statement provided to the consumer prior to the month in which the proposed change would take effect.

(2) Notice of new insurance coverage

In any case in which a proposed change described in paragraph (1) occurs, the insured consumer shall be given the name and address of the new guarantor or insurer and a copy of the policy or group certificate containing the basic terms and conditions, including the premium rate to be charged.

(3) Right to discontinue guarantee or insurance

The notices required under paragraphs (1) and (2) shall each include a statement that the consumer has the option to discontinue the insurance or guarantee.

(4) No preemption of State law

No provision of this subsection shall be construed as superseding any provision of State law which is applicable to the regulation of insurance.

(5) Bureau definition of substantial decrease in coverage or service

The Bureau shall define, in regulations, what constitutes a "substantial decrease in coverage or service" for purposes of paragraph (1).

(h) Prohibition on certain actions for failure to incur finance charges

A creditor of an account under an open end consumer credit plan may not terminate an account prior to its expiration date solely because the consumer has not incurred finance charges on the account. Nothing in this subsection shall prohibit a creditor from terminating an account for inactivity in 3 or more consecutive months.

(i) Advance notice of rate increase and other changes required

(1) Advance notice of increase in interest rate required

In the case of any credit card account under an open end consumer credit plan, a creditor shall provide a written notice of an increase in an annual percentage rate (except in the case of an increase described in paragraph (1), (2), or (3) of section 1666i–1(b) of this title) not later than 45 days prior to the effective date of the increase.

(2) Advance notice of other significant changes required

In the case of any credit card account under an open end consumer credit plan, a creditor shall provide a written notice of any significant change, as determined by rule of the Bureau, in the terms (including an increase in any fee or finance charge, other than as provided in paragraph (1)) of the cardholder agreement between the creditor and the obligor, not later than 45 days prior to the effective date of the change.

(3) Notice of right to cancel

Each notice required by paragraph (1) or (2) shall be made in a clear and conspicuous manner, and shall contain a brief statement of the right of the obligor to cancel the account pursuant to rules established by the Bureau before the effective date of the subject rate increase or other change.

(4) Rule of construction

Closure or cancellation of an account by the obligor shall not constitute a default under an existing cardholder agreement, and shall not trigger an obligation to immediately repay the obligation in full or through a method that is less beneficial to the obligor than one of the methods described in section 1666i–1(c)(2) of this title, or the imposition of any other penalty or fee.

(j) Prohibition on penalties for on-time payments

(1) Prohibition on double-cycle billing and penalties for on-time payments

Except as provided in paragraph (2), a creditor may not impose any finance charge on a credit card account under an open end consumer credit plan as a result of the loss of any time period provided by the creditor within which the obligor may repay any portion of the credit extended without incurring a finance charge, with respect to—
    (A) any balances for days in billing cycles that precede the most recent billing cycle; or
    (B) any balances or portions thereof in the current billing cycle that were repaid within such time period.

(2) Exceptions

Paragraph (1) does not apply to—
    (A) any adjustment to a finance charge as a result of the resolution of a dispute; or
    (B) any adjustment to a finance charge as a result of the return of a payment for insufficient funds.

(k) Opt-in required for over-the-limit transactions if fees are imposed

(1) In general

In the case of any credit card account under an open end consumer credit plan under which an over-the-limit fee may be imposed by the creditor for any extension of credit in excess of the amount of credit authorized to be extended under such account, no such fee shall be charged, unless the consumer has expressly elected to permit the creditor, with respect to such account, to complete transactions involving the extension of credit under such account in excess of the amount of credit authorized.

(2) Disclosure by creditor

No election by a consumer under paragraph (1) shall take effect unless the consumer, before making such election, received a notice from the creditor of any over-the-limit fee in the form and manner, and at the time, determined by the Bureau. If the consumer makes the election referred to in paragraph (1), the creditor shall provide notice to the consumer of the right to revoke the election, in the form prescribed by the Bureau, in any periodic statement that includes notice of the imposition of an over-the-limit fee during the period covered by the statement.

(3) Form of election

A consumer may make or revoke the election referred to in paragraph (1) orally, electronically, or in writing, pursuant to regulations prescribed by the Bureau. The Bureau shall prescribe regulations to ensure that the same options are available for both making and revoking such election.

(4) Time of election

A consumer may make the election referred to in paragraph (1) at any time, and such election shall be effective until the election is revoked in the manner prescribed under paragraph (3).

(5) Regulations

The Bureau shall prescribe regulations—
    (A) governing disclosures under this subsection; and
    (B) that prevent unfair or deceptive acts or practices in connection with the manipulation of credit limits designed to increase over-the-limit fees or other penalty fees.

(6) Rule of construction

Nothing in this subsection shall be construed to prohibit a creditor from completing an over-the-limit transaction, provided that a consumer who has not made a valid election under paragraph (1) is not charged an over-the-limit fee for such transaction.

(7) Restriction on fees charged for an over-the-limit transaction

With respect to a credit card account under an open end consumer credit plan, an over-the-limit fee may be imposed only once during a billing cycle if the credit limit on the account is exceeded, and an over-the-limit fee, with respect to such excess credit, may be imposed only once in each of the 2 subsequent billing cycles, unless the consumer has obtained an additional extension of credit in excess of such credit limit during any such subsequent cycle or the consumer reduces the outstanding balance below the credit limit as of the end of such billing cycle.

(l) Limit on fees related to method of payment

With respect to a credit card account under an open end consumer credit plan, the creditor may not impose a separate fee to allow the obligor to repay an extension of credit or finance charge, whether such repayment is made by mail, electronic transfer, telephone authorization, or other means, unless such payment involves an expedited service by a service representative of the creditor.

(m) Use of term "fixed rate"

With respect to the terms of any credit card account under an open end consumer credit plan, the term "fixed", when appearing in conjunction with a reference to the annual percentage rate or interest rate applicable with respect to such account, may only be used to refer to an annual percentage rate or interest rate that will not change or vary for any reason over the period specified clearly and conspicuously in the terms of the account.

(n) Standards applicable to initial issuance of subprime or "fee harvester" cards

(1) In general

If the terms of a credit card account under an open end consumer credit plan require the payment of any fees (other than any late fee, over-the-limit fee, or fee for a payment returned for insufficient funds) by the consumer in the first year during which the account is opened in an aggregate amount in excess of 25 percent of the total amount of credit authorized under the account when the account is opened, no payment of any fees (other than any late fee, over-the-limit fee, or fee for a payment returned for insufficient funds) may be made from the credit made available under the terms of the account.

(2) Rule of construction

No provision of this subsection may be construed as authorizing any imposition or payment of advance fees otherwise prohibited by any provision of law.

(o) Due dates for credit card accounts

(1) In general

The payment due date for a credit card account under an open end consumer credit plan shall be the same day each month.

(2) Weekend or holiday due dates

If the payment due date for a credit card account under an open end consumer credit plan is a day on which the creditor does not receive or accept payments by mail (including weekends and holidays), the creditor may not treat a payment received on the next business day as late for any purpose.

(p) Parental approval required to increase credit lines for accounts for which parent is jointly liable

No increase may be made in the amount of credit authorized to be extended under a credit card account for which a parent, legal guardian, or spouse of the consumer, or any other individual has assumed joint liability for debts incurred by the consumer in connection with the account before the consumer attains the age of 21, unless that parent, guardian, or spouse approves in writing, and assumes joint liability for, such increase.

(r) [2] College card agreements

(1) Definitions

For purposes of this subsection, the following definitions shall apply:

(A) College affinity card

The term "college affinity card" means a credit card issued by a credit card issuer under an open end consumer credit plan in conjunction with an agreement between the issuer and an institution of higher education, or an alumni organization or foundation affiliated with or related to such institution, under which such cards are issued to college students who have an affinity with such institution, organization and—
(i) the creditor has agreed to donate a portion of the proceeds of the credit card to the institution, organization, or foundation (including a lump sum or 1-time payment of money for access);
(ii) the creditor has agreed to offer discounted terms to the consumer; or
(iii) the credit card bears the name, emblem, mascot, or logo of such institution, organization, or foundation, or other words, pictures, or symbols readily identified with such institution, organization, or foundation.

(B) College student credit card account

The term "college student credit card account" means a credit card account under an open end consumer credit plan established or maintained for or on behalf of any college student.

(C) College student

The term "college student" means an individual who is a full-time or a part-time student attending an institution of higher education.

(D) Institution of higher education

The term "institution of higher education" has the same meaning as in section [3] 1001 and 1002 of title 20.

(2) Reports by creditors

(A) In general

Each creditor shall submit an annual report to the Bureau containing the terms and conditions of all business, marketing, and promotional agreements and college affinity card agreements with an institution of higher education, or an alumni organization or foundation affiliated with or related to such institution, with respect to any college student credit card issued to a college student at such institution.

(B) Details of report

The information required to be reported under subparagraph (A) includes—

(i) any memorandum of understanding between or among a creditor, an institution of higher education, an alumni association, or foundation that directly or indirectly relates to any aspect of any agreement referred to in such subparagraph or controls or directs any obligations or distribution of benefits between or among any such entities;

(ii) the amount of any payments from the creditor to the institution, organization, or foundation during the period covered by the report, and the precise terms of any agreement under which such amounts are determined; and

(iii) the number of credit card accounts covered by any such agreement that were opened during the period covered by the report, and the total number of credit card accounts covered by the agreement that were outstanding at the end of such period.

(C) Aggregation by institution

The information required to be reported under subparagraph (A) shall be aggregated with respect to each institution of higher education or alumni organization or foundation affiliated with or related to such institution.

(D) Initial report

The initial report required under subparagraph (A) shall be submitted to the Bureau before the end of the 9-month period beginning on May 22, 2009.

(3) Reports by Bureau

The Bureau shall submit to the Congress, and make available to the public, an annual report that lists the information concerning credit card agreements submitted to the Bureau under paragraph (2) by each institution of higher education, alumni organization, or foundation.

(Pub. L. 90–321, title I, §127, May 29, 1968, 82 Stat. 153; Pub. L. 93–495, title III, §§304, 305, title IV, §§411, 415, Oct. 28, 1974, 88 Stat. 1511, 1519, 1521; Pub. L. 96–221, title VI, §613(a)–(e), Mar. 31, 1980, 94 Stat. 176, 177; Pub. L. 100–583, §§2(a), 6, Nov. 3, 1988, 102 Stat. 2960, 2968; Pub. L. 100–709, §2(b), Nov. 23, 1988, 102 Stat. 4729; Pub. L. 109–8, title XIII, §§1301(a), 1303(a), 1304(a), 1305(a), 1306(a), Apr. 20, 2005, 119 Stat. 204, 209, 211, 212; Pub. L. 111–24, title I, §§101(a)(1), 102(a), 103, 105, 106(a), title II, §§201(a), 202, 203, title III, §§301, 303, 305(a), May 22, 2009, 123 Stat. 1735, 1738, 1741-1743, 1745-1749; Pub. L. 111–203, title X, §1100A(2), July 21, 2010, 124 Stat. 2107.)

EDITORIAL NOTES

AMENDMENTS

2010—Pub. L. 111–203 substituted "Bureau" for "Board" wherever appearing.

2009—Subsec. (b)(11). Pub. L. 111–24, §201(a), amended par. (11) generally, revising the minimum payment disclosures required from creditors.

Subsec. (b)(12). Pub. L. 111–24, §202, amended par. (12) generally. Prior to amendment, par. (12) read as follows: "If a late payment fee is to be imposed due to the failure of the obligor to make payment on or before a required payment due date, the following shall be stated clearly and conspicuously on the billing statement:

"(A) The date on which that payment is due or, if different, the earliest date on which a late payment fee may be charged.

"(B) The amount of the late payment fee to be imposed if payment is made after such date."

Subsec. (c)(8). Pub. L. 111–24, §301, added par. (8).

Subsec. (d)(1). Pub. L. 111–24, §203(3), substituted "A card issuer that has changed or amended any term of the account since the last renewal that has not been previously disclosed or" for "Except as provided in paragraph (2), a card issuer" in introductory provisions.

Subsec. (d)(2), (3). Pub. L. 111–24, §203(1), (2), redesignated par. (3) as (2) and struck out former par. (2) which provided a special rule for certain disclosures.

Subsec. (i). Pub. L. 111–24, §101(a)(1), added subsec. (i).

Subsecs. (j) to (l). Pub. L. 111–24, §102(a), added subsecs. (j) to (l).

Subsec. (m). Pub. L. 111–24, §103, added subsec. (m).

Subsec. (n). Pub. L. 111–24, §105, added subsec. (n).

Subsec. (o). Pub. L. 111–24, §106(a), added subsec. (o).

Subsec. (p). Pub. L. 111–24, §303, added subsec. (p).

Subsec. (r). Pub. L. 111–24, §305(a), added subsec. (r).

2005—Subsec. (b)(11). Pub. L. 109–8, §1301(a), added par. (11).

Subsec. (b)(12). Pub. L. 109–8, §1305(a), added par. (12).

Subsec. (c)(6). Pub. L. 109–8, §1303(a), added par. (6).

Subsec. (c)(7). Pub. L. 109–8, §1304(a), added par. (7).

Subsec. (h). Pub. L. 109–8, §1306(a), added subsec. (h).

1988—Subsec. (a)(8). Pub. L. 100–709 added par. (8).

Subsecs. (c) to (f). Pub. L. 100–583, §2(a), added subsecs. (c) to (f).

Subsec. (g). Pub. L. 100–583, §6, added subsec. (g).

1980—Subsec. (a)(1). Pub. L. 96–221, §613(a)(1), inserted provisions requiring the creditor to disclose that no time period is provided.

Subsec. (a)(5). Pub. L. 96–221, §613(a)(2), (3), redesignated par. (6) as (5) and inserted provisions relating to identification of other charges, and regulations by the Board. Former par. (5), relating to elective rights of the creditor, was struck out.

Subsec. (a)(6). Pub. L. 96–221, §613(a)(2), (3), redesignated par. (7) as (6) and revised nomenclature and expanded statement requirements. Former par. (6) redesignated (5).

Subsec. (a)(7), (8). Pub. L. 96–221, §613(a)(2), (d), redesignated par. (8) as (7) and substituted provisions relating to one billing cycle per calendar year, for provisions relating to each of two billing cycles per year. Former par. (7) redesignated (6).

Subsec. (b)(2). Pub. L. 96–221, §613(b), inserted provisions relating to failure of the creditor to disclose information in accordance with this paragraph, and made minor changes in phraseology.

Subsec. (b)(7) to (11). Pub. L. 96–221, §613(c), struck out par. (7) which related to elective rights of the creditor, and redesignated pars. (8) to (11) as (7) to (10), respectively.

Subsec. (c). Pub. L. 96–221, §613(e), struck out subsec. (c) which related to the time for making disclosures with respect to open end consumer credit plans having an outstanding balance of more than $1 at or after the close of the first full billing cycle.

1974—Subsec. (a)(1). Pub. L. 93–495, §415(1), inserted exception relating to nonimposition of a finance charge at the election of the creditor and without disclosure.

Subsec. (a)(8). Pub. L. 93–495, §304(a), added par. (8).

Subsec. (b)(2). Pub. L. 93–495, §411, substituted provisions requiring a brief identification on or accompanying the statement of credit extension sufficient to enable the obligor to identify the transaction or relate it to copies of sales vouchers or similar instruments previously furnished, for provisions requiring for purchases a brief identification, unless previously furnished, of the goods or services purchased.

Subsec. (b)(10). Pub. L. 93–495, §415(2), inserted exception relating to nonimposition of additional finance charge at the election of the creditor and without disclosure.

Subsec. (b)(11). Pub. L. 93–495, §305, added par. (11).

Subsec. (c). Pub. L. 93–495, §304(b), substituted provisions relating to disclosure requirements in a notice mailed or delivered to the obligor not later than the time of mailing the next statement required by subsec. (b) of this section, for provisions relating to disclosure requirements in a notice mailed or delivered to the obligor not later than thirty days after July 1, 1969.

STATUTORY NOTES AND RELATED SUBSIDIARIES

EFFECTIVE DATE OF 2010 AMENDMENT

Amendment by Pub. L. 111–203 effective on the designated transfer date, see section 1100H of Pub. L. 111–203, set out as a note under section 552a of Title 5, Government Organization and Employees.

EFFECTIVE DATE OF 2009 AMENDMENT

Amendment by Pub. L. 111–24 effective 9 months after May 22, 2009, except as otherwise specifically provided, see section 3 of Pub. L. 111–24, set out as a note under section 1602 of this title.

Pub. L. 111–24, title I, §101(a)(2), May 22, 2009, 123 Stat. 1736, provided that: "Notwithstanding section 3 [see Effective Date of 2009 Amendment note set out under section 1602 of this title], section 127(i) of the Truth in Lending Act [15 U.S.C. 1637(i)], as added by this subsection, shall become effective 90 days after the date of enactment of this Act [May 22, 2009]."

EFFECTIVE DATE OF 2005 AMENDMENT

Pub. L. 109–8, title XIII, §1301(b)(2), Apr. 20, 2005, 119 Stat. 207, provided that: "Section 127(b)(11) of the Truth in Lending Act [subsec. (b)(11) of this section], as added by subsection (a) of this section, and the regulations issued under paragraph (1) of this subsection [set out as a note under this section] shall not take effect until the later of—

"(A) 18 months after the date of enactment of this Act [Apr. 20, 2005]; or

"(B) 12 months after the publication of such final regulations by the Board [of Governors of the Federal Reserve System] [Jan. 29, 2009, see 74 F.R. 5244]."

Pub. L. 109–8, title XIII, §1303(b)(2), Apr. 20, 2005, 119 Stat. 211, provided that: "Section 127(c)(6) of the Truth in Lending Act [subsec. (c)(6) of this section], as added by this section, and regulations issued under paragraph (1) of this subsection [set out as a note under this section] shall not take effect until the later of—

"(A) 12 months after the date of enactment of this Act [Apr. 20, 2005]; or

"(B) 12 months after the date of publication of such final regulations by the Board [of Governors of the Federal Reserve System] [Jan. 29, 2009, see 74 F.R. 5244]."

Pub. L. 109–8, title XIII, §1304(b)(2), Apr. 20, 2005, 119 Stat. 212, provided that: "The amendment made by subsection (a) [amending this section] and the regulations issued under paragraph (1) of this subsection [set out as a note under this section] shall not take effect until the later of—

"(A) 12 months after the date of enactment of this Act [Apr. 20, 2005]; or

"(B) 12 months after the date of publication of such final regulations by the Board [of Governors of the Federal Reserve System] [Jan. 29, 2009, see 74 F.R. 5244]."

Pub. L. 109–8, title XIII, §1305(b)(2), Apr. 20, 2005, 119 Stat. 212, provided that: "The amendment made by subsection (a) [amending this section] and regulations issued under paragraph (1) of this subsection [set out as a note under this section] shall not take effect until the later of—

"(A) 12 months after the date of enactment of this Act [Apr. 20, 2005]; or

"(B) 12 months after the date of publication of such final regulations by the Board [of Governors of the Federal Reserve System] [Jan. 29, 2009, see 74 F.R. 5244]."

Pub. L. 109–8, title XIII, §1306(b)(2), Apr. 20, 2005, 119 Stat. 212, provided that: "The amendment made by subsection (a) [amending this section] and regulations issued under paragraph (1) of this subsection [set out as a note under this section] shall not take effect until the later of—

"(A) 12 months after the date of enactment of this Act [Apr. 20, 2005]; or

"(B) 12 months after the date of publication of such final regulations by the Board [of Governors of the Federal Reserve System] [Jan. 29, 2009, see 74 F.R. 5244]."

EFFECTIVE DATE OF 1988 AMENDMENT

For effective date of amendments by Pub. L. 100–709, see Regulations; Effective Date note below.

EFFECTIVE DATE OF 1980 AMENDMENT

Amendment by Pub. L. 96–221 effective on expiration of two years and six months after Mar. 31, 1980, with all regulations, forms, and clauses required to be prescribed to be promulgated at least one year prior to such effective date, and allowing any creditor to comply with any amendments, in accordance with the regulations, forms, and clauses prescribed by the Board prior to such effective date, see section 625 of Pub. L. 96–221, set out as a note under section 1602 of this title.

EFFECTIVE DATE OF 1974 AMENDMENT

For effective date of amendment by sections 304 and 305 of Pub. L. 93–495, see section 308 of Pub. L. 93–495, set out as an Effective Date note under section 1666 of this title.

For effective date of amendment by section 411 of Pub. L. 93–495, see section 416 of Pub. L. 93–495, set out as an Effective Date note under section 1665a of this title.

Amendment by section 415 of Pub. L. 93–495 effective Oct. 28, 1974, see section 416 of Pub. L. 93–495, set out as an Effective Date note under section 1665a of this title.

REGULATIONS

Pub. L. 111–24, title II, §201(c), May 22, 2009, 123 Stat. 1745, provided that:

"(1) IN GENERAL.—Not later than 6 months after the date of enactment of this Act [May 22, 2009], the Board [of Governors of the Federal Reserve System] shall issue guidelines, by rule, in consultation with the Secretary of the Treasury, for the establishment and maintenance by creditors of a toll-free telephone number for purposes of providing information about accessing credit counseling and debt management services, as required under section 127(b)(11)(B)(iv) of the Truth in Lending Act [15 U.S.C. 1637(b)(11)(B)(iv)], as added by this section.

"(2) APPROVED AGENCIES.—Guidelines issued under this subsection shall ensure that referrals provided by the toll-free number referred to in paragraph (1) include only those nonprofit budget and credit counseling agencies approved by a United States bankruptcy trustee pursuant to section 111(a) of title 11, United States Code."

Pub. L. 109–8, title XIII, §1301(b)(1), Apr. 20, 2005, 119 Stat. 207, provided that: "The Board of Governors of the Federal Reserve System (hereafter in this title [amending this section and sections 1637a, 1638, 1664, and 1665b of this title and enacting provisions set out as notes under this section and section 1637a of this title] referred to as the 'Board') shall promulgate regulations implementing the requirements of section 127(b)(11) of the Truth in Lending Act [subsec. (b)(11) of this section], as added by subsection (a) of this section."

Pub. L. 109–8, title XIII, §1303(b)(1), Apr. 20, 2005, 119 Stat. 211, provided that: "The Board [of Governors of the Federal Reserve System] shall promulgate regulations implementing the requirements of section 127(c)(6) of the Truth in Lending Act [subsec. (c)(6) of this section], as added by this section."

Pub. L. 109–8, title XIII, §1304(b)(1), Apr. 20, 2005, 119 Stat. 211, provided that: "The Board [of Governors of the Federal Reserve System] shall promulgate regulations implementing the requirements of section 127(c)(7) of the Truth in Lending Act [subsec. (c)(7) of this section], as added by this section."

Pub. L. 109–8, title XIII, §1305(b)(1), Apr. 20, 2005, 119 Stat. 212, provided that: "The Board [of Governors of the Federal Reserve System] shall promulgate regulations implementing the requirements of section 127(b)(12) of the Truth in Lending Act [subsec. (b)(12) of this section], as added by this section."

Pub. L. 109–8, title XIII, §1306(b)(1), Apr. 20, 2005, 119 Stat. 212, provided that: "The Board [of Governors of the Federal Reserve System] shall promulgate regulations implementing the requirements of section 127(h) of the Truth in Lending Act [subsec. (h) of this section], as added by this section."

Pub. L. 109–8, title XIII, §1309, Apr. 20, 2005, 119 Stat. 213, provided that:

"(a) REGULATIONS.—Not later than 6 months after the date of enactment of this Act [Apr. 20, 2005], the Board [of Governors of the Federal Reserve System], in consultation with the other Federal banking agencies (as defined in section 3 of the Federal Deposit Insurance Act [12 U.S.C. 1813]), the National Credit Union Administration Board, and the Federal Trade Commission, shall promulgate regulations to provide guidance regarding the meaning of the term 'clear and conspicuous', as used in subparagraphs (A), (B), and (C) of section 127(b)(11) and clauses (ii) and (iii) of section 127(c)(6)(A) of the Truth in Lending Act [subsecs. (b)(11) and (c)(6)(A) of this section].

"(b) EXAMPLES.—Regulations promulgated under subsection (a) shall include examples of clear and conspicuous model disclosures for the purposes of disclosures required by the provisions of the Truth in Lending Act [15 U.S.C. 1601 et seq.] referred to in subsection (a).

"(c) STANDARDS.—In promulgating regulations under this section, the Board [of Governors of the Federal Reserve System] shall ensure that the clear and conspicuous standard required for disclosures made under the provisions of the Truth in Lending Act referred to in subsection (a) can be implemented in a manner which results in disclosures which are reasonably understandable and designed to call attention to the nature and significance of the information in the notice."

REGULATIONS; EFFECTIVE DATE

For provisions relating to promulgation of regulations to implement amendment by Pub. L. 100–709, and effective date of such amendment in connection with those regulations, see section 7 of Pub. L. 100–709, set out as a note under section 1637a of this title.

Pub. L. 100–583, §7, Nov. 3, 1988, 102 Stat. 2968, provided that: "Any regulation required to be prescribed by the Board under the amendments made by section 2 [amending this section and section 1632 of this title] shall—

"(1) take effect not later than the end of the 150-day period beginning on the date of the enactment of this Act [Nov. 3, 1988]; and

"(2) apply only with respect to applications, solicitations, and other material distributed after the end of the 150-day period beginning after the end of the period referred to in paragraph (1), except that—

"(A) in the case of applications and solicitations subject to paragraph (3) or (4)(C) of section 127(c) of the Truth in Lending Act [15 U.S.C. 1637(c)(3), (4)(C)] (as added by section 2), such period shall be 240 days; and

"(B) any card issuer may, at its option, comply with the requirements of the amendments made by this Act [see Short Title of 1988 Amendment note under section 1601 of this title] prior to the applicable effective date, in which case the amendments made by this Act shall be fully applicable to such card issuer."

REPORTS TO CONGRESS

Pub. L. 111–24, title III, §305(b), May 22, 2009, 123 Stat. 1750, provided that:

"(1) STUDY.—The Comptroller General of the United States shall, from time to time, review the reports submitted by creditors under section 127(r) of the Truth in Lending Act [15 U.S.C. 1637(r)], as added by this section, and the marketing practices of creditors to determine the impact that college affinity card agreements and college student card agreements have on credit card debt.

"(2) REPORT.—Upon completion of any study under paragraph (1), the Comptroller General shall periodically submit a report to the Congress on the findings and conclusions of the study, together with such recommendations for administrative or legislative action as the Comptroller General determines to be appropriate."

Pub. L. 100–583, §8, Nov. 3, 1988, 102 Stat. 2969, provided that: "Not later than 1 year after the regulations prescribed under section 7 of this Act [set out as a note above] become effective and annually thereafter, the Board of Governors of the Federal Reserve System shall transmit to the Congress a report containing an assessment by the Board of the profitability of credit card operations of depository institutions, including an analysis of any impact of the amendments made by this Act [see Short Title of 1988 Amendment note under section 1601 of this title] on such profitability."

¹ *So in original. Probably should be "conspicuously".*

² *So in original. No subsec. (q) has been enacted.*

³ *So in original. Probably should be "sections".*

§1637a. Disclosure requirements for open end consumer credit plans secured by consumer's principal dwelling

(a) Application disclosures

In the case of any open end consumer credit plan which provides for any extension of credit which is secured by the consumer's principal dwelling, the creditor shall make the following disclosures in accordance with subsection (b):

(1) Fixed annual percentage rate

Each annual percentage rate imposed in connection with extensions of credit under the plan and a statement that such rate does not include costs other than interest.

(2) Variable percentage rate

In the case of a plan which provides for variable rates of interest on credit extended under the plan—
    (A) a description of the manner in which such rate will be computed and a statement that such rate does not include costs other than interest;
    (B) a description of the manner in which any changes in the annual percentage rate will be made, including—
        (i) any negative amortization and interest rate carryover;
        (ii) the timing of any such changes;
        (iii) any index or margin to which such changes in the rate are related; and
        (iv) a source of information about any such index;

    (C) if an initial annual percentage rate is offered which is not based on an index—
        (i) a statement of such rate and the period of time such initial rate will be in effect; and
        (ii) a statement that such rate does not include costs other than interest;

    (D) a statement that the consumer should ask about the current index value and interest rate;
    (E) a statement of the maximum amount by which the annual percentage rate may change in any 1-year period or a statement that no such limit exists;
    (F) a statement of the maximum annual percentage rate that may be imposed at any time under the plan;
    (G) subject to subsection (b)(3), a table, based on a $10,000 extension of credit, showing how the annual percentage rate and the minimum periodic payment amount under each repayment option of the plan would have been affected during the preceding 15-year period by changes in any index used to compute such rate;
    (H) a statement of—
        (i) the maximum annual percentage rate which may be imposed under each repayment option of the plan;
        (ii) the minimum amount of any periodic payment which may be required, based on a $10,000 outstanding balance, under each such option when such maximum annual percentage rate is in effect; and
        (iii) the earliest date by which such maximum annual interest rate may be imposed; and

    (I) a statement that interest rate information will be provided on or with each periodic statement.

(3) Other fees imposed by the creditor

An itemization of any fees imposed by the creditor in connection with the availability or use of credit under such plan, including annual fees, application fees, transaction fees, and closing costs (including costs commonly described as "points"), and the time when such fees are payable.

(4) Estimates of fees which may be imposed by third parties

(A) Aggregate amount

An estimate, based on the creditor's experience with such plans and stated as a single amount or as a reasonable range, of the aggregate amount of additional fees that may be imposed by third parties (such as governmental authorities, appraisers, and attorneys) in connection with opening an account under the plan.

(B) Statement of availability

A statement that the consumer may ask the creditor for a good faith estimate by the creditor of the fees that may be imposed by third parties.

(5) Statement of risk of loss of dwelling

A statement that—

(A) any extension of credit under the plan is secured by the consumer's dwelling; and

(B) in the event of any default, the consumer risks the loss of the dwelling.

(6) Conditions to which disclosed terms are subject

(A) Period during which such terms are available

A clear and conspicuous statement—

(i) of the time by which an application must be submitted to obtain the terms disclosed; or

(ii) if applicable, that the terms are subject to change.

(B) Right of refusal if certain terms change

A statement that—

(i) the consumer may elect not to enter into an agreement to open an account under the plan if any term changes (other than a change contemplated by a variable feature of the plan) before any such agreement is final; and

(ii) if the consumer makes an election described in clause (i), the consumer is entitled to a refund of all fees paid in connection with the application.

(C) Retention of information

A statement that the consumer should make or otherwise retain a copy of information disclosed under this subparagraph.

(7) Rights of creditor with respect to extensions of credit

A statement that—

(A) under certain conditions, the creditor may terminate any account under the plan and require immediate repayment of any outstanding balance, prohibit any additional extension of credit to the account, or reduce the credit limit applicable to the account; and

(B) the consumer may receive, upon request, more specific information about the conditions under which the creditor may take any action described in subparagraph (A).

(8) Repayment options and minimum periodic payments

The repayment options under the plan, including—

(A) if applicable, any differences in repayment options with regard to—

(i) any period during which additional extensions of credit may be obtained; and

(ii) any period during which repayment is required to be made and no additional extensions of credit may be obtained;

(B) the length of any repayment period, including any differences in the length of any repayment period with regard to the periods described in clauses (i) and (ii) of subparagraph (A); and

(C) an explanation of how the amount of any minimum monthly or periodic payment will be determined under each such option, including any differences in the determination of any such amount with regard to the periods described in clauses (i) and (ii) of subparagraph (A).

(9) Example of minimum payments and maximum repayment period

An example, based on a $10,000 outstanding balance and the interest rate (other than a rate not based on the index under the plan) which is, or was recently, in effect under such plan, showing the minimum monthly or periodic payment, and the time it would take to repay the entire $10,000 if the consumer paid only the minimum periodic payments and obtained no additional extensions of credit.

(10) Statement concerning balloon payments

If, under any repayment option of the plan, the payment of not more than the minimum periodic payments required under such option over the length of the repayment period—

(A) would not repay any of the principal balance; or

(B) would repay less than the outstanding balance by the end of such period,

as the case may be, a statement of such fact, including an explicit statement that at the end of such repayment period a balloon payment (as defined in section 1665b(f) of this title) would result which would be required to be paid in full at that time.

(11) Negative amortization

If applicable, a statement that—

(A) any limitation in the plan on the amount of any increase in the minimum payments may result in negative amortization;

(B) negative amortization increases the outstanding principal balance of the account; and

(C) negative amortization reduces the consumer's equity in the consumer's dwelling.

(12) Limitations and minimum amount requirements on extensions of credit

(A) Number and dollar amount limitations

Any limitation contained in the plan on the number of extensions of credit and the amount of credit which may be obtained during any month or other defined time period.

(B) Minimum balance and other transaction amount requirements

Any requirement which establishes a minimum amount for—

(i) the initial extension of credit to an account under the plan;

(ii) any subsequent extension of credit to an account under the plan; or

(iii) any outstanding balance of an account under the plan.

(13) Statement regarding tax deductibility

A statement that—

(A) the consumer should consult a tax advisor regarding the deductibility of interest and charges under the plan; and

(B) in any case in which the extension of credit exceeds the fair market value (as defined under title 26) of the dwelling, the interest on the portion of the credit extension that is greater than the fair market value of the dwelling is not tax deductible for Federal income tax purposes.

(14) Disclosure requirements established by Bureau

Any other term which the Bureau requires, in regulations, to be disclosed.

(b) Time and form of disclosures

(1) Time of disclosure

(A) In general

The disclosures required under subsection (a) with respect to any open end consumer credit plan which provides for any extension of credit which is secured by the consumer's principal dwelling and the pamphlet required under subsection (e) shall be provided to any consumer at the time the creditor distributes an application to establish an account under such plan to such consumer.

(B) Telephone, publications, and third party applications

In the case of telephone applications, applications contained in magazines or other publications, or applications provided by a third party, the disclosures required under subsection (a) and the pamphlet required under subsection (e) shall be provided by the creditor before the end of the 3-day period beginning on the date the creditor receives a completed application from a consumer.

(2) Form

(A) In general

Except as provided in paragraph (1)(B), the disclosures required under subsection (a) shall be provided on or with any application to establish an account under an open end consumer credit plan which provides for any extension of credit which is secured by the consumer's principal dwelling.

(B) Segregation of required disclosures from other information

The disclosures required under subsection (a) shall be conspicuously segregated from all other terms, data, or additional information provided in connection with the application, either by grouping the disclosures separately on the application form or by providing the disclosures on a separate form, in accordance with regulations of the Bureau.

(C) Precedence of certain information

The disclosures required by paragraphs (5), (6), and (7) of subsection (a) shall precede all of the other required disclosures.

(D) Special provision relating to variable interest rate information

Whether or not the disclosures required under subsection (a) are provided on the application form, the variable rate information described in subsection (a)(2) may be provided separately from the other information required to be disclosed.

(3) Requirement for historical table

In preparing the table required under subsection (a)(2)(G), the creditor shall consistently select one rate of interest for each year and the manner of selecting the rate from year to year shall be consistent with the plan.

(c) Third party applications

In the case of an application to open an account under any open end consumer credit plan described in subsection (a) which is provided to a consumer by any person other than the creditor—

(1) such person shall provide such consumer with—

 (A) the disclosures required under subsection (a) with respect to such plan, in accordance with subsection (b); and

 (B) the pamphlet required under subsection (e); or

(2) if such person cannot provide specific terms about the plan because specific information about the plan terms is not available, no nonrefundable fee may be imposed in connection with such application before the end of the 3-day period beginning on the date the consumer receives the disclosures required under subsection (a) with respect to the application.

(d) "Principal dwelling" defined

For purposes of this section and sections 1647 and 1665b of this title, the term "principal dwelling" includes any second or vacation home of the consumer.

(e) Pamphlet

In addition to the disclosures required under subsection (a) with respect to an application to open an account under any open end consumer credit plan described in such subsection, the creditor or other person providing such disclosures to the consumer shall provide—

 (1) a pamphlet published by the Bureau pursuant to section 4 of the Home Equity [1] Consumer Protection Act of 1988; or

 (2) any pamphlet which provides substantially similar information to the information described in such section, as determined by the Bureau.

(Pub. L. 90–321, title I, §127A, as added Pub. L. 100–709, §2(a), Nov. 23, 1988, 102 Stat. 4725; amended Pub. L. 109–8, title XIII, §1302(a)(1), Apr. 20, 2005, 119 Stat. 208; Pub. L. 111–203, title X, §1100A(2), July 21, 2010, 124 Stat. 2107.)

EDITORIAL NOTES

REFERENCES IN TEXT

Section 4 of the Home Equity Loan Consumer Protection Act of 1988, referred to in subsec. (e)(1), is section 4 of Pub. L. 100–709, which is set out as a note below.

AMENDMENTS

2010—Subsecs. (a)(14), (b)(2)(B), (e). Pub. L. 111–203 substituted "Bureau" for "Board" wherever appearing.

2005—Subsec. (a)(13). Pub. L. 109–8 substituted "tax deductibility" for "consultation of tax advisor" in heading, designated existing provisions as introductory provisions and subpar. (A), inserted dash, substituted "; and" for period at end of subpar. (A), and added subpar. (B).

STATUTORY NOTES AND RELATED SUBSIDIARIES

EFFECTIVE DATE OF 2010 AMENDMENT

Amendment by Pub. L. 111–203 effective on the designated transfer date, see section 1100H of Pub. L. 111–203, set out as a note under section 552a of Title 5, Government Organization and Employees.

EFFECTIVE DATE OF 2005 AMENDMENT

Amendment by Pub. L. 109–8 effective 180 days after Apr. 20, 2005, and not applicable with respect to cases commenced under Title 11, Bankruptcy, before such effective date, except as otherwise provided, see section 1501 of Pub. L. 109–8, set out as a note under section 101 of Title 11.

EFFECTIVE DATE

For effective date of section, see Regulations; Effective Date note below.

REGULATIONS

Pub. L. 109–8, title XIII, §1302(c), Apr. 20, 2005, 119 Stat. 209, provided that:

"(1) IN GENERAL.—The Board [of Governors of the Federal Reserve System] shall promulgate regulations implementing the amendments made by this section [amending this section and sections 1638, 1664, and 1665b of this title].

"(2) EFFECTIVE DATE.—Regulations issued under paragraph (1) shall not take effect until the later of—

 "(A) 12 months after the date of enactment of this Act [Apr. 20, 2005]; or

"(B) 12 months after the date of publication of such final regulations by the Board."

REGULATIONS; EFFECTIVE DATE

Pub. L. 100–709, §7, Nov. 23, 1988, 102 Stat. 4734, provided that:

"(a) REGULATIONS.—Before the end of the 60-day period beginning on the date of the enactment of this Act [Nov. 23, 1988], the Board of Governors of the Federal Reserve System shall prescribe such regulations as may be necessary to carry out the proposes [sic] of the amendments made by this Act [enacting this section and sections 1647 and 1665b of this title, amending sections 1632 and 1637 of this title, and enacting provisions set out as notes under this section and section 1601 of this title].

"(b) EFFECTIVE DATE.—The amendments made by this Act, and the regulations prescribed pursuant to subsection (a) with respect to such amendments, shall apply to—

"(1) any agreement to open an account under an open end consumer credit plan under which extensions of credit are secured by a consumer's principal dwelling which is entered into after the end of the 5-month period beginning on the date on which the regulations prescribed under subsection (a) become final; and

"(2) any application to open such an account which is distributed by, or received by a creditor, after the end of such 5-month period.

"(c) VOLUNTARY COMPLIANCE.—Notwithstanding subsection (b), any creditor may comply with the amendments made by this Act, in accordance with the regulations prescribed by the Board, before the effective date established under such subsection."

CONSUMER EDUCATION

Pub. L. 100–709, §4, Nov. 23, 1988, 102 Stat. 4733, provided that: "The Board of Governors of the Federal Reserve System shall develop and prepare a pamphlet for distribution to consumers which contains—

"(1) a general description of open end consumer credit plans secured by the consumer's principal dwelling and the terms and conditions under which such loans are generally extended; and

"(2) a discussion of the potential advantages and disadvantages of such plans, including how to compare among home equity plans and between home equity and closed end credit plans."

---

[1] So in original. Probably should be followed by "Loan".

§1638. Transactions other than under an open end credit plan

(a) Required disclosures by creditor

For each consumer credit transaction other than under an open end credit plan, the creditor shall disclose each of the following items, to the extent applicable:

(1) The identity of the creditor required to make disclosure.

(2)(A) The "amount financed", using that term, which shall be the amount of credit of which the consumer has actual use. This amount shall be computed as follows, but the computations need not be disclosed and shall not be disclosed with the disclosures conspicuously segregated in accordance with subsection (b)(1):

(i) take the principal amount of the loan or the cash price less downpayment and trade-in;

(ii) add any charges which are not part of the finance charge or of the principal amount of the loan and which are financed by the consumer, including the cost of any items excluded from the finance charge pursuant to section 1605 of this title; and

(iii) subtract any charges which are part of the finance charge but which will be paid by the consumer before or at the time of the consummation of the transaction, or have been withheld from the proceeds of the credit.

(B) In conjunction with the disclosure of the amount financed, a creditor shall provide a statement of the consumer's right to obtain, upon a written request, a written itemization of the amount financed. The statement shall include spaces for a "yes" and "no" indication to be initialed by the consumer to indicate whether the consumer wants a written itemization of the amount financed. Upon receiving an affirmative indication, the creditor shall provide, at the time other disclosures are required to be furnished, a written itemization of the amount financed. For the purposes of this subparagraph, "itemization of the amount financed" means a disclosure of the following items, to the extent applicable:

(i) the amount that is or will be paid directly to the consumer;

(ii) the amount that is or will be credited to the consumer's account to discharge obligations owed to the creditor;

(iii) each amount that is or will be paid to third persons by the creditor on the consumer's behalf, together with an identification of or reference to the third person; and

(iv) the total amount of any charges described in the preceding subparagraph (A)(iii).

(3) The "finance charge", not itemized, using that term.

(4) The finance charge expressed as an "annual percentage rate", using that term. This shall not be required if the amount financed does not exceed $75 and the finance charge does not exceed $5, or if the amount financed exceeds $75 and the finance charge does not exceed $7.50.

(5) The sum of the amount financed and the finance charge, which shall be termed the "total of payments".

(6) The number, amount, and due dates or period of payments scheduled to repay the total of payments.

(7) In a sale of property or services in which the seller is the creditor required to disclose pursuant to section 1631(b) of this title, the "total sale price", using that term, which shall be the total of the cash price of the property or services, additional charges, and the finance charge.

(8) Descriptive explanations of the terms "amount financed", "finance charge", "annual percentage rate", "total of payments", and "total sale price" as specified by the Bureau. The descriptive explanation of "total sale price" shall include reference to the amount of the downpayment.

(9) Where the credit is secured, a statement that a security interest has been taken in (A) the property which is purchased as part of the credit transaction, or (B) property not purchased as part of the credit transaction identified by item or type.

(10) Any dollar charge or percentage amount which may be imposed by a creditor solely on account of a late payment, other than a deferral or extension charge.

(11) A statement indicating whether or not the consumer is entitled to a rebate of any finance charge upon refinancing or prepayment in full pursuant to acceleration or otherwise, if the obligation involves a precomputed finance charge. A statement indicating whether or not a penalty will be imposed in those same circumstances if the obligation involves a finance charge computed from time to time by application of a rate to the unpaid principal balance.

(12) A statement that the consumer should refer to the appropriate contract document for any information such document provides about nonpayment, default, the right to accelerate the maturity of the debt, and prepayment rebates and penalties.

(13) In any residential mortgage transaction, a statement indicating whether a subsequent purchaser or assignee of the consumer may assume the debt obligation on its original terms and conditions.

(14) In the case of any variable interest rate residential mortgage transaction, in disclosures provided at application as prescribed by the Bureau for a variable rate transaction secured by the consumer's principal dwelling, at the option of the creditor, a statement that the periodic payments may increase or decrease substantially, and the maximum interest rate and payment for a $10,000 loan originated at a recent interest rate, as determined by the Bureau, assuming the maximum periodic increases in rates and payments under the program, or a historical example illustrating the effects of interest rate changes implemented according to the loan program.

(15) In the case of a consumer credit transaction that is secured by the principal dwelling of the consumer, in which the extension of credit may exceed the fair market value of the dwelling, a clear and conspicuous statement that—

(A) the interest on the portion of the credit extension that is greater than the fair market value of the dwelling is not tax deductible for Federal income tax purposes; and

(B) the consumer should consult a tax adviser for further information regarding the deductibility of interest and charges.

(16) In the case of a variable rate residential mortgage loan for which an escrow or impound account will be established for the payment of all applicable taxes, insurance, and assessments—

(A) the amount of initial monthly payment due under the loan for the payment of principal and interest, and the amount of such initial monthly payment including the monthly payment deposited in the account for the payment of all applicable taxes, insurance, and assessments; and

(B) the amount of the fully indexed monthly payment due under the loan for the payment of principal and interest, and the amount of such fully indexed monthly payment including the monthly payment deposited in the account for the payment of all applicable taxes, insurance, and assessments.

(17) In the case of a residential mortgage loan, the aggregate amount of settlement charges for all settlement services provided in connection with the loan, the amount of charges that are included in the loan and the amount of such charges the borrower must pay at closing, the approximate amount of the wholesale rate of funds in connection with the loan, and the aggregate amount of other fees or required payments in connection with the loan.

(18) In the case of a residential mortgage loan, the aggregate amount of fees paid to the mortgage originator in connection with the loan, the amount of such fees paid directly by the consumer, and any additional amount received by the originator from the creditor.

(19) In the case of a residential mortgage loan, the total amount of interest that the consumer will pay over the life of the loan as a percentage of the principal of the loan. Such amount shall be computed assuming the consumer makes each monthly payment in full and on-time, and does not make any over-payments.

(b) Form and timing of disclosures; residential mortgage transaction requirements

(1) Except as otherwise provided in this part, the disclosures required under subsection (a) shall be made before the credit is extended. Except for the disclosures required by subsection (a)(1) of this section, all disclosures required under subsection (a) and any disclosure provided for in subsection (b), (c), or (d) of section 1605 of this title shall be

conspicuously segregated from all other terms, data, or information provided in connection with a transaction, including any computations or itemization.

(2)(A) Except as provided in subparagraph (G), in the case of any extension of credit that is secured by the dwelling of a consumer, which is also subject to the Real Estate Settlement Procedures Act [12 U.S.C. 2601 et seq.], good faith estimates of the disclosures required under subsection (a) shall be made in accordance with regulations of the Bureau under section 1631(c) of this title and shall be delivered or placed in the mail not later than three business days after the creditor receives the consumer's written application, which shall be at least 7 business days before consummation of the transaction.

(B) In the case of an extension of credit that is secured by the dwelling of a consumer, the disclosures provided under subparagraph (A),[1] shall be in addition to the other disclosures required by subsection (a), and shall—

(i) state in conspicuous type size and format, the following: "You are not required to complete this agreement merely because you have received these disclosures or signed a loan application."; and

(ii) be provided in the form of final disclosures at the time of consummation of the transaction, in the form and manner prescribed by this section.

(C) In the case of an extension of credit that is secured by the dwelling of a consumer, under which the annual rate of interest is variable, or with respect to which the regular payments may otherwise be variable, in addition to the other disclosures required by subsection (a), the disclosures provided under this subsection shall do the following:

(i) Label the payment schedule as follows: "Payment Schedule: Payments Will Vary Based on Interest Rate Changes".

(ii) State in conspicuous type size and format examples of adjustments to the regular required payment on the extension of credit based on the change in the interest rates specified by the contract for such extension of credit. Among the examples required to be provided under this clause is an example that reflects the maximum payment amount of the regular required payments on the extension of credit, based on the maximum interest rate allowed under the contract, in accordance with the rules of the Bureau. Prior to issuing any rules pursuant to this clause, the Bureau shall conduct consumer testing to determine the appropriate format for providing the disclosures required under this subparagraph to consumers so that such disclosures can be easily understood, including the fact that the initial regular payments are for a specific time period that will end on a certain date, that payments will adjust afterwards potentially to a higher amount, and that there is no guarantee that the borrower will be able to refinance to a lower amount.

(D) In any case in which the disclosure statement under subparagraph (A) contains an annual percentage rate of interest that is no longer accurate, as determined under section 1606(c) of this title, the creditor shall furnish an additional, corrected statement to the borrower, not later than 3 business days before the date of consummation of the transaction.

(E) The consumer shall receive the disclosures required under this paragraph before paying any fee to the creditor or other person in connection with the consumer's application for an extension of credit that is secured by the dwelling of a consumer. If the disclosures are mailed to the consumer, the consumer is considered to have received them 3 business days after they are mailed. A creditor or other person may impose a fee for obtaining the consumer's credit report before the consumer has received the disclosures under this paragraph, provided the fee is bona fide and reasonable in amount.

(F) WAIVER OF TIMELINESS OF DISCLOSURES.—To expedite consummation of a transaction, if the consumer determines that the extension of credit is needed to meet a bona fide personal financial emergency, the consumer may waive or modify the timing requirements for disclosures under subparagraph (A), provided that—

(i) the term "bona fide personal emergency" may be further defined in regulations issued by the Bureau;

(ii) the consumer provides to the creditor a dated, written statement describing the emergency and specifically waiving or modifying those timing requirements, which statement shall bear the signature of all consumers entitled to receive the disclosures required by this paragraph; and

(iii) the creditor provides to the consumers at or before the time of such waiver or modification, the final disclosures required by paragraph (1).

(G)(i) In the case of an extension of credit relating to a plan described in section 101(53D) of title 11—

(I) the requirements of subparagraphs (A) through (E) shall not apply; and

(II) a good faith estimate of the disclosures required under subsection (a) shall be made in accordance with regulations of the Bureau under section 1631(c) of this title before such credit is extended, or shall be delivered or placed in the mail not later than 3 business days after the date on which the creditor receives the written application of the consumer for such credit, whichever is earlier.

(ii) If a disclosure statement furnished within 3 business days of the written application (as provided under clause (i)(II)) contains an annual percentage rate which is subsequently rendered inaccurate, within the meaning of section 1606(c) of this title, the creditor shall furnish another disclosure statement at the time of settlement or consummation of the transaction.

(3) In the case of a credit transaction described in paragraph (15) of subsection (a), disclosures required by that paragraph shall be made to the consumer at the time of application for such extension of credit.

(4) Repayment analysis required to include escrow payments.—

(A) In general.—In the case of any consumer credit transaction secured by a first mortgage or lien on the principal dwelling of the consumer, other than a consumer credit transaction under an open end credit plan or a reverse mortgage, for which an impound, trust, or other type of account has been or will be established in connection with the transaction for the payment of property taxes, hazard and flood (if any) insurance premiums, or other periodic payments or premiums with respect to the property, the information required to be provided under subsection (a) with respect to the number, amount, and due dates or period of payments scheduled to repay the total of payments shall take into account the amount of any monthly payment to such account for each such repayment in accordance with section 10(a)(2) of the Real Estate Settlement Procedures Act of 1974 [12 U.S.C. 2609(a)(2)].

(B) Assessment value.—The amount taken into account under subparagraph (A) for the payment of property taxes, hazard and flood (if any) insurance premiums, or other periodic payments or premiums with respect to the property shall reflect the taxable assessed value of the real property securing the transaction after the consummation of the transaction, including the value of any improvements on the property or to be constructed on the property (whether or not such construction will be financed from the proceeds of the transaction), if known, and the replacement costs of the property for hazard insurance, in the initial year after the transaction.

(c) Timing of disclosures on unsolicited mailed or telephone purchase orders or loan requests

(1) If a creditor receives a purchase order by mail or telephone without personal solicitation, and the cash price and the total sale price and the terms of financing, including the annual percentage rate, are set forth in the creditor's catalog or other printed material distributed to the public, then the disclosures required under subsection (a) may be made at any time not later than the date the first payment is due.

(2) If a creditor receives a request for a loan by mail or telephone without personal solicitation and the terms of financing, including the annual percentage rate for representative amounts of credit, are set forth in the creditor's printed material distributed to the public, or in the contract of loan or other printed material delivered to the obligor, then the disclosures required under subsection (a) may be made at any time not later than the date the first payment is due.

(d) Timing of disclosure in cases of an addition of a deferred payment price to an existing outstanding balance

If a consumer credit sale is one of a series of consumer credit sales transactions made pursuant to an agreement providing for the addition of the deferred payment price of that sale to an existing outstanding balance, and the person to whom the credit is extended has approved in writing both the annual percentage rate or rates and the method of computing the finance charge or charges, and the creditor retains no security interest in any property as to which he has received payments aggregating the amount of the sales price including any finance charges attributable thereto, then the disclosure required under subsection (a) for the particular sale may be made at any time not later than the date the first payment for that sale is due. For the purposes of this subsection, in the case of items purchased on different dates, the first purchased shall be deemed first paid for, and in the case of items purchased on the same date, the lowest price shall be deemed first paid for.

(e) Terms and disclosure with respect to private education loans

(1) Disclosures required in private education loan applications and solicitations

In any application for a private education loan, or a solicitation for a private education loan without requiring an application, the private educational lender shall disclose to the borrower, clearly and conspicuously—

(A) the potential range of rates of interest applicable to the private education loan;

(B) whether the rate of interest applicable to the private education loan is fixed or variable;

(C) limitations on interest rate adjustments, both in terms of frequency and amount, or the lack thereof, if applicable;

(D) requirements for a co-borrower, including any changes in the applicable interest rates without a co-borrower;

(E) potential finance charges, late fees, penalties, and adjustments to principal, based on defaults or late payments of the borrower;

(F) fees or range of fees applicable to the private education loan;

(G) the term of the private education loan;

(H) whether interest will accrue while the student to whom the private education loan relates is enrolled at a covered educational institution;

(I) payment deferral options;

(J) general eligibility criteria for the private education loan;

(K) an example of the total cost of the private education loan over the life of the loan—

(i) which shall be calculated using the principal amount and the maximum rate of interest actually offered by the private educational lender; and

(ii) calculated both with and without capitalization of interest, if an option exists for postponing interest payments;

(L) that a covered educational institution may have school-specific education loan benefits and terms not detailed on the disclosure form;

(M) that the borrower may qualify for Federal student financial assistance through a program under title IV of the Higher Education Act of 1965 (20 U.S.C. 1070 et seq.), in lieu of, or in addition to, a loan from a non-Federal source;

(N) the interest rates available with respect to such Federal student financial assistance through a program under title IV of the Higher Education Act of 1965 (20 U.S.C. 1070 et seq.);

(O) that, as provided in paragraph (6)—

(i) the borrower shall have the right to accept the terms of the loan and consummate the transaction at any time within 30 calendar days (or such longer period as the private educational lender may provide) following the date on which the application for the private education loan is approved and the borrower receives the disclosure documents required under this subsection for the loan; and

(ii) except for changes based on adjustments to the index used for a loan, the rates and terms of the loan may not be changed by the private educational lender during the period described in clause (i);

(P) that, before a private education loan may be consummated, the borrower must obtain from the relevant institution of higher education the form required under paragraph (3), and complete, sign, and return such form to the private educational lender;

(Q) that the consumer may obtain additional information concerning such Federal student financial assistance from their institution of higher education, or at the website of the Department of Education; and

(R) such other information as the Bureau shall prescribe, by rule, as necessary or appropriate for consumers to make informed borrowing decisions.

(2) Disclosures at the time of private education loan approval

Contemporaneously with the approval of a private education loan application, and before the loan transaction is consummated, the private educational lender shall disclose to the borrower, clearly and conspicuously—

(A) the applicable rate of interest in effect on the date of approval;

(B) whether the rate of interest applicable to the private education loan is fixed or variable;

(C) limitations on interest rate adjustments, both in terms of frequency and amount, or the lack thereof, if applicable;

(D) the initial approved principal amount;

(E) applicable finance charges, late fees, penalties, and adjustments to principal, based on borrower defaults or late payments, including limitations on the discharge of a private education loan in bankruptcy;

(F) fees or range of fees applicable to the private education loan;

(G) the maximum term under the private education loan program;

(H) an estimate of the total amount for repayment, at both the interest rate in effect on the date of approval and at the maximum possible rate of interest offered by the private educational lender and applicable to the borrower, to the extent that such maximum rate may be determined, or if not, a good faith estimate thereof;

(I) any principal and interest payments required while the student for whom the private education loan is intended is enrolled at a covered educational institution and unpaid interest that will accrue during such enrollment;

(J) payment deferral options applicable to the borrower;

(K) whether monthly payments are graduated;

(L) that, as provided in paragraph (6)—

(i) the borrower shall have the right to accept the terms of the loan and consummate the transaction at any time within 30 calendar days (or such longer period as the private educational lender may provide) following the date on which the application for the private education loan is approved and the borrower receives the disclosure documents required under this subsection for the loan; and

(ii) except for changes based on adjustments to the index used for a loan, the rates and terms of the loan may not be changed by the private educational lender during the period described in clause (i);

(M) that the borrower—

(i) may qualify for Federal financial assistance through a program under title IV of the Higher Education Act of 1965 (20 U.S.C. 1070 et seq.), in lieu of, or in addition to, a loan from a non-Federal source; and

(ii) may obtain additional information concerning such assistance from their institution of higher education or the website of the Department of Education;

(N) the interest rates available with respect to such Federal financial assistance through a program under title IV of the Higher Education Act of 1965 (20 U.S.C. 1070 et seq.);

(O) the maximum monthly payment, calculated using the maximum rate of interest actually offered by the private educational lender and applicable to the borrower, to the extent that such maximum rate may be determined, or if not, a good faith estimate thereof; and

(P) such other information as the Bureau shall prescribe, by rule, as necessary or appropriate for consumers to make informed borrowing decisions.

(3) Self-certification of information

(A) In general

Before a private educational lender may consummate a private education loan with respect to a student attending an institution of higher education, the lender shall obtain from the applicant for the private education loan the form developed by the Secretary of Education under section 155 of the Higher Education Act of 1965 [20 U.S.C. 1019d], signed by the applicant, in written or electronic form.

(B) Rule of construction

No other provision of this subsection shall be construed to require a private educational lender to perform any additional duty under this paragraph, other than collecting the form required under subparagraph (A).

(4) Disclosures at the time of private education loan consummation

Contemporaneously with the consummation of a private education loan, a private educational lender shall make to the borrower each of the disclosures described in—

(A) paragraph (2)(A) (adjusted, as necessary, for the rate of interest in effect on the date of consummation, based on the index used for the loan);

(B) subparagraphs (B) through (K) and (M) through (P) of paragraph (2); and

(C) paragraph (7).

(5) Format of disclosures

(A) Model form

Not later than 2 years after August 14, 2008, the Bureau shall, based on consumer testing, and in consultation with the Secretary of Education, develop and issue model forms that may be used, at the option of the private educational lender, for the provision of disclosures required under this subsection.

(B) Format

Model forms developed under this paragraph shall—

(i) be comprehensible to borrowers, with a clear format and design;

(ii) provide for clear and conspicuous disclosures;

(iii) enable borrowers easily to identify material terms of the loan and to compare such terms among private education loans; and

(iv) be succinct, and use an easily readable type font.

(C) Safe harbor

Any private educational lender that elects to provide a model form developed under this subsection that accurately reflects the practices of the private educational lender shall be deemed to be in compliance with the disclosures required under this subsection.

(6) Effective period of approved rate of interest and loan terms

(A) In general

With respect to a private education loan, the borrower shall have the right to accept the terms of the loan and consummate the transaction at any time within 30 calendar days (or such longer period as the private educational lender may provide) following the date on which the application for the private education loan is approved and the borrower receives the disclosure documents required under this subsection for the loan, and the rates and terms of the loan may not be changed by the private educational lender during that period.

(B) Prohibition on changes

Except for changes based on adjustments to the index used for a loan, the rates and terms of the loan may not be changed by the private educational lender prior to the earlier of—

(i) the date of acceptance of the terms of the loan and consummation of the transaction by the borrower, as described in subparagraph (A); or

(ii) the expiration of the period described in subparagraph (A).

(7) Right to cancel

With respect to a private education loan, the borrower may cancel the loan, without penalty to the borrower, at any time within 3 business days of the date on which the loan is consummated, and the private educational lender shall disclose such right to the borrower in accordance with paragraph (4).

(8) Prohibition on disbursement

No funds may be disbursed with respect to a private education loan until the expiration of the 3-day period described in paragraph (7).

(9) Bureau regulations

In issuing regulations under this subsection, the Bureau shall prevent, to the extent possible, duplicative disclosure requirements for private educational lenders that are otherwise required to make disclosures under this subchapter, except that in any case in which the disclosure requirements of this subsection differ or conflict with the disclosure requirements of any other provision of this subchapter, the requirements of this subsection shall be controlling.

(10) Definitions

For purposes of this subsection, the terms "covered educational institution", "private educational lender", and "private education loan" have the same meanings as in section 1650 of this title.

(11) Duties of lenders participating in preferred lender arrangements

Each private educational lender that has a preferred lender arrangement with a covered educational institution shall annually, by a date determined by the Bureau, in consultation with the Secretary of Education, provide to the covered educational institution such information as the Bureau determines to include in the model form developed under paragraph (5) for each type of private education loan that the lender plans to offer to students attending the covered educational institution, or to the families of such students, for the next award year (as that term is defined in section 481 of the Higher Education Act of 1965 [20 U.S.C. 1088]).

(f) Periodic statements for residential mortgage loans

(1) In general

The creditor, assignee, or servicer with respect to any residential mortgage loan shall transmit to the obligor, for each billing cycle, a statement setting forth each of the following items, to the extent applicable, in a conspicuous and prominent manner:

(A) The amount of the principal obligation under the mortgage.

(B) The current interest rate in effect for the loan.

(C) The date on which the interest rate may next reset or adjust.

(D) The amount of any prepayment fee to be charged, if any.

(E) A description of any late payment fees.

(F) A telephone number and electronic mail address that may be used by the obligor to obtain information regarding the mortgage.

(G) The names, addresses, telephone numbers, and Internet addresses of counseling agencies or programs reasonably available to the consumer that have been certified or approved and made publicly available by the Secretary of Housing and Urban Development or a State housing finance authority (as defined in section 1441a–1 of title 12).

(H) Such other information as the Board [2] may prescribe in regulations.

(2) Development and use of standard form

The Board [2] shall develop and prescribe a standard form for the disclosure required under this subsection, taking into account that the statements required may be transmitted in writing or electronically.

(3) Exception

Paragraph (1) shall not apply to any fixed rate residential mortgage loan where the creditor, assignee, or servicer provides the obligor with a coupon book that provides the obligor with substantially the same information as required in paragraph (1).

(Pub. L. 90–321, title I, §128, May 29, 1968, 82 Stat. 155; Pub. L. 96–221, title VI, §614(a)–(c), Mar. 31, 1980, 94 Stat. 178, 179; Pub. L. 104–208, div. A, title II, §2105, Sept. 30, 1996, 110 Stat. 3009–402; Pub. L. 109–8, title XIII, §1302(b)(1), Apr. 20, 2005, 119 Stat. 208; Pub. L. 110–289, div. B, title V, §2502(a), July 30, 2008, 122 Stat. 2855; Pub. L. 110–315, title X, §1021(a), Aug. 14, 2008, 122 Stat. 3483; Pub. L. 110–343, div. A, title I, §130(a), Oct. 3, 2008, 122 Stat. 3797; Pub. L. 111–203, title X, §1100A(2), title XIV, §§1419, 1420, 1465, July 21, 2010, 124 Stat. 2107, 2154, 2155, 2185.)

EDITORIAL NOTES

REFERENCES IN TEXT

The Real Estate Settlement Procedures Act, referred to in subsec. (b)(2)(A), probably refers to the Real Estate Settlement Procedures Act of 1974, Pub. L. 93–533, Dec. 22, 1974, 88 Stat. 1724, which is classified principally to chapter 27 (§2601 et seq.) of Title 12, Banks and Banking. For complete classification of this Act to the Code, see Short Title note set out under section 2601 of Title 12 and Tables.

The Higher Education Act of 1965, referred to in subsec. (e)(1)(M), (N), (2)(M)(i), (N), is Pub. L. 89–329, Nov. 8, 1965, 79 Stat. 1219. Title IV of the Act is classified generally to subchapter IV (§1070 et seq.) of chapter 28 of Title 20, Education. For complete classification of this Act to the Code, see Short Title note set out under section 1001 of Title 20 and Tables.

AMENDMENTS

2010—Pub. L. 111–203, §1100A(2), substituted "Bureau" for "Board" wherever appearing.

Subsec. (a)(16) to (19). Pub. L. 111–203, §1419, added pars. (16) to (19).

Subsec. (b)(4). Pub. L. 111–203, §1465, added par. (4).

Subsec. (f). Pub. L. 111–203, §1420, added subsec. (f).

2008—Subsec. (b)(2). Pub. L. 110–289, §2502(a)(1), designated existing provisions as subpar. (A).

Subsec. (b)(2)(A). Pub. L. 110–343, §130(a)(1), substituted "Except as provided in subparagraph (G), in the case" for "In the case".

Pub. L. 110–289, §2502(a)(5), (6), struck out ", whichever is earlier" after "consummation of the transaction" and "If the disclosure statement furnished within three days of the written application contains an annual percentage rate which is subsequently rendered inaccurate within the meaning of section 1606(c) of this title, the creditor shall furnish another statement at the time of settlement or consummation." at the end.

Pub. L. 110–289, §2502(a)(4), which directed insertion of ", which shall be at least 7 business days before consummation of the transaction" after "written application", was executed by making the insertion after "written application" the first place appearing.

Pub. L. 110–289, §2502(a)(2), (3), substituted "any extension of credit that is secured by the dwelling of a consumer" for "a residential mortgage transaction, as defined in section 1602(w) of this title" and "and" for "before the credit is extended, or".

Subsec. (b)(2)(B) to (F). Pub. L. 110–289, §2502(a)(6), added subpars. (B) to (F).

Subsec. (b)(2)(G). Pub. L. 110–343, §130(a)(2), amended subpar. (G) generally. Prior to amendment, subpar. (G) read as follows: "The requirements of subparagraphs (B), (C), (D) and (E) shall not apply to extensions of credit relating to plans described in section 101(53D) of title 11."

Pub. L. 110–289, §2502(a)(6), added subpar. (G).

Subsec. (e). Pub. L. 110–315 added subsec. (e).

2005—Subsec. (a)(15). Pub. L. 109–8, §1302(b)(1)(A), added par. (15).

Subsec. (b)(3). Pub. L. 109–8, §1302(b)(1)(B), added par. (3).

1996—Subsec. (a)(14). Pub. L. 104–208 added par. (14).

1980—Subsec. (a). Pub. L. 96–221, §614(a), substituted provisions setting forth required disclosures by the creditor for transactions other than under an open end credit plan, for provisions setting forth required disclosures by the creditor for sales not under open end credit plans.

Subsec. (b). Pub. L. 96–221, §614(b), designated existing provisions as par. (1), inserted provisions relating to the conspicuous segregation of required disclosures, and struck out provisions authorizing the required information to be disclosed in the signed evidence of indebtedness, and added par. (2).

Subsec. (c). Pub. L. 96–221, §614(c), designated existing provisions as par. (1), substituted "total sale" for "deferred payment", and added par. (2).

STATUTORY NOTES AND RELATED SUBSIDIARIES

EFFECTIVE DATE OF 2010 AMENDMENT

Amendment by section 1100A(2) of Pub. L. 111–203 effective on the designated transfer date, see section 1100H of Pub. L. 111–203, set out as a note under section 552a of Title 5, Government Organization and Employees.

Amendment by sections 1419, 1420, and 1465 of Pub. L. 111–203 effective on the date on which final regulations implementing that amendment take effect, or on the date that is 18 months after the designated transfer date if such regulations have not been issued by that date, see section 1400(c) of Pub. L. 111–203, set out as a note under section 1601 of this title.

EFFECTIVE DATE OF 2008 AMENDMENT

Pub. L. 110–343, div. A, title I, §130(b), Oct. 3, 2008, 122 Stat. 3797, provided that: "The amendments made by subsection (a) [amending this section] shall take effect as if included in the amendments made by section 2502 of the Mortgage Disclosure Improvement Act of 2008 (Public Law 110–289) [amending this section and section 1640 of this title]."

Pub. L. 110–315, title X, §1003, Aug. 14, 2008, 122 Stat. 3478, provided that:

"(a) IN GENERAL.—Except as provided in subsection (b) and as otherwise provided in this title [see Short Title of 2008 Amendment note set out under section 1601 of this title], this title and the amendments made by this title shall become effective on the date of enactment of this Act [Aug. 14, 2008].

"(b) EFFECT NOTWITHSTANDING REGULATIONS.—Paragraphs (1), (2), (3), (4), (6), (7), and (8) of section 128(e) [15 U.S.C. 1638(e)] and section 140(c) of the Truth in Lending Act [15 U.S.C. 1650(c)], as added by this title, shall become effective on the earlier of the date on which regulations issued under section 1002 [set out as a note below] become effective [Such regulations were issued effective Sept. 14, 2009, with compliance optional until Feb. 14, 2010. See 74 F.R. 41194.] or 18 months after the date of enactment of this Act [Aug. 14, 2008]."

Pub. L. 110–289, div. B, title V, §2502(c), July 30, 2008, 122 Stat. 2857, provided that:

"(1) GENERAL DISCLOSURES.—Except as provided in paragraph (2), the amendments made by subsection (a) [amending this section] shall become effective 12 months after the date of enactment of this Act [July 30, 2008].

"(2) Variable interest rates.—Subparagraph (C) of section 128(b)(2) of the Truth in Lending Act (15 U.S.C. 1638(b)(2)(C)), as added by subsection (a) of this section, shall become effective on the earlier of—
    "(A) the compliance date established by the Board for such purpose, by regulation; or
    "(B) 30 months after the date of enactment of this Act [July 30, 2008]."

EFFECTIVE DATE OF 2005 AMENDMENT

Amendment by Pub. L. 109–8 effective 180 days after Apr. 20, 2005, and not applicable with respect to cases commenced under Title 11, Bankruptcy, before such effective date, except as otherwise provided, see section 1501 of Pub. L. 109–8, set out as a note under section 101 of Title 11.

EFFECTIVE DATE OF 1980 AMENDMENT

Amendment by Pub. L. 96–221 effective on expiration of two years and six months after Mar. 31, 1980, with all regulations, forms, and clauses required to be prescribed to be promulgated at least one year prior to such effective date, and allowing any creditor to comply with any amendments, in accordance with the regulations, forms, and clauses prescribed by the Board prior to such effective date, see section 625 of Pub. L. 96–221, set out as a note under section 1602 of this title.

REGULATIONS

Pub. L. 110–315, title X, §1002, Aug. 14, 2008, 122 Stat. 3478, provided that: "Not later than 365 days after the date of enactment of this Act [Aug. 14, 2008], the Board of Governors of the Federal Reserve System shall issue regulations in final form to implement paragraphs (1), (2), (3), (4), (6), (7), and (8) of section 128(e) [15 U.S.C. 1638(e)] and section 140(c) of the Truth in Lending Act [15 U.S.C. 1650(c)], as added by this title, which regulations shall become effective not later than 6 months after their date of issuance."

[1] So in original. The comma probably should not appear.

[2] So in original. Probably should be "Bureau".

§1638a. Reset of hybrid adjustable rate mortgages

(a) Hybrid adjustable rate mortgages defined

For purposes of this section, the term "hybrid adjustable rate mortgage" means a consumer credit transaction secured by the consumer's principal residence with a fixed interest rate for an introductory period that adjusts or resets to a variable interest rate after such period.

(b) Notice of reset and alternatives

During the 1-month period that ends 6 months before the date on which the interest rate in effect during the introductory period of a hybrid adjustable rate mortgage adjusts or resets to a variable interest rate or, in the case of such an adjustment or resetting that occurs within the first 6 months after consummation of such loan, at consummation, the creditor or servicer of such loan shall provide a written notice, separate and distinct from all other correspondence to the consumer, that includes the following:

(1) Any index or formula used in making adjustments to or resetting the interest rate and a source of information about the index or formula.

(2) An explanation of how the new interest rate and payment would be determined, including an explanation of how the index was adjusted, such as by the addition of a margin.

(3) A good faith estimate, based on accepted industry standards, of the creditor or servicer of the amount of the monthly payment that will apply after the date of the adjustment or reset, and the assumptions on which this estimate is based.

(4) A list of alternatives consumers may pursue before the date of adjustment or reset, and descriptions of the actions consumers must take to pursue these alternatives, including—
    (A) refinancing;
    (B) renegotiation of loan terms;
    (C) payment forbearances; and
    (D) pre-foreclosure sales.

(5) The names, addresses, telephone numbers, and Internet addresses of counseling agencies or programs reasonably available to the consumer that have been certified or approved and made publicly available by the Secretary of Housing and Urban Development or a State housing finance authority (as defined in section 1441a–1 of title 12).

(6) The address, telephone number, and Internet address for the State housing finance authority (as so defined) for the State in which the consumer resides.

(c) Savings clause

The Board may require the notice in paragraph (b) or other notice consistent with this chapter for adjustable rate mortgage loans that are not hybrid adjustable rate mortgage loans.

(Pub. L. 90–321, title I, §128A, as added Pub. L. 111–203, title XIV, §1418(a), July 21, 2010, 124 Stat. 2153.)

EDITORIAL NOTES

REFERENCES IN TEXT

This chapter, referred to in subsec. (c), was in the original "this Act" meaning Pub. L. 90–321, May 29, 1968, 82 Stat. 146, which is classified principally to this chapter. For complete classification of this Act to the Code, see Short Title note set out under section 1601 of this title and Tables.

STATUTORY NOTES AND RELATED SUBSIDIARIES

EFFECTIVE DATE

Section effective on the date on which final regulations implementing such section take effect, or on the date that is 18 months after the designated transfer date, if such regulations have not been issued by that date, see section 1400(c) of Pub. L. 111–203, set out as an Effective Date of 2010 Amendment note under section 1601 of this title.

§1639. Requirements for certain mortgages

(a) Disclosures

(1) Specific disclosures

In addition to other disclosures required under this subchapter, for each mortgage referred to in section 1602(aa) [1] of this title, the creditor shall provide the following disclosures in conspicuous type size:

(A) "You are not required to complete this agreement merely because you have received these disclosures or have signed a loan application.".

(B) "If you obtain this loan, the lender will have a mortgage on your home. You could lose your home, and any money you have put into it, if you do not meet your obligations under the loan.".

(2) Annual percentage rate

In addition to the disclosures required under paragraph (1), the creditor shall disclose—

(A) in the case of a credit transaction with a fixed rate of interest, the annual percentage rate and the amount of the regular monthly payment; or

(B) in the case of any other credit transaction, the annual percentage rate of the loan, the amount of the regular monthly payment, a statement that the interest rate and monthly payment may increase, and the amount of the maximum monthly payment, based on the maximum interest rate allowed pursuant to section 3806 of title 12.

(b) Time of disclosures

(1) In general

The disclosures required by this section shall be given not less than 3 business days prior to consummation of the transaction.

(2) New disclosures required

(A) In general

After providing the disclosures required by this section, a creditor may not change the terms of the extension of credit if such changes make the disclosures inaccurate, unless new disclosures are provided that meet the requirements of this section.

(B) Telephone disclosure

A creditor may provide new disclosures pursuant to subparagraph (A) by telephone, if—

(i) the change is initiated by the consumer; and

(ii) at the consummation of the transaction under which the credit is extended—

(I) the creditor provides to the consumer the new disclosures, in writing; and

(II) the creditor and consumer certify in writing that the new disclosures were provided by telephone, by not later than 3 days prior to the date of consummation of the transaction.

(3) No wait for lower rate

If a creditor extends to a consumer a second offer of credit with a lower annual percentage rate, the transaction may be consummated without regard to the period specified in paragraph (1) with respect to the second offer.

(4) Modifications

The Bureau may, if it finds that such action is necessary to permit homeowners to meet bona fide personal financial emergencies, prescribe regulations authorizing the modification or waiver of rights created under this subsection, to the extent and under the circumstances set forth in those regulations.

(c) No prepayment penalty

(1) In general [2]

(A) Limitation on terms

A mortgage referred to in section 1602(aa) [1] of this title may not contain terms under which a consumer must pay a prepayment penalty for paying all or part of the principal before the date on which the principal is due.

(B) Construction

For purposes of this subsection, any method of computing a refund of unearned scheduled interest is a prepayment penalty if it is less favorable to the consumer than the actuarial method (as that term is defined in section 1615(d) of this title).

(d) Limitations after default

A mortgage referred to in section 1602(aa) [1] of this title may not provide for an interest rate applicable after default that is higher than the interest rate that applies before default. If the date of maturity of a mortgage referred to in subsection [3] 1602(aa) [1] of this title is accelerated due to default and the consumer is entitled to a rebate of interest, that rebate shall be computed by any method that is not less favorable than the actuarial method (as that term is defined in section 1615(d) of this title).

(e) No balloon payments

No high-cost mortgage may contain a scheduled payment that is more than twice as large as the average of earlier scheduled payments. This subsection shall not apply when the payment schedule is adjusted to the seasonal or irregular income of the consumer.

(f) No negative amortization

A mortgage referred to in section 1602(aa) [1] of this title may not include terms under which the outstanding principal balance will increase at any time over the course of the loan because the regular periodic payments do not cover the full amount of interest due.

(g) No prepaid payments

A mortgage referred to in section 1602(aa) [1] of this title may not include terms under which more than 2 periodic payments required under the loan are consolidated and paid in advance from the loan proceeds provided to the consumer.

(h) Prohibition on extending credit without regard to payment ability of consumer

A creditor shall not engage in a pattern or practice of extending credit to consumers under mortgages referred to in section 1602(aa) [1] of this title based on the consumers' collateral without regard to the consumers' repayment ability, including the consumers' current and expected income, current obligations, and employment.

(i) Requirements for payments under home improvement contracts

A creditor shall not make a payment to a contractor under a home improvement contract from amounts extended as credit under a mortgage referred to in section 1602(aa) [1] of this title, other than—

(1) in the form of an instrument that is payable to the consumer or jointly to the consumer and the contractor; or
(2) at the election of the consumer, by a third party escrow agent in accordance with terms established in a written agreement signed by the consumer, the creditor, and the contractor before the date of payment.

(j) Recommended default

No creditor shall recommend or encourage default on an existing loan or other debt prior to and in connection with the closing or planned closing of a high-cost mortgage that refinances all or any portion of such existing loan or debt.

(k) Late fees

(1) In general

No creditor may impose a late payment charge or fee in connection with a high-cost mortgage—
(A) in an amount in excess of 4 percent of the amount of the payment past due;
(B) unless the loan documents specifically authorize the charge or fee;
(C) before the end of the 15-day period beginning on the date the payment is due, or in the case of a loan on which interest on each installment is paid in advance, before the end of the 30-day period beginning on the date

the payment is due; or

(D) more than once with respect to a single late payment.

(2) Coordination with subsequent late fees

If a payment is otherwise a full payment for the applicable period and is paid on its due date or within an applicable grace period, and the only delinquency or insufficiency of payment is attributable to any late fee or delinquency charge assessed on any earlier payment, no late fee or delinquency charge may be imposed on such payment.

(3) Failure to make installment payment

If, in the case of a loan agreement the terms of which provide that any payment shall first be applied to any past due principal balance, the consumer fails to make an installment payment and the consumer subsequently resumes making installment payments but has not paid all past due installments, the creditor may impose a separate late payment charge or fee for any principal due (without deduction due to late fees or related fees) until the default is cured.

(l) Acceleration of debt

No high-cost mortgage may contain a provision which permits the creditor to accelerate the indebtedness, except when repayment of the loan has been accelerated by default in payment, or pursuant to a due-on-sale provision, or pursuant to a material violation of some other provision of the loan document unrelated to payment schedule.

(m) Restriction on financing points and fees

No creditor may directly or indirectly finance, in connection with any high-cost mortgage, any of the following:

(1) Any prepayment fee or penalty payable by the consumer in a refinancing transaction if the creditor or an affiliate of the creditor is the noteholder of the note being refinanced.

(2) Any points or fees.

(n) Consequence of failure to comply

Any mortgage that contains a provision prohibited by this section shall be deemed a failure to deliver the material disclosures required under this subchapter, for the purpose of section 1635 of this title.

(o) "Affiliate" defined

For purposes of this section, the term "affiliate" has the same meaning as in section 1841(k) of title 12.

(p) Discretionary regulatory authority of Bureau

(1) Exemptions

The Bureau may, by regulation or order, exempt specific mortgage products or categories of mortgages from any or all of the prohibitions specified in subsections (c) through (i), if the Bureau finds that the exemption—

(A) is in the interest of the borrowing public; and

(B) will apply only to products that maintain and strengthen home ownership and equity protection.

(2) Prohibitions

The Bureau, by regulation or order, shall prohibit acts or practices in connection with—

(A) mortgage loans that the Bureau finds to be unfair, deceptive, or designed to evade the provisions of this section; and

(B) refinancing of mortgage loans that the Bureau finds to be associated with abusive lending practices, or that are otherwise not in the interest of the borrower.

(q) Civil penalties in Federal Trade Commission enforcement actions

For purposes of enforcement by the Federal Trade Commission, any violation of a regulation issued by the Bureau pursuant to subsection (l)(2) shall be treated as a violation of a rule promulgated under section 57a of this title regarding unfair or deceptive acts or practices.

(r) Prohibitions on evasions, structuring of transactions, and reciprocal arrangements

A creditor may not take any action in connection with a high-cost mortgage—

(1) to structure a loan transaction as an open-end credit plan or another form of loan for the purpose and with the intent of evading the provisions of this subchapter; or

(2) to divide any loan transaction into separate parts for the purpose and with the intent of evading provisions of this subchapter.

(s) Modification and deferral fees prohibited

A creditor, successor in interest, assignee, or any agent of any of the above, may not charge a consumer any fee to modify, renew, extend, or amend a high-cost mortgage, or to defer any payment due under the terms of such mortgage.

(t) Payoff statement

(1) Fees

(A) In general

Except as provided in subparagraph (B), no creditor or servicer may charge a fee for informing or transmitting to any person the balance due to pay off the outstanding balance on a high-cost mortgage.

(B) Transaction fee

When payoff information referred to in subparagraph (A) is provided by facsimile transmission or by a courier service, a creditor or servicer may charge a processing fee to cover the cost of such transmission or service in an amount not to exceed an amount that is comparable to fees imposed for similar services provided in connection with consumer credit transactions that are secured by the consumer's principal dwelling and are not high-cost mortgages.

(C) Fee disclosure

Prior to charging a transaction fee as provided in subparagraph (B), a creditor or servicer shall disclose that payoff balances are available for free pursuant to subparagraph (A).

(D) Multiple requests

If a creditor or servicer has provided payoff information referred to in subparagraph (A) without charge, other than the transaction fee allowed by subparagraph (B), on 4 occasions during a calendar year, the creditor or servicer may thereafter charge a reasonable fee for providing such information during the remainder of the calendar year.

(2) Prompt delivery

Payoff balances shall be provided within 5 business days after receiving a request by a consumer or a person authorized by the consumer to obtain such information.

(u) Pre-loan counseling

(1) In general

A creditor may not extend credit to a consumer under a high-cost mortgage without first receiving certification from a counselor that is approved by the Secretary of Housing and Urban Development, or at the discretion of the Secretary, a State housing finance authority, that the consumer has received counseling on the advisability of the mortgage. Such counselor shall not be employed by the creditor or an affiliate of the creditor or be affiliated with the creditor.

(2) Disclosures required prior to counseling

No counselor may certify that a consumer has received counseling on the advisability of the high-cost mortgage unless the counselor can verify that the consumer has received each statement required (in connection with such loan) by this section or the Real Estate Settlement Procedures Act of 1974 [12 U.S.C. 2601 et seq.] with respect to the transaction.

(3) Regulations

The Board [4] may prescribe such regulations as the Board determines to be appropriate to carry out the requirements of paragraph (1).

(v) Corrections and unintentional violations

A creditor or assignee in a high-cost mortgage who, when acting in good faith, fails to comply with any requirement under this section will not be deemed to have violated such requirement if the creditor or assignee establishes that either—

(1) within 30 days of the loan closing and prior to the institution of any action, the consumer is notified of or discovers the violation, appropriate restitution is made, and whatever adjustments are necessary are made to the loan to either, at the choice of the consumer—

  (A) make the loan satisfy the requirements of this part; or

  (B) in the case of a high-cost mortgage, change the terms of the loan in a manner beneficial to the consumer so that the loan will no longer be a high-cost mortgage; or

(2) within 60 days of the creditor's discovery or receipt of notification of an unintentional violation or bona fide error and prior to the institution of any action, the consumer is notified of the compliance failure, appropriate restitution is made, and whatever adjustments are necessary are made to the loan to either, at the choice of the consumer—

  (A) make the loan satisfy the requirements of this part; or

  (B) in the case of a high-cost mortgage, change the terms of the loan in a manner beneficial so that the loan will no longer be a high-cost mortgage.

(Pub. L. 90–321, title I, §129, as added Pub. L. 103–325, title I, §152(d), Sept. 23, 1994, 108 Stat. 2191; amended Pub. L. 111–8, div. D, title VI, §626(c), Mar. 11, 2009, 123 Stat. 679; Pub. L. 111–203, title X, §1100A(2), (9), title XIV, §§1432, 1433, July 21, 2010, 124 Stat. 2107, 2109, 2160; Pub. L. 115–174, title I, §109(a), May 24, 2018, 132 Stat. 1305.)

EDITORIAL NOTES

Section 1602(aa) of this title, referred to in text, was redesignated section 1602(bb) of this title by Pub. L. 111–203, title X, §1100A(1)(A), July 21, 2010, 124 Stat. 2107.

The Real Estate Settlement Procedures Act of 1974, referred to in subsec. (u)(2), is Pub. L. 93–533, Dec. 22, 1974, 88 Stat. 1724, which is classified principally to chapter 27 (§2601 et seq.) of Title 12, Banks and Banking. For complete classification of this Act to the Code, see Short Title note set out under section 2601 of Title 12 and Tables.

PRIOR PROVISIONS

A prior section 1639, Pub. L. 90–321, title I, §129, May 29, 1968, 82 Stat. 156, related to consumer loans not under open end credit plans, prior to repeal by Pub. L. 96–221, title VI, §614(d)(1), Mar. 31, 1980, 94 Stat. 180. Repeal effective on expiration of two years and six months after Mar. 31, 1980, with all regulations, forms, and clauses required to be prescribed to be promulgated at least one year prior to such effective date, and allowing any creditor to comply with any amendments, in accordance with the regulations, forms, and clauses prescribed by the Board prior to such effective date, see section 625 of Pub. L. 96–221, set out as an Effective Date of 1980 Amendment note under section 1602 of this title.

AMENDMENTS

2018—Subsec. (b)(3), (4). Pub. L. 115–174 added par. (3) and redesignated former par. (3) as (4).

2010—Pub. L. 111–203, §1100A(2), substituted "Bureau" for "Board" wherever appearing.

Subsec. (c)(2). Pub. L. 111–203, §1432(a), struck out par. (2) which related to exception to prepayment penalty prohibition.

Subsec. (e). Pub. L. 111–203, §1432(b), amended subsec. (e) generally. Prior to amendment, text read as follows: "A mortgage referred to in section 1602(aa) of this title having a term of less than 5 years may not include terms under which the aggregate amount of the regular periodic payments would not fully amortize the outstanding principal balance."

Subsecs. (j) to (l). Pub. L. 111–203, §1433(a)(2), added subsecs. (j) to (l). Former subsecs. (j) to (l) redesignated (n) to (p), respectively.

Subsec. (m). Pub. L. 111–203, §1433(a)(2), added subsec. (m). Former subsec. (m) redesignated (q).

Pub. L. 111–203, §1100A(9), added subsec. (m) and struck out former subsec. (m). Prior to amendment, text read as follows: "For purposes of enforcement by the Federal Trade Commission, any violation of a regulation issued by the Federal Reserve Board pursuant to subsection (l)(2) of this section shall be treated as a violation of a rule promulgated under section 57a of this title regarding unfair or deceptive acts or practices."

Subsecs. (n) to (q). Pub. L. 111–203, §1433(a)(1), redesignated former subsecs. (j) to (m) as (n) to (q), respectively.

Subsecs. (r) to (v). Pub. L. 111–203, §1433(b)–(f), added subsecs. (r) to (v).

2009—Subsec. (m). Pub. L. 111–8 added subsec. (m).

EFFECTIVE DATE OF 2010 AMENDMENT

Amendment by section 1100A(2), (9) of Pub. L. 111–203 effective on the designated transfer date, see section 1100H of Pub. L. 111–203, set out as a note under section 552a of Title 5, Government Organization and Employees.

Amendment by sections 1432 and 1433 of Pub. L. 111–203 effective on the date on which final regulations implementing that amendment take effect, or on the date that is 18 months after the designated transfer date if such regulations have not been issued by that date, see section 1400(c) of Pub. L. 111–203, set out as a note under section 1601 of this title.

[1] *See References in Text note below.*

[2] *So in original. There is no par. (2).*

[3] *So in original. Probably should be "section".*

[4] *So in original. Probably should be "Bureau".*

§1639a. Duty of servicers of residential mortgages

(a) In general

Notwithstanding any other provision of law, whenever a servicer of residential mortgages agrees to enter into a qualified loss mitigation plan with respect to 1 or more residential mortgages originated before May 20, 2009, including mortgages held in a securitization or other investment vehicle—

(1) to the extent that the servicer owes a duty to investors or other parties to maximize the net present value of such mortgages, the duty shall be construed to apply to all such investors and parties, and not to any individual party or group of parties; and

(2) the servicer shall be deemed to have satisfied the duty set forth in paragraph (1) if, before December 31, 2012, the servicer implements a qualified loss mitigation plan that meets the following criteria:

(A) Default on the payment of such mortgage has occurred, is imminent, or is reasonably foreseeable, as such terms are defined by guidelines issued by the Secretary of the Treasury or his designee under the Emergency Economic Stabilization Act of 2008 [12 U.S.C. 5201 et seq.].

(B) The mortgagor occupies the property securing the mortgage as his or her principal residence.

(C) The servicer reasonably determined, consistent with the guidelines issued by the Secretary of the Treasury or his designee, that the application of such qualified loss mitigation plan to a mortgage or class of mortgages will likely provide an anticipated recovery on the outstanding principal mortgage debt that will exceed the anticipated recovery through foreclosures.

(b) No liability

A servicer that is deemed to be acting in the best interests of all investors or other parties under this section shall not be liable to any party who is owed a duty under subsection (a)(1), and shall not be subject to any injunction, stay, or other equitable relief to such party, based solely upon the implementation by the servicer of a qualified loss mitigation plan.

(c) Standard industry practice

The qualified loss mitigation plan guidelines issued by the Secretary of the Treasury under the Emergency Economic Stabilization Act of 2008 [12 U.S.C. 5201 et seq.] shall constitute standard industry practice for purposes of all Federal and State laws.

(d) Scope of safe harbor

Any person, including a trustee, issuer, and loan originator, shall not be liable for monetary damages or be subject to an injunction, stay, or other equitable relief, based solely upon the cooperation of such person with a servicer when such cooperation is necessary for the servicer to implement a qualified loss mitigation plan that meets the requirements of subsection (a).

(e) Reporting

Each servicer that engages in qualified loss mitigation plans under this section shall regularly report to the Secretary of the Treasury the extent, scope, and results of the servicer's modification activities. The Secretary of the Treasury shall prescribe regulations or guidance specifying the form, content, and timing of such reports.

(f) Definitions

As used in this section—

(1) the term "qualified loss mitigation plan" means—

(A) a residential loan modification, workout, or other loss mitigation plan, including to the extent that the Secretary of the Treasury determines appropriate, a loan sale, real property disposition, trial modification, pre-foreclosure sale, and deed in lieu of foreclosure, that is described or authorized in guidelines issued by the Secretary of the Treasury or his designee under the Emergency Economic Stabilization Act of 2008 [12 U.S.C. 5201 et seq.]; and

(B) a refinancing of a mortgage under the Hope for Homeowners program;

(2) the term "servicer" means the person responsible for the servicing for others of residential mortgage loans (including of a pool of residential mortgage loans); and

(3) the term "securitization vehicle" means a trust, special purpose entity, or other legal structure that is used to facilitate the issuing of securities, participation certificates, or similar instruments backed by or referring to a pool of assets that includes residential mortgages (or instruments that are related to residential mortgages such as credit-linked notes).

(g) Rule of construction

No provision of subsection (b) or (d) shall be construed as affecting the liability of any servicer or person as described in subsection (d) for actual fraud in the origination or servicing of a loan or in the implementation of a qualified loss mitigation plan, or for the violation of a State or Federal law, including laws regulating the origination of mortgage loans, commonly referred to as predatory lending laws.

(Pub. L. 90–321, title I, §129A, as added Pub. L. 110–289, div. A, title IV, §1403, July 30, 2008, 122 Stat. 2809; renumbered §129 and amended Pub. L. 111–22, div. A, title II, §201(b), May 20, 2009, 123 Stat. 1638; renumbered §129A, Pub. L. 111–203, title XIV, §1402(a)(1), July 21, 2010, 124 Stat. 2138.)

EDITORIAL NOTES

REFERENCES IN TEXT

The Emergency Economic Stabilization Act of 2008, referred to in subsecs. (a)(2)(A), (c), (f)(1)(A), is div. A of Pub. L. 110–343, Oct. 3, 2008, 122 Stat. 3765, which is classified principally to chapter 52 (§5201 et seq.) of Title 12, Banks and Banking. For complete classification of this Act to the Code, see Short Title note set out under section 5201 of Title 12 and Tables.

AMENDMENTS

2009—Pub. L. 111–22 amended section generally. Prior to amendment, section related to fiduciary duty of servicers of pooled residential mortgages without providing for date limitation for implementing modifications or workout plans.

STATUTORY NOTES AND RELATED SUBSIDIARIES

FINDINGS

Pub. L. 111–22, div. A, title II, §201(a), May 20, 2009, 123 Stat. 1638, provided that: "Congress finds the following:

"(1) Increasing numbers of mortgage foreclosures are not only depriving many Americans of their homes, but are also destabilizing property values and negatively affecting State and local economies as well as the national economy.

"(2) In order to reduce the number of foreclosures and to stabilize property values, local economies, and the national economy, servicers must be given—

"(A) authorization to—

"(i) modify mortgage loans and engage in other loss mitigation activities consistent with applicable guidelines issued by the Secretary of the Treasury or his designee under the Emergency Economic Stabilization Act of 2008 [12 U.S.C. 5201 et seq.]; and

"(ii) refinance mortgage loans under the Hope for Homeowners program; and

"(B) a safe harbor to enable such servicers to exercise these authorities."

§1639b. Residential mortgage loan origination

(a) Finding and purpose

(1) Finding

The Congress finds that economic stabilization would be enhanced by the protection, limitation, and regulation of the terms of residential mortgage credit and the practices related to such credit, while ensuring that responsible, affordable mortgage credit remains available to consumers.

(2) Purpose

It is the purpose of this section and section 1639c of this title to assure that consumers are offered and receive residential mortgage loans on terms that reasonably reflect their ability to repay the loans and that are understandable and not unfair, deceptive or abusive.

(b) Duty of care

(1) Standard

Subject to regulations prescribed under this subsection, each mortgage originator shall, in addition to the duties imposed by otherwise applicable provisions of State or Federal law—

(A) be qualified and, when required, registered and licensed as a mortgage originator in accordance with applicable State or Federal law, including the Secure and Fair Enforcement for Mortgage Licensing Act of 2008 [12 U.S.C. 5101 et seq.]; and

(B) include on all loan documents any unique identifier of the mortgage originator provided by the Nationwide Mortgage Licensing System and Registry.

(2) Compliance procedures required

The Bureau shall prescribe regulations requiring depository institutions to establish and maintain procedures reasonably designed to assure and monitor the compliance of such depository institutions, the subsidiaries of such institutions, and the employees of such institutions or subsidiaries with the requirements of this section and the registration procedures established under section 1507 of the Secure and Fair Enforcement for Mortgage Licensing Act of 2008 [12 U.S.C. 5106].

(c) Prohibition on steering incentives

(1) In general

For any residential mortgage loan, no mortgage originator shall receive from any person and no person shall pay to a mortgage originator, directly or indirectly, compensation that varies based on the terms of the loan (other than the amount of the principal).

(2) Restructuring of financing origination fee

(A) In general

For any mortgage loan, a mortgage originator may not receive from any person other than the consumer and no person, other than the consumer, who knows or has reason to know that a consumer has directly compensated or will directly compensate a mortgage originator may pay a mortgage originator any origination fee or charge except bona fide third party charges not retained by the creditor, mortgage originator, or an affiliate of the creditor or mortgage originator.

(B) Exception

Notwithstanding subparagraph (A), a mortgage originator may receive from a person other than the consumer an origination fee or charge, and a person other than the consumer may pay a mortgage originator an origination fee or charge, if—

(i) the mortgage originator does not receive any compensation directly from the consumer; and

(ii) the consumer does not make an upfront payment of discount points, origination points, or fees, however denominated (other than bona fide third party charges not retained by the mortgage originator, creditor, or an affiliate of the creditor or originator), except that the Bureau may, by rule, waive or provide exemptions to this clause if the Bureau determines that such waiver or exemption is in the interest of consumers and in the public interest.

(3) Regulations

The Bureau shall prescribe regulations to prohibit—

(A) mortgage originators from steering any consumer to a residential mortgage loan that—

(i) the consumer lacks a reasonable ability to repay (in accordance with regulations prescribed under section 1639c(a) of this title); or

(ii) has predatory characteristics or effects (such as equity stripping, excessive fees, or abusive terms);

(B) mortgage originators from steering any consumer from a residential mortgage loan for which the consumer is qualified that is a qualified mortgage (as defined in section 1639c(b)(2) of this title) to a residential mortgage loan that is not a qualified mortgage;

(C) abusive or unfair lending practices that promote disparities among consumers of equal credit worthiness but of different race, ethnicity, gender, or age; and

(D) mortgage originators from—

(i) mischaracterizing the credit history of a consumer or the residential mortgage loans available to a consumer;

(ii) mischaracterizing or suborning the mischaracterization of the appraised value of the property securing the extension of credit; or

(iii) if unable to suggest, offer, or recommend to a consumer a loan that is not more expensive than a loan for which the consumer qualifies, discouraging a consumer from seeking a residential mortgage loan secured by a consumer's principal dwelling from another mortgage originator.

(4) Rules of construction

No provision of this subsection shall be construed as—

(A) permitting any yield spread premium or other similar compensation that would, for any residential mortgage loan, permit the total amount of direct and indirect compensation from all sources permitted to a mortgage originator to vary based on the terms of the loan (other than the amount of the principal);

(B) limiting or affecting the amount of compensation received by a creditor upon the sale of a consummated loan to a subsequent purchaser;

(C) restricting a consumer's ability to finance, at the option of the consumer, including through principal or rate, any origination fees or costs permitted under this subsection, or the mortgage originator's right to receive such fees or costs (including compensation) from any person, subject to paragraph (2)(B), so long as such fees or costs do not vary based on the terms of the loan (other than the amount of the principal) or the consumer's decision about whether to finance such fees or costs; or

(D) prohibiting incentive payments to a mortgage originator based on the number of residential mortgage loans originated within a specified period of time.

(d) Liability for violations

(1) In general

For purposes of providing a cause of action for any failure by a mortgage originator, other than a creditor, to comply with any requirement imposed under this section and any regulation prescribed under this section, section 1640 of this title shall be applied with respect to any such failure by substituting "mortgage originator" for "creditor" each place such term appears in each such subsection.[1]

(2) Maximum

The maximum amount of any liability of a mortgage originator under paragraph (1) to a consumer for any violation of this section shall not exceed the greater of actual damages or an amount equal to 3 times the total amount of direct and indirect compensation or gain accruing to the mortgage originator in connection with the residential mortgage loan involved in the violation, plus the costs to the consumer of the action, including a reasonable attorney's fee.

(e) Discretionary regulatory authority

(1) In general

The Bureau shall, by regulations, prohibit or condition terms, acts or practices relating to residential mortgage loans that the Bureau finds to be abusive, unfair, deceptive, predatory, necessary or proper to ensure that responsible, affordable mortgage credit remains available to consumers in a manner consistent with the purposes of this section and section 1639c of this title, necessary or proper to effectuate the purposes of this section and section 1639c of this title, to prevent circumvention or evasion thereof, or to facilitate compliance with such sections, or are not in the interest of the borrower.

(2) Application

The regulations prescribed under paragraph (1) shall be applicable to all residential mortgage loans and shall be applied in the same manner as regulations prescribed under section 1604 of this title.

(f) Timeshare plans

This section and any regulations promulgated thereunder do not apply to an extension of credit relating to a plan described in section 101(53D) of title 11.

(Pub. L. 90–321, title I, §129B, as added and amended Pub. L. 111–203, title X, §1100A(2), title XIV, §§1402(a)(2), 1403–1405(a), July 21, 2010, 124 Stat. 2107, 2139-2141.)

EDITORIAL NOTES

REFERENCES IN TEXT

The Secure and Fair Enforcement for Mortgage Licensing Act of 2008, referred to in subsec. (b)(1)(A), is title V of div. A of Pub. L. 110–289, July 30, 2008, 122 Stat. 2810, also known as the S.A.F.E. Mortgage Licensing Act of 2008, which is classified generally to chapter 51 (§5101 et seq.) of Title 12, Banks and Banking. For complete classification of this Act to the Code, see Short Title note set out under section 5101 of Title 12 and Tables.

AMENDMENTS

2010—Pub. L. 111–203, §1100A(2), substituted "Bureau" for "Board" wherever appearing.
Subsec. (c). Pub. L. 111–203, §1403, added subsec. (c).
Subsec. (d). Pub. L. 111–203, §1404, added subsec. (d).
Subsecs. (e), (f). Pub. L. 111–203, §1405(a), added subsecs. (e) and (f).

EFFECTIVE DATE OF 2010 AMENDMENT

Amendment by section 1100A(2) of Pub. L. 111–203 effective on the designated transfer date, see section 1100H of Pub. L. 111–203, set out as a note under section 552a of Title 5, Government Organization and Employees.

Amendment by sections 1403–1405(a) of Pub. L. 111–203 effective on the date on which final regulations implementing that amendment take effect, or on the date that is 18 months after the designated transfer date if such regulations have not been issued by that date, see section 1400(c) of Pub. L. 111–203, set out as a note under section 1601 of this title.

STATUTORY NOTES AND RELATED SUBSIDIARIES

EFFECTIVE DATE

Section effective on the date on which final regulations implementing such section take effect, or on the date that is 18 months after the designated transfer date if such regulations have not been issued by that date, see section 1400(c) of Pub. L. 111–203, set out as an Effective Date of 2010 Amendment note under section 1601 of this title.

RULE OF CONSTRUCTION

Pub. L. 111–203, title XIV, §1415, July 21, 2010, 124 Stat. 2153, provided that: "Except as otherwise expressly provided in section 129B or 129C of the Truth in Lending Act [15 U.S.C. 1639b, 1639c] (as added by this title), no provision of such section 129B or 129C shall be construed as superseding, repealing, or affecting any duty, right, obligation, privilege, or remedy of any person under any other provision of the Truth in Lending Act [15 U.S.C. 1601 et seq.] or any other provision of Federal or State law."

[For definition of "State" as used in section 1415 of Pub. L. 111–203, set out above, see section 5301 of Title 12, Banks and Banking.]

---

[1] So in original. Probably should be "in such section."

---

§1639c. Minimum standards for residential mortgage loans

(a) Ability to repay

(1) In general

In accordance with regulations prescribed by the Bureau, no creditor may make a residential mortgage loan unless the creditor makes a reasonable and good faith determination based on verified and documented information that, at the time the loan is consummated, the consumer has a reasonable ability to repay the loan, according to its terms, and all applicable taxes, insurance (including mortgage guarantee insurance), and assessments.

(2) Multiple loans

If the creditor knows, or has reason to know, that 1 or more residential mortgage loans secured by the same dwelling will be made to the same consumer, the creditor shall make a reasonable and good faith determination, based on verified and documented information, that the consumer has a reasonable ability to repay the combined payments of all loans on the same dwelling according to the terms of those loans and all applicable taxes, insurance (including mortgage guarantee insurance), and assessments.

(3) Basis for determination

A determination under this subsection of a consumer's ability to repay a residential mortgage loan shall include consideration of the consumer's credit history, current income, expected income the consumer is reasonably assured of receiving, current obligations, debt-to-income ratio or the residual income the consumer will have after paying non-mortgage debt and mortgage-related obligations, employment status, and other financial resources other than the consumer's equity in the dwelling or real property that secures repayment of the loan. A creditor shall determine the ability of the consumer to repay using a payment schedule that fully amortizes the loan over the term of the loan.

(4) Income verification

A creditor making a residential mortgage loan shall verify amounts of income or assets that such creditor relies on to determine repayment ability, including expected income or assets, by reviewing the consumer's Internal Revenue Service Form W–2, tax returns, payroll receipts, financial institution records, or other third-party documents that provide reasonably reliable evidence of the consumer's income or assets. In order to safeguard against fraudulent reporting, any consideration of a consumer's income history in making a determination under this subsection shall include the verification of such income by the use of—

(A) Internal Revenue Service transcripts of tax returns; or

(B) a method that quickly and effectively verifies income documentation by a third party subject to rules prescribed by the Bureau.

(5) Exemption

With respect to loans made, guaranteed, or insured by Federal departments or agencies identified in subsection (b)(3)(B)(ii), such departments or agencies may exempt refinancings under a streamlined refinancing from this income verification requirement as long as the following conditions are met:

(A) The consumer is not 30 days or more past due on the prior existing residential mortgage loan.

(B) The refinancing does not increase the principal balance outstanding on the prior existing residential mortgage loan, except to the extent of fees and charges allowed by the department or agency making, guaranteeing, or insuring the refinancing.

(C) Total points and fees (as defined in section 1602(aa)(4) [1] of this title, other than bona fide third party charges not retained by the mortgage originator, creditor, or an affiliate of the creditor or mortgage originator) payable in connection with the refinancing do not exceed 3 percent of the total new loan amount.

(D) The interest rate on the refinanced loan is lower than the interest rate of the original loan, unless the borrower is refinancing from an adjustable rate to a fixed-rate loan, under guidelines that the department or agency shall establish for loans they make, guarantee, or issue.

(E) The refinancing is subject to a payment schedule that will fully amortize the refinancing in accordance with the regulations prescribed by the department or agency making, guaranteeing, or insuring the refinancing.

(F) The terms of the refinancing do not result in a balloon payment, as defined in subsection (b)(2)(A)(ii).

(G) Both the residential mortgage loan being refinanced and the refinancing satisfy all requirements of the department or agency making, guaranteeing, or insuring the refinancing.

(6) Nonstandard loans

(A) Variable rate loans that defer repayment of any principal or interest

For purposes of determining, under this subsection, a consumer's ability to repay a variable rate residential mortgage loan that allows or requires the consumer to defer the repayment of any principal or interest, the creditor shall use a fully amortizing repayment schedule.

(B) Interest-only loans

For purposes of determining, under this subsection, a consumer's ability to repay a residential mortgage loan that permits or requires the payment of interest only, the creditor shall use the payment amount required to amortize the loan by its final maturity.

(C) Calculation for negative amortization

In making any determination under this subsection, a creditor shall also take into consideration any balance increase that may accrue from any negative amortization provision.

(D) Calculation process

For purposes of making any determination under this subsection, a creditor shall calculate the monthly payment amount for principal and interest on any residential mortgage loan by assuming—

(i) the loan proceeds are fully disbursed on the date of the consummation of the loan;

(ii) the loan is to be repaid in substantially equal monthly amortizing payments for principal and interest over the entire term of the loan with no balloon payment, unless the loan contract requires more rapid repayment (including balloon payment), in which case the calculation shall be made (I) in accordance with regulations prescribed by the Bureau, with respect to any loan which has an annual percentage rate that does not exceed the average prime offer rate for a comparable transaction, as of the date the interest rate is set, by 1.5 or more percentage points for a first lien residential mortgage loan; and by 3.5 or more percentage points for a subordinate lien residential mortgage loan; or (II) using the contract's repayment schedule, with respect to a loan which has an annual percentage rate, as of the date the interest rate is set, that is at least 1.5 percentage points above the average prime offer rate for a first lien residential mortgage loan; and 3.5 percentage points above the average prime offer rate for a subordinate lien residential mortgage loan; and

(iii) the interest rate over the entire term of the loan is a fixed rate equal to the fully indexed rate at the time of the loan closing, without considering the introductory rate.

(E) Refinance of hybrid loans with current lender

In considering any application for refinancing an existing hybrid loan by the creditor into a standard loan to be made by the same creditor in any case in which there would be a reduction in monthly payment and the mortgagor has not been delinquent on any payment on the existing hybrid loan, the creditor may—

(i) consider the mortgagor's good standing on the existing mortgage;

(ii) consider if the extension of new credit would prevent a likely default should the original mortgage reset and give such concerns a higher priority as an acceptable underwriting practice; and

(iii) offer rate discounts and other favorable terms to such mortgagor that would be available to new customers with high credit ratings based on such underwriting practice.

(7) Fully-indexed rate defined

For purposes of this subsection, the term "fully indexed rate" means the index rate prevailing on a residential mortgage loan at the time the loan is made plus the margin that will apply after the expiration of any introductory interest rates.

(8) Reverse mortgages and bridge loans

This subsection shall not apply with respect to any reverse mortgage or temporary or bridge loan with a term of 12 months or less, including to any loan to purchase a new dwelling where the consumer plans to sell a different dwelling within 12 months.

(9) Seasonal income

If documented income, including income from a small business, is a repayment source for a residential mortgage loan, a creditor may consider the seasonality and irregularity of such income in the underwriting of and scheduling of payments for such credit.

(b) Presumption of ability to repay

(1) In general

Any creditor with respect to any residential mortgage loan, and any assignee of such loan subject to liability under this subchapter, may presume that the loan has met the requirements of subsection (a), if the loan is a qualified mortgage.

(2) Definitions

For purposes of this subsection, the following definitions shall apply:

(A) Qualified mortgage

The term "qualified mortgage" means any residential mortgage loan—

(i) for which the regular periodic payments for the loan may not—

(I) result in an increase of the principal balance; or

(II) except as provided in subparagraph (E), allow the consumer to defer repayment of principal;

(ii) except as provided in subparagraph (E), the terms of which do not result in a balloon payment, where a "balloon payment" is a scheduled payment that is more than twice as large as the average of earlier scheduled payments;

(iii) for which the income and financial resources relied upon to qualify the obligors on the loan are verified and documented;

(iv) in the case of a fixed rate loan, for which the underwriting process is based on a payment schedule that fully amortizes the loan over the loan term and takes into account all applicable taxes, insurance, and assessments;

(v) in the case of an adjustable rate loan, for which the underwriting is based on the maximum rate permitted under the loan during the first 5 years, and a payment schedule that fully amortizes the loan over the loan term and takes into account all applicable taxes, insurance, and assessments;

(vi) that complies with any guidelines or regulations established by the Bureau relating to ratios of total monthly debt to monthly income or alternative measures of ability to pay regular expenses after payment of total monthly debt, taking into account the income levels of the borrower and such other factors as the Bureau may determine relevant and consistent with the purposes described in paragraph (3)(B)(i);

(vii) for which the total points and fees (as defined in subparagraph (C)) payable in connection with the loan do not exceed 3 percent of the total loan amount;

(viii) for which the term of the loan does not exceed 30 years, except as such term may be extended under paragraph (3), such as in high-cost areas; and

(ix) in the case of a reverse mortgage (except for the purposes of subsection (a) of this section, to the extent that such mortgages are exempt altogether from those requirements), a reverse mortgage which meets the standards for a qualified mortgage, as set by the Bureau in rules that are consistent with the purposes of this subsection.

(B) Average prime offer rate

The term "average prime offer rate" means the average prime offer rate for a comparable transaction as of the date on which the interest rate for the transaction is set, as published by the Bureau..[2]

(C) Points and fees

(i) In general

For purposes of subparagraph (A), the term "points and fees" means points and fees as defined by section 1602(aa)(4) [1] of this title (other than bona fide third party charges not retained by the mortgage originator, creditor, or an affiliate of the creditor or mortgage originator).

(ii) Computation

For purposes of computing the total points and fees under this subparagraph, the total points and fees shall exclude either of the amounts described in the following subclauses, but not both:

(I) Up to and including 2 bona fide discount points payable by the consumer in connection with the mortgage, but only if the interest rate from which the mortgage's interest rate will be discounted does not exceed by more than 1 percentage point the average prime offer rate.

(II) Unless 2 bona fide discount points have been excluded under subclause (I), up to and including 1 bona fide discount point payable by the consumer in connection with the mortgage, but only if the interest rate from which the mortgage's interest rate will be discounted does not exceed by more than 2 percentage points the average prime offer rate.

(iii) Bona fide discount points defined

For purposes of clause (ii), the term "bona fide discount points" means loan discount points which are knowingly paid by the consumer for the purpose of reducing, and which in fact result in a bona fide reduction of, the interest rate or time-price differential applicable to the mortgage.

(iv) Interest rate reduction

Subclauses (I) and (II) of clause (ii) shall not apply to discount points used to purchase an interest rate reduction unless the amount of the interest rate reduction purchased is reasonably consistent with established industry norms and practices for secondary mortgage market transactions.

(D) Smaller loans

The Bureau shall prescribe rules adjusting the criteria under subparagraph (A)(vii) in order to permit lenders that extend smaller loans to meet the requirements of the presumption of compliance under paragraph (1). In prescribing such rules, the Bureau shall consider the potential impact of such rules on rural areas and other areas where home values are lower.

(E) Balloon loans

The Bureau may, by regulation, provide that the term "qualified mortgage" includes a balloon loan—

(i) that meets all of the criteria for a qualified mortgage under subparagraph (A) (except clauses (i)(II), (ii), (iv), and (v) of such subparagraph);

(ii) for which the creditor makes a determination that the consumer is able to make all scheduled payments, except the balloon payment, out of income or assets other than the collateral;

(iii) for which the underwriting is based on a payment schedule that fully amortizes the loan over a period of not more than 30 years and takes into account all applicable taxes, insurance, and assessments; and

(iv) that is extended by a creditor that—

(I) operates in rural or underserved areas;

(II) together with all affiliates, has total annual residential mortgage loan originations that do not exceed a limit set by the Bureau;

(III) retains the balloon loans in portfolio; and

(IV) meets any asset size threshold and any other criteria as the Bureau may establish, consistent with the purposes of this part.

(F) Safe harbor

(i) Definitions

In this subparagraph—

(I) the term "covered institution" means an insured depository institution or an insured credit union that, together with its affiliates, has less than $10,000,000,000 in total consolidated assets;

(II) the term "insured credit union" has the meaning given the term in section 1752 of title 12;

(III) the term "insured depository institution" has the meaning given the term in section 1813 of title 12;

(IV) the term "interest-only" means that, under the terms of the legal obligation, one or more of the periodic payments may be applied solely to accrued interest and not to loan principal; and

(V) the term "negative amortization" means payment of periodic payments that will result in an increase in the principal balance under the terms of the legal obligation.

(ii) Safe harbor

In this section—

(I) the term "qualified mortgage" includes any residential mortgage loan—

(aa) that is originated and retained in portfolio by a covered institution;

(bb) that is in compliance with the limitations with respect to prepayment penalties described in subsections (c)(1) and (c)(3);

(cc) that is in compliance with the requirements of clause (vii) of subparagraph (A);

(dd) that does not have negative amortization or interest-only features; and

(ee) for which the covered institution considers and documents the debt, income, and financial resources of the consumer in accordance with clause (iv); and

(II) a residential mortgage loan described in subclause (I) shall be deemed to meet the requirements of subsection (a).

(iii) Exception for certain transfers

A residential mortgage loan described in clause (ii)(I) shall not qualify for the safe harbor under clause (ii) if the legal title to the residential mortgage loan is sold, assigned, or otherwise transferred to another person unless the residential mortgage loan is sold, assigned, or otherwise transferred—

(I) to another person by reason of the bankruptcy or failure of a covered institution;

(II) to a covered institution so long as the loan is retained in portfolio by the covered institution to which the loan is sold, assigned, or otherwise transferred;

(III) pursuant to a merger of a covered institution with another person or the acquisition of a covered institution by another person or of another person by a covered institution, so long as the loan is retained in portfolio by the person to whom the loan is sold, assigned, or otherwise transferred; or

(IV) to a wholly owned subsidiary of a covered institution, provided that, after the sale, assignment, or transfer, the residential mortgage loan is considered to be an asset of the covered institution for regulatory accounting purposes.

(iv) Consideration and documentation requirements

The consideration and documentation requirements described in clause (ii)(I)(ee) shall—

(I) not be construed to require compliance with, or documentation in accordance with, appendix Q to part 1026 of title 12, Code of Federal Regulations, or any successor regulation; and

(II) be construed to permit multiple methods of documentation.

(3) Regulations

(A) In general

The Bureau shall prescribe regulations to carry out the purposes of this subsection.

(B) Revision of safe harbor criteria

(i) In general

The Bureau may prescribe regulations that revise, add to, or subtract from the criteria that define a qualified mortgage upon a finding that such regulations are necessary or proper to ensure that responsible, affordable mortgage credit remains available to consumers in a manner consistent with the purposes of this section, necessary and appropriate to effectuate the purposes of this section and section 1639b of this title, to prevent circumvention or evasion thereof, or to facilitate compliance with such sections.

(ii) Loan definition

The following agencies shall, in consultation with the Bureau, prescribe rules defining the types of loans they insure, guarantee, or administer, as the case may be, that are qualified mortgages for purposes of paragraph (2)(A), and such rules may revise, add to, or subtract from the criteria used to define a qualified mortgage under paragraph (2)(A), upon a finding that such rules are consistent with the purposes of this section and section 1639b of this title, to prevent circumvention or evasion thereof, or to facilitate compliance with such sections:

(I) The Department of Housing and Urban Development, with regard to mortgages insured under the National Housing Act [12 U.S.C. 1701 et seq.].

(II) The Department of Veterans Affairs, with regard to a loan made or guaranteed by the Secretary of Veterans Affairs.

(III) The Department of Agriculture, with regard [3] loans guaranteed by the Secretary of Agriculture pursuant to section 1472(h) of title 42.

(IV) The Rural Housing Service, with regard to loans insured by the Rural Housing Service.

(C) Consideration of underwriting requirements for Property Assessed Clean Energy financing

(i) Definition

In this subparagraph, the term "Property Assessed Clean Energy financing" means financing to cover the costs of home improvements that results in a tax assessment on the real property of the consumer.

(ii) Regulations

The Bureau shall prescribe regulations that carry out the purposes of subsection (a) and apply section 1640 of this title with respect to violations under subsection (a) of this section with respect to Property Assessed Clean Energy financing, which shall account for the unique nature of Property Assessed Clean Energy financing.

(iii) Collection of information and consultation

In prescribing the regulations under this subparagraph, the Bureau—

(I) may collect such information and data that the Bureau determines is necessary; and

(II) shall consult with State and local governments and bond-issuing authorities.

(c) Prohibition on certain prepayment penalties

(1) Prohibited on certain loans

(A) In general

A residential mortgage loan that is not a "qualified mortgage", as defined under subsection (b)(2), may not contain terms under which a consumer must pay a prepayment penalty for paying all or part of the principal after the loan is consummated.

(B) Exclusions

For purposes of this subsection, a "qualified mortgage" may not include a residential mortgage loan that—

(i) has an adjustable rate; or

(ii) has an annual percentage rate that exceeds the average prime offer rate for a comparable transaction, as of the date the interest rate is set—

(I) by 1.5 or more percentage points, in the case of a first lien residential mortgage loan having a original principal obligation amount that is equal to or less than the amount of the maximum limitation on the original principal obligation of mortgage in effect for a residence of the applicable size, as of the date of such interest rate set, pursuant to the 6th sentence of section 1454(a)(2) of title 12;

(II) by 2.5 or more percentage points, in the case of a first lien residential mortgage loan having a original principal obligation amount that is more than the amount of the maximum limitation on the original principal obligation of mortgage in effect for a residence of the applicable size, as of the date of such interest rate set, pursuant to the 6th sentence of section 1454(a)(2) of title 12; and

(III) by 3.5 or more percentage points, in the case of a subordinate lien residential mortgage loan.

(2) Publication of average prime offer rate and APR thresholds

The Bureau—

    (A) shall publish, and update at least weekly, average prime offer rates;

    (B) may publish multiple rates based on varying types of mortgage transactions; and

    (C) shall adjust the thresholds established under subclause (I), (II), and (III) of paragraph (1)(B)(ii) as necessary to reflect significant changes in market conditions and to effectuate the purposes of the Mortgage Reform and Anti-Predatory Lending Act.

(3) Phased-out penalties on qualified mortgages

A qualified mortgage (as defined in subsection (b)(2)) may not contain terms under which a consumer must pay a prepayment penalty for paying all or part of the principal after the loan is consummated in excess of the following limitations:

    (A) During the 1-year period beginning on the date the loan is consummated, the prepayment penalty shall not exceed an amount equal to 3 percent of the outstanding balance on the loan.

    (B) During the 1-year period beginning after the period described in subparagraph (A), the prepayment penalty shall not exceed an amount equal to 2 percent of the outstanding balance on the loan.

    (C) During the 1-year period beginning after the 1-year period described in subparagraph (B), the prepayment penalty shall not exceed an amount equal to 1 percent of the outstanding balance on the loan.

    (D) After the end of the 3-year period beginning on the date the loan is consummated, no prepayment penalty may be imposed on a qualified mortgage.

(4) Option for no prepayment penalty required

A creditor may not offer a consumer a residential mortgage loan product that has a prepayment penalty for paying all or part of the principal after the loan is consummated as a term of the loan without offering the consumer a residential mortgage loan product that does not have a prepayment penalty as a term of the loan.

(d) Single premium credit insurance prohibited

No creditor may finance, directly or indirectly, in connection with any residential mortgage loan or with any extension of credit under an open end consumer credit plan secured by the principal dwelling of the consumer, any credit life, credit disability, credit unemployment, or credit property insurance, or any other accident, loss-of-income, life, or health insurance, or any payments directly or indirectly for any debt cancellation or suspension agreement or contract, except that—

    (1) insurance premiums or debt cancellation or suspension fees calculated and paid in full on a monthly basis shall not be considered financed by the creditor; and

    (2) this subsection shall not apply to credit unemployment insurance for which the unemployment insurance premiums are reasonable, the creditor receives no direct or indirect compensation in connection with the unemployment insurance premiums, and the unemployment insurance premiums are paid pursuant to another insurance contract and not paid to an affiliate of the creditor.

(e) Arbitration

(1) In general

No residential mortgage loan and no extension of credit under an open end consumer credit plan secured by the principal dwelling of the consumer may include terms which require arbitration or any other nonjudicial procedure as the method for resolving any controversy or settling any claims arising out of the transaction.

(2) Post-controversy agreements

Subject to paragraph (3), paragraph (1) shall not be construed as limiting the right of the consumer and the creditor or any assignee to agree to arbitration or any other nonjudicial procedure as the method for resolving any controversy at any time after a dispute or claim under the transaction arises.

(3) No waiver of statutory cause of action

No provision of any residential mortgage loan or of any extension of credit under an open end consumer credit plan secured by the principal dwelling of the consumer, and no other agreement between the consumer and the creditor relating to the residential mortgage loan or extension of credit referred to in paragraph (1), shall be applied or interpreted so as to bar a consumer from bringing an action in an appropriate district court of the United States, or any other court of competent jurisdiction, pursuant to section 1640 of this title or any other provision of law, for damages or other relief in connection with any alleged violation of this section, any other provision of this subchapter, or any other Federal law.

(f) Mortgages with negative amortization

No creditor may extend credit to a borrower in connection with a consumer credit transaction under an open or closed end consumer credit plan secured by a dwelling or residential real property that includes a dwelling, other than a reverse mortgage, that provides or permits a payment plan that may, at any time over the term of the extension of credit, result in negative amortization unless, before such transaction is consummated—

    (1) the creditor provides the consumer with a statement that—

        (A) the pending transaction will or may, as the case may be, result in negative amortization;

        (B) describes negative amortization in such manner as the Bureau shall prescribe;

(C) negative amortization increases the outstanding principal balance of the account; and

(D) negative amortization reduces the consumer's equity in the dwelling or real property; and

(2) in the case of a first-time borrower with respect to a residential mortgage loan that is not a qualified mortgage, the first-time borrower provides the creditor with sufficient documentation to demonstrate that the consumer received homeownership counseling from organizations or counselors certified by the Secretary of Housing and Urban Development as competent to provide such counseling.

(g) Protection against loss of anti-deficiency protection

(1) Definition

For purposes of this subsection, the term "anti-deficiency law" means the law of any State which provides that, in the event of foreclosure on the residential property of a consumer securing a mortgage, the consumer is not liable, in accordance with the terms and limitations of such State law, for any deficiency between the sale price obtained on such property through foreclosure and the outstanding balance of the mortgage.

(2) Notice at time of consumation

In the case of any residential mortgage loan that is, or upon consummation will be, subject to protection under an anti-deficiency law, the creditor or mortgage originator shall provide a written notice to the consumer describing the protection provided by the anti-deficiency law and the significance for the consumer of the loss of such protection before such loan is consummated.

(3) Notice before refinancing that would cause loss of protection

In the case of any residential mortgage loan that is subject to protection under an anti-deficiency law, if a creditor or mortgage originator provides an application to a consumer, or receives an application from a consumer, for any type of refinancing for such loan that would cause the loan to lose the protection of such anti-deficiency law, the creditor or mortgage originator shall provide a written notice to the consumer describing the protection provided by the anti-deficiency law and the significance for the consumer of the loss of such protection before any agreement for any such refinancing is consummated.

(h) Policy regarding acceptance of partial payment

In the case of any residential mortgage loan, a creditor shall disclose prior to settlement or, in the case of a person becoming a creditor with respect to an existing residential mortgage loan, at the time such person becomes a creditor
—

(1) the creditor's policy regarding the acceptance of partial payments; and

(2) if partial payments are accepted, how such payments will be applied to such mortgage and if such payments will be placed in escrow.

(i) Timeshare plans

This section and any regulations promulgated under this section do not apply to an extension of credit relating to a plan described in section 101(53D) of title 11.

(Pub. L. 90–321, title I, §129C, as added and amended Pub. L. 111–203, title X, §1100A(2), title XIV, §§1411(a)(2), 1412, 1414(a), (c), (d), July 21, 2010, 124 Stat. 2107, 2142, 2145, 2149, 2152; Pub. L. 114–94, div. G, title LXXXIX, §89003(1), Dec. 4, 2015, 129 Stat. 1800; Pub. L. 115–174, title I, §101, title III, §307, May 24, 2018, 132 Stat. 1297, 1347.)

EDITORIAL NOTES

REFERENCES IN TEXT

Section 1602(aa)(4) of this title, referred to in subsecs. (a)(5)(C) and (b)(2)(C)(i), was redesignated section 1602(bb)(4) of this title by Pub. L. 111–203, title X, §1100A(1)(A), July 21, 2010, 124 Stat. 2107.

This part, referred to in subsec. (b)(2)(E)(iv)(IV), was in the original "this subtitle", and was translated as reading "this chapter", meaning chapter 2 of title I of Pub. L. 90–321, to reflect the probable intent of Congress. Title I of Pub. L. 90–321 does not contain subtitles.

The National Housing Act, referred to in subsec. (b)(3)(B)(ii)(I), is act June 27, 1934, ch. 847, 48 Stat. 246, which is classified principally to chapter 13 (§1701 et seq.) of Title 12, Banks and Banking. For complete classification of this Act to the Code, see section 1701 of Title 12 and Tables.

The Mortgage Reform and Anti-Predatory Lending Act, referred to in subsec. (c)(2)(C), is title XIV of Pub. L. 111–203, July 21, 2010, 124 Stat. 2136. For complete classification of this Act to the Code, see Short Title of 2010 Amendment note set out under section 1601 of this title and Tables.

AMENDMENTS

2018—Subsec. (b)(2)(F). Pub. L. 115–174, §101, added subpar. (F).
Subsec. (b)(3)(C). Pub. L. 115–174, §307, added subpar. (C).

2015—Subsec. (b)(2)(E)(iv)(I). Pub. L. 114–94 struck out "predominantly" after "operates".
2010—Pub. L. 111–203, §1100A(2), substituted "Bureau" for "Board" wherever appearing.
Subsec. (b). Pub. L. 111–203, §1412, added subsec. (b).
Subsecs. (c) to (f). Pub. L. 111–203, §1414(a), added subsecs. (c) to (f).
Subsec. (g). Pub. L. 111–203, §1414(c), added subsec. (g).
Subsecs. (h), (i). Pub. L. 111–203, §1414(d), added subsecs. (h) and (i).

STATUTORY NOTES AND RELATED SUBSIDIARIES

EFFECTIVE DATE OF 2010 AMENDMENT

Amendment by section 1100A(2) of Pub. L. 111–203 effective on the designated transfer date, see section 1100H of Pub. L. 111–203, set out as a note under section 552a of Title 5, Government Organization and Employees.
Amendment by sections 1412 and 1414(a), (c), (d) of Pub. L. 111–203 effective on the date on which final regulations implementing that amendment take effect, or on the date that is 18 months after the designated transfer date, if such regulations have not been issued by that date, see section 1400(c) of Pub. L. 111–203, set out as a note under section 1601 of this title.

EFFECTIVE DATE

Section effective on the date on which final regulations implementing such section take effect, or on the date that is 18 months after the designated transfer date if such regulations have not been issued by that date, see section 1400(c) of Pub. L. 111–203, set out as an Effective Date of 2010 Amendment note under section 1601 of this title.

RULE OF CONSTRUCTION

Pub. L. 111–203, title XIV, §1411(a)(1), July 21, 2010, 124 Stat. 2142, provided that: "No regulation, order, or guidance issued by the Bureau under this title [see Tables for classification] shall be construed as requiring a depository institution to apply mortgage underwriting standards that do not meet the minimum underwriting standards required by the appropriate prudential regulator of the depository institution."
[For definitions of "Bureau" and "depository institution" as used in section 1411(a)(1) of Pub. L. 111–203, set out above, see section 5301 of Title 12, Banks and Banking.]

1 See References in Text note below.

2 So in original.

3 So in original. Probably should be followed by "to".

§1639d. Escrow or impound accounts relating to certain consumer credit transactions

(a) In general

Except as provided in subsection (b), (c), (d), or (e), a creditor, in connection with the consummation of a consumer credit transaction secured by a first lien on the principal dwelling of the consumer, other than a consumer credit transaction under an open end credit plan or a reverse mortgage, shall establish, before the consummation of such transaction, an escrow or impound account for the payment of taxes and hazard insurance, and, if applicable, flood insurance, mortgage insurance, ground rents, and any other required periodic payments or premiums with respect to the property or the loan terms, as provided in, and in accordance with, this section.

(b) When required

No impound, trust, or other type of account for the payment of property taxes, insurance premiums, or other purposes relating to the property may be required as a condition of a real property sale contract or a loan secured by a first deed of trust or mortgage on the principal dwelling of the consumer, other than a consumer credit transaction under an open end credit plan or a reverse mortgage, except when—
(1) any such impound, trust, or other type of escrow or impound account for such purposes is required by Federal or State law;
(2) a loan is made, guaranteed, or insured by a State or Federal governmental lending or insuring agency;
(3) the transaction is secured by a first mortgage or lien on the consumer's principal dwelling having an original principal obligation amount that—

(A) does not exceed the amount of the maximum limitation on the original principal obligation of mortgage in effect for a residence of the applicable size, as of the date such interest rate set, pursuant to the sixth sentence of section 1454(a)(2) of title 12, and the annual percentage rate will exceed the average prime offer rate as defined in section 1639c of this title by 1.5 or more percentage points; or

(B) exceeds the amount of the maximum limitation on the original principal obligation of mortgage in effect for a residence of the applicable size, as of the date such interest rate set, pursuant to the sixth sentence of section 1454(a)(2) of title 12, and the annual percentage rate will exceed the average prime offer rate as defined in section 1639c of this title by 2.5 or more percentage points; or

(4) so required pursuant to regulation.

(c) Exemptions

(1) In general

The Bureau may, by regulation, exempt from the requirements of subsection (a) a creditor that—

(A) operates in rural or underserved areas;

(B) together with all affiliates, has total annual mortgage loan originations that do not exceed a limit set by the Bureau;

(C) retains its mortgage loan originations in portfolio; and

(D) meets any asset size threshold and any other criteria the Bureau may establish, consistent with the purposes of this part.

(2) Treatment of loans held by smaller institutions

The Bureau shall, by regulation, exempt from the requirements of subsection (a) any loan made by an insured depository institution or an insured credit union secured by a first lien on the principal dwelling of a consumer if—

(A) the insured depository institution or insured credit union has assets of $10,000,000,000 or less;

(B) during the preceding calendar year, the insured depository institution or insured credit union and its affiliates originated 1,000 or fewer loans secured by a first lien on a principal dwelling; and

(C) the transaction satisfies the criteria in sections 1026.35(b)(2)(iii)(A), 1026.35(b)(2)(iii)(D), and 1026.35(b)(2)(v) of title 12, Code of Federal Regulations, or any successor regulation.

(d) Duration of mandatory escrow or impound account

An escrow or impound account established pursuant to subsection (b) shall remain in existence for a minimum period of 5 years, beginning with the date of the consummation of the loan, unless and until—

(1) such borrower has sufficient equity in the dwelling securing the consumer credit transaction so as to no longer be required to maintain private mortgage insurance;

(2) such borrower is delinquent;

(3) such borrower otherwise has not complied with the legal obligation, as established by rule; or

(4) the underlying mortgage establishing the account is terminated.

(e) Limited exemptions for loans secured by shares in a cooperative or in which an association must maintain a master insurance policy

Escrow accounts need not be established for loans secured by shares in a cooperative. Insurance premiums need not be included in escrow accounts for loans secured by dwellings or units, where the borrower must join an association as a condition of ownership, and that association has an obligation to the dwelling or unit owners to maintain a master policy insuring the dwellings or units.

(f) Clarification on escrow accounts for loans not meeting statutory test

For mortgages not covered by the requirements of subsection (b), no provision of this section shall be construed as precluding the establishment of an impound, trust, or other type of account for the payment of property taxes, insurance premiums, or other purposes relating to the property—

(1) on terms mutually agreeable to the parties to the loan;

(2) at the discretion of the lender or servicer, as provided by the contract between the lender or servicer and the borrower; or

(3) pursuant to the requirements for the escrowing of flood insurance payments for regulated lending institutions in section 102(d) of the Flood Disaster Protection Act of 1973 [42 U.S.C. 4012a(d)].

(g) Administration of mandatory escrow or impound accounts

(1) In general

Except as may otherwise be provided for in this subchapter or in regulations prescribed by the Bureau, escrow or impound accounts established pursuant to subsection (b) shall be established in a federally insured depository institution or credit union.

(2) Administration

Except as provided in this section or regulations prescribed under this section, an escrow or impound account subject to this section shall be administered in accordance with—

(A) the Real Estate Settlement Procedures Act of 1974 [12 U.S.C. 2601 et seq.] and regulations prescribed under such Act;

(B) the Flood Disaster Protection Act of 1973 and regulations prescribed under such Act; and

(C) the law of the State, if applicable, where the real property securing the consumer credit transaction is located.

(3) Applicability of payment of interest

If prescribed by applicable State or Federal law, each creditor shall pay interest to the consumer on the amount held in any impound, trust, or escrow account that is subject to this section in the manner as prescribed by that applicable State or Federal law.

(4) Penalty coordination with RESPA

Any action or omission on the part of any person which constitutes a violation of the Real Estate Settlement Procedures Act of 1974 or any regulation prescribed under such Act for which the person has paid any fine, civil money penalty, or other damages shall not give rise to any additional fine, civil money penalty, or other damages under this section, unless the action or omission also constitutes a direct violation of this section.

(h) Disclosures relating to mandatory escrow or impound account

In the case of any impound, trust, or escrow account that is required under subsection (b), the creditor shall disclose by written notice to the consumer at least 3 business days before the consummation of the consumer credit transaction giving rise to such account or in accordance with timeframes established in prescribed regulations the following information:

(1) The fact that an escrow or impound account will be established at consummation of the transaction.

(2) The amount required at closing to initially fund the escrow or impound account.

(3) The amount, in the initial year after the consummation of the transaction, of the estimated taxes and hazard insurance, including flood insurance, if applicable, and any other required periodic payments or premiums that reflects, as appropriate, either the taxable assessed value of the real property securing the transaction, including the value of any improvements on the property or to be constructed on the property (whether or not such construction will be financed from the proceeds of the transaction) or the replacement costs of the property.

(4) The estimated monthly amount payable to be escrowed for taxes, hazard insurance (including flood insurance, if applicable) and any other required periodic payments or premiums.

(5) The fact that, if the consumer chooses to terminate the account in the future, the consumer will become responsible for the payment of all taxes, hazard insurance, and flood insurance, if applicable, as well as any other required periodic payments or premiums on the property unless a new escrow or impound account is established.

(6) Such other information as the Bureau determines necessary for the protection of the consumer.

(i) Definitions

For purposes of this section, the following definitions shall apply:

(1) Flood insurance

The term "flood insurance" means flood insurance coverage provided under the national flood insurance program pursuant to the National Flood Insurance Act of 1968 [42 U.S.C. 4001 et seq.].

(2) Hazard insurance

The term "hazard insurance" shall have the same meaning as provided for "hazard insurance", "casualty insurance", "homeowner's insurance", or other similar term under the law of the State where the real property securing the consumer credit transaction is located.

(3) Insured credit union

The term "insured credit union" has the meaning given the term in section 1752 of title 12.

(4) Insured depository institution

The term "insured depository institution" has the meaning given the term in section 1813 of title 12.

(j) Disclosure notice required for consumers who waive escrow services

(1) In general

If—

(A) an impound, trust, or other type of account for the payment of property taxes, insurance premiums, or other purposes relating to real property securing a consumer credit transaction is not established in connection with the transaction; or

(B) a consumer chooses, and provides written notice to the creditor or servicer of such choice, at any time after such an account is established in connection with any such transaction and in accordance with any statute, regulation, or contractual agreement, to close such account,

the creditor or servicer shall provide a timely and clearly written disclosure to the consumer that advises the consumer of the responsibilities of the consumer and implications for the consumer in the absence of any such account.

(2) Disclosure requirements

Any disclosure provided to a consumer under paragraph (1) shall include the following:

(A) Information concerning any applicable fees or costs associated with either the non-establishment of any such account at the time of the transaction, or any subsequent closure of any such account.

(B) A clear and prominent statement that the consumer is responsible for personally and directly paying the non-escrowed items, in addition to paying the mortgage loan payment, in the absence of any such account, and the fact that the costs for taxes, insurance, and related fees can be substantial.

(C) A clear explanation of the consequences of any failure to pay non-escrowed items, including the possible requirement for the forced placement of insurance by the creditor or servicer and the potentially higher cost (including any potential commission payments to the servicer) or reduced coverage for the consumer in the event of any such creditor-placed insurance.

(D) Such other information as the Bureau determines necessary for the protection of the consumer.

(Pub. L. 90–321, title I, §129D, as added and amended Pub. L. 111–203, title X, §1100A(2), title XIV, §§1461(a), 1462, July 21, 2010, 124 Stat. 2107, 2178, 2181; Pub. L. 114–94, div. G, title LXXXIX, §89003(2), Dec. 4, 2015, 129 Stat. 1801; Pub. L. 115–174, title I, §108, May 24, 2018, 132 Stat. 1304.)

EDITORIAL NOTES

REFERENCES IN TEXT

This part, referred to in subsec. (c)(1)(D), was in the original "this subtitle", and was translated as reading "this chapter", meaning chapter 2 of title I of Pub. L. 90–321, to reflect the probable intent of Congress. Title I of Pub. L. 90–321 does not contain subtitles.

The Real Estate Settlement Procedures Act of 1974, referred to in subsec. (g)(2)(A), (4), is Pub. L. 93–533, Dec. 22, 1974, 88 Stat. 1724, which is classified principally to chapter 27 (§2601 et seq.) of Title 12, Banks and Banking. For complete classification of this Act to the Code, see Short Title note set out under section 2601 of Title 12 and Tables.

The Flood Disaster Protection Act of 1973, referred to in subsec. (g)(2)(B), is Pub. L. 93–234, Dec. 31, 1973, 87 Stat. 975. For complete classification of this Act to the Code, see Short Title of 1973 Amendment note set out under section 4001 of Title 42, The Public Health and Welfare, and Tables.

The National Flood Insurance Act of 1968, referred to in subsec. (i)(1), is title XIII of Pub. L. 90–448, Aug. 1, 1968, 82 Stat. 572, which is classified principally to chapter 50 (§4001 et seq.) of Title 42, The Public Health and Welfare. For complete classification of this Act to the Code, see Short Title note set out under section 4001 of Title 42 and Tables.

AMENDMENTS

2018—Subsec. (c). Pub. L. 115–174, §108(1)(A), (B), (D), designated existing provisions as par. (1) and inserted heading, redesignated former pars. (1) to (4) as subpars. (A) to (D), respectively, of par. (1) and realigned margins, and added par. (2).

Subsec. (c)(1). Pub. L. 115–174, §108(1)(B), (C), which directed substitution of "The Bureau" for "The Board" in introductory provisions, and "the Bureau" for "the Board" wherever appearing, duplicated the amendment made by Pub. L. 111–203, §1100A(2), which had already been executed. See 2010 Amendment note below.

Subsec. (i)(3), (4). Pub. L. 115–174, §108(2), added pars. (3) and (4).

2015—Subsec. (c)(1). Pub. L. 114–94 struck out "predominantly" after "operates".

2010—Pub. L. 111–203, §1100A(2), which directed substitution of "Bureau" for "Board" wherever appearing in Pub. L. 90–321, was executed to this section, which was added to Pub. L. 90–321 by section 1461(a) of Pub. L. 111–203.

Subsec. (j). Pub. L. 111–203, §1462, added subsec. (j).

STATUTORY NOTES AND RELATED SUBSIDIARIES

EFFECTIVE DATE OF 2010 AMENDMENT

Amendment by section 1100A(2) of Pub. L. 111–203 effective on the designated transfer date, see section 1100H of Pub. L. 111–203, set out as a note under section 552a of Title 5, Government Organization and Employees.

Amendment by section 1462 of Pub. L. 111–203 effective on the date on which final regulations implementing that amendment take effect, or on the date that is 18 months after the designated transfer date if such regulations have not been issued by that date, see section 1400(c) of Pub. L. 111–203, set out as a note under section 1601 of this title.

Section effective on the date on which final regulations implementing such section take effect, or on the date that is 18 months after the designated transfer date if such regulations have not been issued by that date, see section 1400(c) of Pub. L. 111–203, set out as an Effective Date of 2010 Amendment note under section 1601 of this title.

EXEMPTIONS AND MODIFICATIONS

Pub. L. 111–203, title XIV, §1461(b), July 21, 2010, 124 Stat. 2181, provided that: "The Board may prescribe rules that revise, add to, or subtract from the criteria of section 129D(b) of the Truth in Lending Act [15 U.S.C. 1639d(b)] if the Board determines that such rules are in the interest of consumers and in the public interest."

§1639e. Appraisal independence requirements

(a) In general

It shall be unlawful, in extending credit or in providing any services for a consumer credit transaction secured by the principal dwelling of the consumer, to engage in any act or practice that violates appraisal independence as described in or pursuant to regulations prescribed under this section.

(b) Appraisal independence

For purposes of subsection (a), acts or practices that violate appraisal independence shall include—

(1) any appraisal of a property offered as security for repayment of the consumer credit transaction that is conducted in connection with such transaction in which a person with an interest in the underlying transaction compensates, coerces, extorts, colludes, instructs, induces, bribes, or intimidates a person, appraisal management company, firm, or other entity conducting or involved in an appraisal, or attempts, to compensate, coerce, extort, collude, instruct, induce, bribe, or intimidate such a person, for the purpose of causing the appraised value assigned, under the appraisal, to the property to be based on any factor other than the independent judgment of the appraiser;

(2) mischaracterizing, or suborning any mischaracterization of, the appraised value of the property securing the extension of the credit;

(3) seeking to influence an appraiser or otherwise to encourage a targeted value in order to facilitate the making or pricing of the transaction; and

(4) withholding or threatening to withhold timely payment for an appraisal report or for appraisal services rendered when the appraisal report or services are provided for in accordance with the contract between the parties.

(c) Exceptions

The requirements of subsection (b) shall not be construed as prohibiting a mortgage lender, mortgage broker, mortgage banker, real estate broker, appraisal management company, employee of an appraisal management company, consumer, or any other person with an interest in a real estate transaction from asking an appraiser to undertake 1 or more of the following:

(1) Consider additional, appropriate property information, including the consideration of additional comparable properties to make or support an appraisal.

(2) Provide further detail, substantiation, or explanation for the appraiser's value conclusion.

(3) Correct errors in the appraisal report.

(d) Prohibitions on conflicts of interest

No certified or licensed appraiser conducting, and no appraisal management company procuring or facilitating, an appraisal in connection with a consumer credit transaction secured by the principal dwelling of a consumer may have a direct or indirect interest, financial or otherwise, in the property or transaction involving the appraisal.

(e) Mandatory reporting

Any mortgage lender, mortgage broker, mortgage banker, real estate broker, appraisal management company, employee of an appraisal management company, or any other person involved in a real estate transaction involving an appraisal in connection with a consumer credit transaction secured by the principal dwelling of a consumer who has a reasonable basis to believe an appraiser is failing to comply with the Uniform Standards of Professional Appraisal Practice, is violating applicable laws, or is otherwise engaging in unethical or unprofessional conduct, shall refer the matter to the applicable State appraiser certifying and licensing agency.

(f) No extension of credit

In connection with a consumer credit transaction secured by a consumer's principal dwelling, a creditor who knows, at or before loan consummation, of a violation of the appraisal independence standards established in subsections [1] (b) or (d) shall not extend credit based on such appraisal unless the creditor documents that the creditor has acted with reasonable diligence to determine that the appraisal does not materially misstate or misrepresent the value of such dwelling.

(g) Rules and interpretive guidelines

(1) In general

Except as provided under paragraph (2), the Board, the Comptroller of the Currency, the Federal Deposit Insurance Corporation, the National Credit Union Administration Board, the Federal Housing Finance Agency, and the Bureau may jointly issue rules, interpretive guidelines, and general statements of policy with respect to acts or practices that violate appraisal independence in the provision of mortgage lending services for a consumer credit transaction secured by the principal dwelling of the consumer and mortgage brokerage services for such a transaction, within the meaning of subsections (a), (b), (c), (d), (e), (f), (h), and (i).

(2) Interim final regulations

The Board shall, for purposes of this section, prescribe interim final regulations no later than 90 days after July 21, 2010, defining with specificity acts or practices that violate appraisal independence in the provision of mortgage lending services for a consumer credit transaction secured by the principal dwelling of the consumer or mortgage brokerage services for such a transaction and defining any terms in this section or such regulations. Rules prescribed by the Board under this paragraph shall be deemed to be rules prescribed by the agencies jointly under paragraph (1).

(h) Appraisal report portability

Consistent with the requirements of this section, the Board, the Comptroller of the Currency, the Federal Deposit Insurance Corporation, the National Credit Union Administration Board, the Federal Housing Finance Agency, and the Bureau may jointly issue regulations that address the issue of appraisal report portability, including regulations that ensure the portability of the appraisal report between lenders for a consumer credit transaction secured by a 1-4 unit single family residence that is the principal dwelling of the consumer, or mortgage brokerage services for such a transaction.

(i) Customary and reasonable fee

(1) In general

Lenders and their agents shall compensate fee appraisers at a rate that is customary and reasonable for appraisal services performed in the market area of the property being appraised. Evidence for such fees may be established by objective third-party information, such as government agency fee schedules, academic studies, and independent private sector surveys. Fee studies shall exclude assignments ordered by known appraisal management companies.

(2) Fee appraiser definition

(A) In general

For purposes of this section, the term "fee appraiser" means a person who is not an employee of the mortgage loan originator or appraisal management company engaging the appraiser and is—

(i) a State licensed or certified appraiser who receives a fee for performing an appraisal and certifies that the appraisal has been prepared in accordance with the Uniform Standards of Professional Appraisal Practice; or

(ii) a company not subject to the requirements of section 3353 of title 12 that utilizes the services of State licensed or certified appraisers and receives a fee for performing appraisals in accordance with the Uniform Standards of Professional Appraisal Practice.

(B) Rule of construction related to appraisal donations

If a fee appraiser voluntarily donates appraisal services to an organization eligible to receive tax-deductible charitable contributions, such voluntary donation shall be considered customary and reasonable for the purposes of paragraph (1).

(3) Exception for complex assignments

In the case of an appraisal involving a complex assignment, the customary and reasonable fee may reflect the increased time, difficulty, and scope of the work required for such an appraisal and include an amount over and above the customary and reasonable fee for non-complex assignments.

(j) Sunset

Effective on the date the interim final regulations are promulgated pursuant to subsection (g), the Home Valuation Code of Conduct announced by the Federal Housing Finance Agency on December 23, 2008, shall have no force or effect.

(k) Penalties

(1) First violation

In addition to the enforcement provisions referred to in section 1640 of this title, each person who violates this section shall forfeit and pay a civil penalty of not more than $10,000 for each day any such violation continues.

(2) Subsequent violations

In the case of any person on whom a civil penalty has been imposed under paragraph (1), paragraph (1) shall be applied by substituting "$20,000" for "$10,000" with respect to all subsequent violations.

(3) Assessment

The agency referred to in subsection (a) or (c) of section 1607 of this title with respect to any person described in paragraph (1) shall assess any penalty under this subsection to which such person is subject.

(Pub. L. 90–321, title I, §129E, as added Pub. L. 111–203, title XIV, §1472(a), July 21, 2010, 124 Stat. 2187; amended Pub. L. 115–174, title I, §102, May 24, 2018, 132 Stat. 1299.)

EDITORIAL NOTES

AMENDMENTS

2018—Subsec. (i)(2). Pub. L. 115–174 designated existing provisions as subpar. (A) and inserted heading, redesignated former subpars. (A) and (B) as cls. (i) and (ii), respectively, of subpar. (A) and realigned margins, and added subpar. (B).

STATUTORY NOTES AND RELATED SUBSIDIARIES

EFFECTIVE DATE

Section effective on the date on which final regulations implementing such section take effect, or on the date that is 18 months after the designated transfer date if such regulations have not been issued by that date, see section 1400(c) of Pub. L. 111–203, set out as an Effective Date of 2010 Amendment note under section 1601 of this title.

---

¹ So in original. Probably should be "subsection".

---

§1639f. Requirements for prompt crediting of home loan payments

(a) In general

In connection with a consumer credit transaction secured by a consumer's principal dwelling, no servicer shall fail to credit a payment to the consumer's loan account as of the date of receipt, except when a delay in crediting does not result in any charge to the consumer or in the reporting of negative information to a consumer reporting agency, except as required in subsection (b).

(b) Exception

If a servicer specifies in writing requirements for the consumer to follow in making payments, but accepts a payment that does not conform to the requirements, the servicer shall credit the payment as of 5 days after receipt.

(Pub. L. 90–321, title I, §129F, as added Pub. L. 111–203, title XIV, §1464(a), July 21, 2010, 124 Stat. 2184.)

STATUTORY NOTES AND RELATED SUBSIDIARIES

EFFECTIVE DATE

Section effective on the date on which final regulations implementing such section take effect, or on the date that is 18 months after the designated transfer date if such regulations have not been issued by that date, see section 1400(c) of Pub. L. 111–203, set out as an Effective Date of 2010 Amendment note under section 1601 of this title.

---

§1639g. Requests for payoff amounts of home loan

A creditor or servicer of a home loan shall send an accurate payoff balance within a reasonable time, but in no case more than 7 business days, after the receipt of a written request for such balance from or on behalf of the borrower.

(Pub. L. 90–321, title I, §129G, as added Pub. L. 111–203, title XIV, §1464(b), July 21, 2010, 124 Stat. 2184.)

STATUTORY NOTES AND RELATED SUBSIDIARIES

EFFECTIVE DATE

Section effective on the date on which final regulations implementing such section take effect, or on the date that is 18 months after the designated transfer date if such regulations have not been issued by that date, see section 1400(c) of Pub. L. 111–203, set out as an Effective Date of 2010 Amendment note under section 1601 of this title.

§1639h. Property appraisal requirements

(a) In general

A creditor may not extend credit in the form of a higher-risk mortgage to any consumer without first obtaining a written appraisal of the property to be mortgaged prepared in accordance with the requirements of this section.

(b) Appraisal requirements

(1) Physical property visit

Subject to the rules prescribed under paragraph (4), an appraisal of property to be secured by a higher-risk mortgage does not meet the requirement of this section unless it is performed by a certified or licensed appraiser who conducts a physical property visit of the interior of the mortgaged property.

(2) Second appraisal under certain circumstances

(A) In general

If the purpose of a higher-risk mortgage is to finance the purchase or acquisition of the mortgaged property from a person within 180 days of the purchase or acquisition of such property by that person at a price that was lower than the current sale price of the property, the creditor shall obtain a second appraisal from a different certified or licensed appraiser. The second appraisal shall include an analysis of the difference in sale prices, changes in market conditions, and any improvements made to the property between the date of the previous sale and the current sale.

(B) No cost to applicant

The cost of any second appraisal required under subparagraph (A) may not be charged to the applicant.

(3) Certified or licensed appraiser defined

For purposes of this section, the term "certified or licensed appraiser" means a person who—
(A) is, at a minimum, certified or licensed by the State in which the property to be appraised is located; and
(B) performs each appraisal in conformity with the Uniform Standards of Professional Appraisal Practice and title XI of the Financial Institutions Reform, Recovery, and Enforcement Act of 1989 [12 U.S.C. 3331 et seq.], and the regulations prescribed under such title, as in effect on the date of the appraisal.

(4) Regulations

(A) In general

The Board, the Comptroller of the Currency, the Federal Deposit Insurance Corporation, the National Credit Union Administration Board, the Federal Housing Finance Agency, and the Bureau shall jointly prescribe regulations to implement this section.

(B) Exemption

The agencies listed in subparagraph (A) may jointly exempt, by rule, a class of loans from the requirements of this subsection or subsection (a) if the agencies determine that the exemption is in the public interest and promotes the safety and soundness of creditors.

(c) Free copy of appraisal

A creditor shall provide 1 copy of each appraisal conducted in accordance with this section in connection with a higher-risk mortgage to the applicant without charge, and at least 3 days prior to the transaction closing date.

(d) Consumer notification

At the time of the initial mortgage application, the applicant shall be provided with a statement by the creditor that any appraisal prepared for the mortgage is for the sole use of the creditor, and that the applicant may choose to have a separate appraisal conducted at the expense of the applicant.

(e) Violations

In addition to any other liability to any person under this subchapter, a creditor found to have willfully failed to obtain an appraisal as required in this section shall be liable to the applicant or borrower for the sum of $2,000.

(f) Higher-risk mortgage defined

For purposes of this section, the term "higher-risk mortgage" means a residential mortgage loan, other than a reverse mortgage loan that is a qualified mortgage, as defined in section 1639c of this title, secured by a principal dwelling—
(1) that is not a qualified mortgage, as defined in section 1639c of this title; and
(2) with an annual percentage rate that exceeds the average prime offer rate for a comparable transaction, as defined in section 1639c of this title, as of the date the interest rate is set—

(A) by 1.5 or more percentage points, in the case of a first lien residential mortgage loan having an original principal obligation amount that does not exceed the amount of the maximum limitation on the original principal obligation of mortgage in effect for a residence of the applicable size, as of the date of such interest rate set, pursuant to the sixth sentence of section 1454(a)(2) of title 12;

(B) by 2.5 or more percentage points, in the case of a first lien residential mortgage loan having an original principal obligation amount that exceeds the amount of the maximum limitation on the original principal obligation of mortgage in effect for a residence of the applicable size, as of the date of such interest rate set, pursuant to the sixth sentence of section 1454(a)(2) of title 12; and

(C) by 3.5 or more percentage points for a subordinate lien residential mortgage loan.

(Pub. L. 90–321, title I, §129H, as added Pub. L. 111–203, title XIV, §1471, July 21, 2010, 124 Stat. 2185.)

EDITORIAL NOTES

REFERENCES IN TEXT

The Financial Institutions Reform, Recovery, and Enforcement Act of 1989, referred to in subsec. (b)(3)(B), is Pub. L. 101–73, Aug. 9, 1989, 103 Stat. 183. Title XI of the Act is classified principally to chapter 34A (§3331 et seq.) of Title 12, Banks and Banking. For complete classification of this Act to the Code, see Short Title of 1989 Amendment note set out under section 1811 of Title 12 and Tables.

STATUTORY NOTES AND RELATED SUBSIDIARIES

EFFECTIVE DATE

Section effective on the date on which final regulations implementing such section take effect, or on the date that is 18 months after the designated transfer date if such regulations have not been issued by that date, see section 1400(c) of Pub. L. 111–203, set out as an Effective Date of 2010 Amendment note under section 1601 of this title.

§1640. Civil liability

(a) Individual or class action for damages; amount of award; factors determining amount of award

Except as otherwise provided in this section, any creditor who fails to comply with any requirement imposed under this part, including any requirement under section 1635 of this title, subsection (f) or (g) of section 1641 of this title, or part D or E of this subchapter with respect to any person is liable to such person in an amount equal to the sum of—

(1) any actual damage sustained by such person as a result of the failure;

(2)(A)(i) in the case of an individual action twice the amount of any finance charge in connection with the transaction, (ii) in the case of an individual action relating to a consumer lease under part E of this subchapter, 25 per centum of the total amount of monthly payments under the lease, except that the liability under this subparagraph shall not be less than $200 nor greater than $2,000, (iii) in the case of an individual action relating to an open end consumer credit plan that is not secured by real property or a dwelling, twice the amount of any finance charge in connection with the transaction, with a minimum of $500 and a maximum of $5,000, or such higher amount as may be appropriate in the case of an established pattern or practice of such failures; [1] or (iv) in the case of an individual action relating to a credit transaction not under an open end credit plan that is secured by real property or a dwelling, not less than $400 or greater than $4,000; or

(B) in the case of a class action, such amount as the court may allow, except that as to each member of the class no minimum recovery shall be applicable, and the total recovery under this subparagraph in any class action or series of class actions arising out of the same failure to comply by the same creditor shall not be more than the lesser of $1,000,000 or 1 per centum of the net worth of the creditor;

(3) in the case of any successful action to enforce the foregoing liability or in any action in which a person is determined to have a right of rescission under section 1635 or 1638(e)(7) of this title, the costs of the action, together with a reasonable attorney's fee as determined by the court; and

(4) in the case of a failure to comply with any requirement under section 1639 of this title, paragraph (1) or (2) of section 1639b(c) of this title, or section 1639c(a) of this title, an amount equal to the sum of all finance charges and fees paid by the consumer, unless the creditor demonstrates that the failure to comply is not material.

In determining the amount of award in any class action, the court shall consider, among other relevant factors, the amount of any actual damages awarded, the frequency and persistence of failures of compliance by the creditor, the resources of the creditor, the number of persons adversely affected, and the extent to which the creditor's failure of compliance was intentional. In connection with the disclosures referred to in subsections (a) and (b) of section 1637 of this title, a creditor shall have a liability determined under paragraph (2) only for failing to comply with the requirement of section 1635 of this title, 1637(a) [2] of this title, or any of paragraphs (4) through (13) of section 1637(b) of this title, or for failing to comply with disclosure requirements under State law for any term or item that the Bureau has determined to be substantially the same in meaning under section 1610(a)(2) of this title as any of the terms or items referred to in section 1637(a) of this title, or any of paragraphs (4) through (13) of section 1637(b) of this title. In connection with the disclosures referred to in subsection (c) or (d) of section 1637 of this title, a card issuer shall have a liability under this section only to a cardholder who pays a fee described in section 1637(c)(1)(A)(ii)(I) or section 1637(c)(4)(A)(i) of this title or who uses the credit card or charge card. In connection with the disclosures referred to in section 1638 of this title, a creditor shall have a liability determined under paragraph (2) only for failing to comply with the requirements of section 1635 of this title, of paragraph (2) (insofar as it requires a disclosure of the "amount financed"), (3), (4), (5), (6), or (9) of section 1638(a) of this title, or section 1638(b)(2)(C)(ii) of this title, of subparagraphs (A), (B), (D), (F), or (J) of section 1638(e)(2) of this title (for purposes of paragraph (2) or (4) of section 1638(e) of this title), or paragraph (4)(C), (6), (7), or (8) of section 1638(e) of this title, or for failing to comply with disclosure requirements under State law for any term which the Bureau has determined to be substantially the same in meaning under section 1610(a)(2) of this title as any of the terms referred to in any of those paragraphs of section 1638(a) of this title or section 1638(b)(2)(C)(ii) of this title. With respect to any failure to make disclosures required under this part or part D or E of this subchapter, liability shall be imposed only upon the creditor required to make disclosure, except as provided in section 1641 of this title.

(b) Correction of errors

A creditor or assignee has no liability under this section or section 1607 of this title or section 1611 of this title for any failure to comply with any requirement imposed under this part or part E, if within sixty days after discovering an error, whether pursuant to a final written examination report or notice issued under section 1607(e)(1) of this title or through the creditor's or assignee's own procedures, and prior to the institution of an action under this section or the receipt of written notice of the error from the obligor, the creditor or assignee notifies the person concerned of the error and makes whatever adjustments in the appropriate account are necessary to assure that the person will not be required to pay an amount in excess of the charge actually disclosed, or the dollar equivalent of the annual percentage rate actually disclosed, whichever is lower.

(c) Unintentional violations; bona fide errors

A creditor or assignee may not be held liable in any action brought under this section or section 1635 of this title for a violation of this subchapter if the creditor or assignee shows by a preponderance of evidence that the violation was not intentional and resulted from a bona fide error notwithstanding the maintenance of procedures reasonably adapted to avoid any such error. Examples of a bona fide error include, but are not limited to, clerical, calculation, computer malfunction and programing, and printing errors, except that an error of legal judgment with respect to a person's obligations under this subchapter is not a bona fide error.

(d) Liability in transaction or lease involving multiple obligors

When there are multiple obligors in a consumer credit transaction or consumer lease, there shall be no more than one recovery of damages under subsection (a)(2) for a violation of this subchapter.

(e) Jurisdiction of courts; limitations on actions; State attorney general enforcement

Except as provided in the subsequent sentence, any action under this section may be brought in any United States district court, or in any other court of competent jurisdiction, within one year from the date of the occurrence of the violation or, in the case of a violation involving a private education loan (as that term is defined in section 1650(a) of this title), 1 year from the date on which the first regular payment of principal is due under the loan. Any action under this section with respect to any violation of section 1639, 1639b, or 1639c of this title may be brought in any United States district court, or in any other court of competent jurisdiction, before the end of the 3-year period beginning on the date of the occurrence of the violation. This subsection does not bar a person from asserting a violation of this subchapter in an action to collect the debt which was brought more than one year from the date of the occurrence of the violation as a matter of defense by recoupment or set-off in such action, except as otherwise provided by State law. An action to enforce a violation of section 1639, 1639b, 1639c, 1639d, 1639e, 1639f, 1639g, or 1639h of this title may also be brought by the appropriate State attorney general in any appropriate United States district court, or any other court of competent jurisdiction, not later than 3 years after the date on which the violation occurs. The State attorney general shall provide prior written notice of any such civil action to the Federal agency responsible for enforcement under section 1607 of this title and shall provide the agency with a copy of the complaint. If prior notice is not feasible, the State attorney general shall provide notice to such agency immediately upon instituting the action. The Federal agency may—

(1) intervene in the action;

(2) upon intervening—

(A) remove the action to the appropriate United States district court, if it was not originally brought there; and

(B) be heard on all matters arising in the action; and

(3) file a petition for appeal.

) Good faith compliance with rule, regulation, or interpretation of Bureau or with interpretation or approval of duly authorized official or employee of Federal Reserve System

No provision of this section, section 1607(b) of this title, section 1607(c) of this title, section 1607(e) of this title, or section 1611 of this title imposing any liability shall apply to any act done or omitted in good faith in conformity with any rule, regulation, or interpretation thereof by the Bureau or in conformity with any interpretation or approval by an official or employee of the Federal Reserve System duly authorized by the Bureau to issue such interpretations or approvals under such procedures as the Bureau may prescribe therefor, notwithstanding that after such act or omission has occurred, such rule, regulation, interpretation, or approval is amended, rescinded, or determined by judicial or other authority to be invalid for any reason.

(g) Recovery for multiple failures to disclose

The multiple failure to disclose to any person any information required under this part or part D or E of this subchapter to be disclosed in connection with a single account under an open end consumer credit plan, other single consumer credit sale, consumer loan, consumer lease, or other extension of consumer credit, shall entitle the person to a single recovery under this section but continued failure to disclose after a recovery has been granted shall give rise to rights to additional recoveries. This subsection does not bar any remedy permitted by section 1635 of this title.

(h) Offset from amount owed to creditor or assignee; rights of defaulting consumer

A person may not take any action to offset any amount for which a creditor or assignee is potentially liable to such person under subsection (a)(2) against any amount owed by such person, unless the amount of the creditor's or assignee's liability under this subchapter has been determined by judgment of a court of competent jurisdiction in an action of which such person was a party. This subsection does not bar a consumer then in default on the obligation from asserting a violation of this subchapter as an original action, or as a defense or counterclaim to an action to collect amounts owed by the consumer brought by a person liable under this subchapter.

(i) Class action moratorium

(1) In general

During the period beginning on May 18, 1995, and ending on October 1, 1995, no court may enter any order certifying any class in any action under this subchapter—

(A) which is brought in connection with any credit transaction not under an open end credit plan which is secured by a first lien on real property or a dwelling and constitutes a refinancing or consolidation of an existing extension of credit; and

(B) which is based on the alleged failure of a creditor—

(i) to include a charge actually incurred (in connection with the transaction) in the finance charge disclosed pursuant to section 1638 of this title;

(ii) to properly make any other disclosure required under section 1638 of this title as a result of the failure described in clause (i); or

(iii) to provide proper notice of rescission rights under section 1635(a) of this title due to the selection by the creditor of the incorrect form from among the model forms prescribed by the Bureau or from among forms based on such model forms.

(2) Exceptions for certain alleged violations

Paragraph (1) shall not apply with respect to any action—

(A) described in clause (i) or (ii) of paragraph (1)(B), if the amount disclosed as the finance charge results in an annual percentage rate that exceeds the tolerance provided in section 1606(c) of this title; or

(B) described in paragraph (1)(B)(iii), if—

(i) no notice relating to rescission rights under section 1635(a) of this title was provided in any form; or

(ii) proper notice was not provided for any reason other than the reason described in such paragraph.

(j) Private educational lender

A private educational lender (as that term is defined in section 1650(a) of this title) has no liability under this section for failure to comply with section 1638(e)(3) of this title.[3]

(k) Defense to foreclosure

(1) In general

Notwithstanding any other provision of law, when a creditor, assignee, or other holder of a residential mortgage loan or anyone acting on behalf of such creditor, assignee, or holder, initiates a judicial or nonjudicial foreclosure of the residential mortgage loan, or any other action to collect the debt in connection with such loan, a consumer may assert a violation by a creditor of paragraph (1) or (2) of section 1639b(c) of this title, or of section 1639c(a) of this title, as a matter of defense by recoupment or set off without regard for the time limit on a private action for damages under subsection (e).

(2) Amount of recoupment or setoff

(A) In general

The amount of recoupment or set-off under paragraph (1) shall equal the amount to which the consumer would be entitled under subsection (a) for damages for a valid claim brought in an original action against the creditor, plus the costs to the consumer of the action, including a reasonable attorney's fee.

(B) Special rule

Where such judgment is rendered after the expiration of the applicable time limit on a private action for damages under subsection (e), the amount of recoupment or set-off under paragraph (1) derived from damages under subsection (a)(4) shall not exceed the amount to which the consumer would have been entitled under subsection (a)(4) for damages computed up to the day preceding the expiration of the applicable time limit.

(l) Exemption from liability and rescission in case of borrower fraud or deception

In addition to any other remedy available by law or contract, no creditor or assignee shall be liable to an obligor under this section, if such obligor, or co-obligor has been convicted of obtaining by actual fraud such residential mortgage loan.

(Pub. L. 90–321, title I, §130, May 29, 1968, 82 Stat. 157; Pub. L. 93–495, title IV, §§406, 407, 408(a)–(d), Oct. 28, 1974, 88 Stat. 1518; Pub. L. 94–222, §3(b), Feb. 27, 1976, 90 Stat. 197; Pub. L. 94–240, §4, Mar. 23, 1976, 90 Stat. 260; Pub. L. 96–221, title VI, §615, Mar. 31, 1980, 94 Stat. 180; Pub. L. 100–583, §3, Nov. 3, 1988, 102 Stat. 2966; Pub. L. 103–325, title I, §153(a), (b), Sept. 23, 1994, 108 Stat. 2195; Pub. L. 104–12, §2, May 18, 1995, 109 Stat. 161; Pub. L. 104–29, §6, Sept. 30, 1995, 109 Stat. 274; Pub. L. 110–289, div. B, title V, §2502(b), July 30, 2008, 122 Stat. 2857; Pub. L. 110–315, title X, §1012(a), Aug. 14, 2008, 122 Stat. 3482; Pub. L. 111–22, div. A, title IV, §404(b), May 20, 2009, 123 Stat. 1658; Pub. L. 111–24, title I, §107, title II, §201(b), May 22, 2009, 123 Stat. 1743, 1745; Pub. L. 111–203, title X, §1100A(2), title XIV, §§1413, 1416, 1417, 1422, July 21, 2010, 124 Stat. 2107, 2148, 2153, 2157.)

Editorial Notes

Amendments

2010—Pub. L. 111–203, §1100A(2), substituted "Bureau" for "Board" wherever appearing.

Subsec. (a)(2)(A)(ii). Pub. L. 111–203, §1416(a)(1), substituted "$200" for "$100" and "$2,000" for "$1,000".

Subsec. (a)(2)(B). Pub. L. 111–203, §1416(a)(2), substituted "$1,000,000" for "$500,000".

Subsec. (a)(4). Pub. L. 111–203, §1416(a)(3), inserted ", paragraph (1) or (2) of section 1639b(c) of this title, or section 1639c(a) of this title" after "section 1639 of this title".

Subsec. (e). Pub. L. 111–203, §1422, substituted "section 1639, 1639b, 1639c, 1639d, 1639e, 1639f, 1639g, or 1639h of this title may also" for "section 1639 of this title may also".

Pub. L. 111–203, §1416(b), in first sentence substituted "Except as provided in the subsequent sentence, any action" for "Any action" and inserted after first sentence "Any action under this section with respect to any violation of section 1639, 1639b, or 1639c of this title may be brought in any United States district court, or in any other court of competent jurisdiction, before the end of the 3-year period beginning on the date of the occurrence of the violation."

Subsec. (k). Pub. L. 111–203, §1413, added subsec. (k).

Subsec. (l). Pub. L. 111–203, §1417, added subsec. (l).

2009—Subsec. (a). Pub. L. 111–24, §201(b), in concluding provisions, substituted "In connection with the disclosures referred to in subsections (a) and (b) of section 1637 of this title, a creditor shall have a liability determined under paragraph (2) only for failing to comply with the requirements of section 1635 of this title, 1637(a) of this title, or any of paragraphs (4) through (13) of section 1637(b) of this title, or for failing to comply with disclosure requirements under State law for any term or item that the Board has determined to be substantially the same in meaning under section 1610(a)(2) of this title as any of the terms or items referred to in section 1637(a) of this title, or any of paragraphs (4) through (13) of section 1637(b) of this title." for "In connection with the disclosures referred to in subsections (a) and (b) of section 1637 of this title, a creditor shall have a liability determined under paragraph (2) only for failing to comply with the requirements of section 1635 of this title, section 1637(a) of this title, or of paragraph (4), (5), (6), (7), (8), (9), or (10) of section 1637(b) of this title or for failing to comply with disclosure requirements under State law for any term or item which the Board has determined to be substantially the same in meaning under section 1610(a)(2) of this title as any of the terms or items referred to in section 1637(a) of this title or any of those paragraphs of section 1637(b) of this title."

Pub. L. 111–22, §404(b), which directed insertion of "subsection (f) or (g) of section 1641 of this title," after "section 1635 of this title,", was executed by making the insertion only in the introductory provisions to reflect the probable intent of Congress.

Subsec. (a)(2)(A)(iii), (iv). Pub. L. 111–24, §107, added cl. (iii) and redesignated former cl. (iii) as (iv).

2008—Subsec. (a). Pub. L. 110–315, §1012(a)(1)(B), in fourth sentence of concluding provisions, substituted "1635 of this title," for "1635 of this title or" and inserted "of subparagraphs (A), (B), (D), (F), or (J) of section 1638(e)(2) of this title (for purposes of paragraph (2) or (4) of section 1638(e) of this title), or paragraph (4)(C), (6), (7), or (8) of section 1638(e) of this title," before "or for failing".

Pub. L. 110–289, §2502(b)(2), in concluding provisions, inserted "or section 1638(b)(2)(C)(ii) of this title," before "or for failing to comply" and "or section 1638(b)(2)(C)(ii) of this title" before ". With respect to".

Subsec. (a)(2)(A)(iii). Pub. L. 110–289, §2502(b)(1), substituted "not less than $400 or greater than $4,000" for "not less than $200 or greater than $2,000".

Subsec. (a)(3). Pub. L. 110–315, §1012(a)(1)(A), inserted "or 1638(e)(7)" after "section 1635".

Subsec. (e). Pub. L. 110–315, §1012(a)(2), inserted before period at end of first sentence "or, in the case of a violation involving a private education loan (as that term is defined in section 1650(a) of this title), 1 year from the date on which the first regular payment of principal is due under the loan".

Subsec. (j). Pub. L. 110–315, §1012(a)(3), added subsec. (j).

1995—Subsec. (a)(2)(A)(iii). Pub. L. 104–29 added cl. (iii).

Subsec. (i). Pub. L. 104–12 added subsec. (i).

1994—Subsec. (a)(4). Pub. L. 103–325, §153(a), added par. (4).

Subsec. (e). Pub. L. 103–325, §153(b), inserted at end "An action to enforce a violation of section 1639 of this title may also be brought by the appropriate State attorney general in any appropriate United States district court, or any other court of competent jurisdiction, not later than 3 years after the date on which the violation occurs. The State attorney general shall provide prior written notice of any such civil action to the Federal agency responsible for enforcement under section 1607 of this title and shall provide the agency with a copy of the complaint. If prior notice is not feasible, the State attorney general shall provide notice to such agency immediately upon instituting the action. The Federal agency may—

"(1) intervene in the action;

"(2) upon intervening—

"(A) remove the action to the appropriate United States district court, if it was not originally brought there; and

"(B) be heard on all matters arising in the action; and

"(3) file a petition for appeal."

1988—Subsec. (a). Pub. L. 100–583 substituted "in subsections (a) and (b) of section 1637" for "in section 1637" in third sentence and inserted provisions limiting liability of card issuer under this section to cardholders who pay fee or use credit card or charge card.

1980—Subsec. (a). Pub. L. 96–221, §615(b), in introductory text inserted provisions respecting applicability of section 1635 of this title, and in text following numbered pars. inserted provisions relating to disclosures required under sections 1637 and 1638 of this title.

Subsec. (a)(2)(B). Pub. L. 96–221, §615(a)(1), substituted provisions respecting recovery under this subparagraph in any class action or series of class actions, for provisions respecting recovery in a class action.

Subsec. (a)(3). Pub. L. 96–221, §615(a)(2), inserted provisions relating to right of rescission under section 1635 of this title.

Subsec. (b). Pub. L. 96–221, §615(a)(3), substituted provisions relating to correction of errors within sixty days by a creditor or assignee, for provisions relating to correction of errors within fifteen days by a creditor.

Subsec. (c). Pub. L. 96–221, §615(a)(3), substituted provisions relating to liability of a creditor or assignee in any action brought under this section or section 1635 of this title, for provisions relating to liability of a creditor in any action brought under this section.

Subsec. (d). Pub. L. 96–221, §615(a)(3), substituted provisions relating to liability in transaction or lease involving multiple obligors, for provisions relating to liability of subsequent assignees original creditor.

Subsec. (e). Pub. L. 96–221, §615(a)(4), inserted provisions relating to limitations on actions.

Subsec. (f). Pub. L. 96–221, §615(a)(5), inserted references to section 1607(b), (c), and (e) of this title.

Subsec. (g). Pub. L. 96–221, §615(a)(6), inserted provisions relating to remedy under section 1635 of this title.

Subsec. (h). Pub. L. 96–221, §615(a)(7), substituted provisions relating to offset from amounts owed to the creditor or assignee, and rights of defaulting consumer, for provisions relating to offset from amounts owed to the creditor.

1976—Subsec. (a). Pub. L. 94–240, §4(1), inserted "or E" after "part D".

Subsec. (a)(2)(A). Pub. L. 94–240, §4(2), designated existing provision as cl. (i) and added cl. (ii).

Subsec. (a)(2)(B). Pub. L. 94–240, §4(3), substituted "lesser of $500,000" for "lesser of $100,000".

Subsec. (b). Pub. L. 94–240, §4(4), inserted "or part E of this subchapter" after "this part" and struck out "finance" after "required to pay a".

Subsec. (f). Pub. L. 94–222 inserted "or in conformity with any interpretation or approval by an official or employee of the Federal Reserve System duly authorized by the Board to issue such interpretations or approvals under such procedures as the Board may prescribe therefor" after "by the Board", and substituted "interpretation, or approval" for "or interpretation" before "is amended".

Subsec. (g). Pub. L. 94–240, §4(5), inserted "or part D or E of this subchapter" after "this part", and "consumer lease" after "consumer loan".

1974—Subsec. (a). Pub. L. 93–495, §408(a), substituted provisions setting forth determination of amount of liability of any creditor failing to comply with any requirement imposed under part D of this subchapter or this part, for provisions setting forth determination of amount of liability of any creditor failing to disclose in connection with any consumer credit transaction any information required under this part to be disclosed to specified persons.

Subsec. (b). Pub. L. 93–495, §408(b), inserted "for any failure to comply with any requirement imposed under this part," before "if within".

Subsec. (c). Pub. L. 93–495, §408(c), substituted "subchapter" for "part".

Subsec. (f). Pub. L. 93–495, §406, added subsec. (f).

Subsec. (g). Pub. L. 93–495, §407, added subsec. (g).

Subsec. (h). Pub. L. 93–495, §408(d), added subsec. (h).

Statutory Notes and Related Subsidiaries

Effective Date of 2010 Amendment

Amendment by section 1100A(2) of Pub. L. 111–203 effective on the designated transfer date, see section 1100H of Pub. L. 111–203, set out as a note under section 552a of Title 5, Government Organization and Employees.

Amendment by sections 1413, 1416, 1417, and 1422 of Pub. L. 111–203 effective on the date on which final regulations implementing that amendment take effect, or on the date that is 18 months after the designated transfer date, if such regulations have not been issued by that date, see section 1400(c) of Pub. L. 111–203, set out as a note under section 1601 of this title.

Effective Date of 2009 Amendment

Amendment by Pub. L. 111–24 effective 9 months after May 22, 2009, except as otherwise specifically provided, see section 3 of Pub. L. 111–24, set out as a note under section 1602 of this title.

Effective Date of 2008 Amendment

Pub. L. 110–315, title X, §1012(b), Aug. 14, 2008, 122 Stat. 3482, provided that: "The amendments made by this section [amending this section] shall have the same effective date as provisions referred to in section 1003(b) [set out as a note under section 1638 of this title]."

Effective Date of 1980 Amendment

Amendment by Pub. L. 96–221 effective on expiration of two years and six months after Mar. 31, 1980, with all regulations, forms, and clauses required to be prescribed to be promulgated at least one year prior to such effective date, and allowing any creditor to comply with any amendments, in accordance with the regulations, forms, and clauses prescribed by the Board prior to such effective date, see section 625 of Pub. L. 96–221, set out as a note under section 1602 of this title.

Effective Date of 1976 Amendment

Amendment by Pub. L. 94–240 effective on expiration of one year after Mar. 23, 1976, see section 6 of Pub. L. 94–240, set out as an Effective Date note under section 1667 of this title.

Effective Date of 1974 Amendment

Amendment by Pub. L. 93–495 effective Oct. 28, 1974, see section 416 of Pub. L. 93–495, set out as an Effective Date note under section 1665a of this title.

Determination of Liability Prior to October 28, 1974

Pub. L. 93–495, title IV, §408(e), Oct. 28, 1974, 88 Stat. 1519, provided that: "The amendments made by sections 406, 407, and 408 [amending this section] shall apply in determining the liability of any person under chapter 2 or 4 of the Truth in Lending Act [this part or part D of this subchapter], unless prior to the date of enactment of this Act [Oct. 28, 1974] such liability has been determined by final judgment of a court of competent jurisdiction and no further review of such judgment may be had by appeal or otherwise."

---

[1] So in original. The semicolon probably should be a comma.

[2] So in original. Probably should be preceded by "section".

§1641. Liability of assignees

(a) Prerequisites

Except as otherwise specifically provided in this subchapter, any civil action for a violation of this subchapter or proceeding under section 1607 of this title which may be brought against a creditor may be maintained against any assignee of such creditor only if the violation for which such action or proceeding is brought is apparent on the face of the disclosure statement, except where the assignment was involuntary. For the purpose of this section, a violation apparent on the face of the disclosure statement includes, but is not limited to (1) a disclosure which can be determined to be incomplete or inaccurate from the face of the disclosure statement or other documents assigned, or (2) a disclosure which does not use the terms required to be used by this subchapter.

(b) Proof of compliance with statutory provisions

Except as provided in section 1635(c) of this title, in any action or proceeding by or against any subsequent assignee of the original creditor without knowledge to the contrary by the assignee when he acquires the obligation, written acknowledgement of receipt by a person to whom a statement is required to be given pursuant to this subchapter shall be conclusive proof of the delivery thereof and, except as provided in subsection (a), of compliance with this part. This section does not affect the rights of the obligor in any action against the original creditor.

(c) Right of rescission by consumer unaffected

Any consumer who has the right to rescind a transaction under section 1635 of this title may rescind the transaction as against any assignee of the obligation.

(d) Rights upon assignment of certain mortgages

(1) In general

Any person who purchases or is otherwise assigned a mortgage referred to in section 1602(aa) [1] of this title shall be subject to all claims and defenses with respect to that mortgage that the consumer could assert against the creditor of the mortgage, unless the purchaser or assignee demonstrates, by a preponderance of the evidence, that a reasonable person exercising ordinary due diligence, could not determine, based on the documentation required by this subchapter, the itemization of the amount financed, and other disclosure of disbursements that the mortgage was a mortgage referred to in section 1602(aa) [1] of this title. The preceding sentence does not affect rights of a consumer under subsection (a), (b), or (c) of this section or any other provision of this subchapter.

(2) Limitation on damages

Notwithstanding any other provision of law, relief provided as a result of any action made permissible by paragraph (1) may not exceed—
  (A) with respect to actions based upon a violation of this subchapter, the amount specified in section 1640 of this title; and
  (B) with respect to all other causes of action, the sum of—
    (i) the amount of all remaining indebtedness; and
    (ii) the total amount paid by the consumer in connection with the transaction.

(3) Offset

The amount of damages that may be awarded under paragraph (2)(B) shall be reduced by the amount of any damages awarded under paragraph (2)(A).

(4) Notice

Any person who sells or otherwise assigns a mortgage referred to in section 1602(aa) [1] of this title shall include a prominent notice of the potential liability under this subsection as determined by the Bureau.

(e) Liability of assignee for consumer credit transactions secured by real property

(1) In general

Except as otherwise specifically provided in this subchapter, any civil action against a creditor for a violation of th subchapter, and any proceeding under section 1607 of this title against a creditor, with respect to a consumer credi transaction secured by real property may be maintained against any assignee of such creditor only if—
    (A) the violation for which such action or proceeding is brought is apparent on the face of the disclosure statement provided in connection with such transaction pursuant to this subchapter; and
    (B) the assignment to the assignee was voluntary.

(2) Violation apparent on the face of the disclosure described

For the purpose of this section, a violation is apparent on the face of the disclosure statement if—
    (A) the disclosure can be determined to be incomplete or inaccurate by a comparison among the disclosure statement, any itemization of the amount financed, the note, or any other disclosure of disbursement; or

(B) the disclosure statement does not use the terms or format required to be used by this subchapter.

(f) Treatment of servicer

(1) In general

A servicer of a consumer obligation arising from a consumer credit transaction shall not be treated as an assignee of such obligation for purposes of this section unless the servicer is or was the owner of the obligation.

(2) Servicer not treated as owner on basis of assignment for administrative convenience

A servicer of a consumer obligation arising from a consumer credit transaction shall not be treated as the owner of the obligation for purposes of this section on the basis of an assignment of the obligation from the creditor or another assignee to the servicer solely for the administrative convenience of the servicer in servicing the obligation. Upon written request by the obligor, the servicer shall provide the obligor, to the best knowledge of the servicer, with the name, address, and telephone number of the owner of the obligation or the master servicer of the obligation.

(3) "Servicer" defined

For purposes of this subsection, the term "servicer" has the same meaning as in section 2605(i)(2) of title 12.

(4) Applicability

This subsection shall apply to all consumer credit transactions in existence or consummated on or after September 30, 1995.

(g) Notice of new creditor

(1) In general

In addition to other disclosures required by this subchapter, not later than 30 days after the date on which a mortgage loan is sold or otherwise transferred or assigned to a third party, the creditor that is the new owner or assignee of the debt shall notify the borrower in writing of such transfer, including—

(A) the identity, address, telephone number of the new creditor;
(B) the date of transfer;
(C) how to reach an agent or party having authority to act on behalf of the new creditor;
(D) the location of the place where transfer of ownership of the debt is recorded; and
(E) any other relevant information regarding the new creditor.

(2) Definition

As used in this subsection, the term "mortgage loan" means any consumer credit transaction that is secured by the principal dwelling of a consumer.

(Pub. L. 90–321, title I, §131, May 29, 1968, 82 Stat. 157; Pub. L. 96–221, title VI, §616(a), Mar. 31, 1980, 94 Stat. 182; Pub. L. 103–325, title I, §153(c), Sept. 23, 1994, 108 Stat. 2195; Pub. L. 104–29, §7, Sept. 30, 1995, 109 Stat. 274; Pub. L. 111–22, div. A, title IV, §404(a), May 20, 2009, 123 Stat. 1658; Pub. L. 111–203, title X, §1100A(2), July 21, 2010, 124 Stat. 2107.)

Editorial Notes

References in Text

Section 1602(aa) of this title, referred to in subsec. (d)(1), (4), was redesignated section 1602(bb) of this title by Pub. L. 111–203, title X, §1100A(1)(A), July 21, 2010, 124 Stat. 2107.

Amendments

2010—Subsec. (d)(4). Pub. L. 111–203 substituted "Bureau" for "Board".
2009—Subsec. (g). Pub. L. 111–22 added subsec. (g).
1995—Subsec. (e). Pub. L. 104–29, §7(a), added subsec. (e).
Subsec. (f). Pub. L. 104–29, §7(b), added subsec. (f).
1994—Subsec. (d). Pub. L. 103–325 added subsec. (d).
1980—Pub. L. 96–221 added subsecs. (a) and (c), designated existing provisions as subsec. (b), substituted "excepted as provided in subsection (a)" for "unless the violation is apparent on the face of the statement", and struck out exception for actions under section 1640(d) of this title.

Statutory Notes and Related Subsidiaries

Effective Date of 2010 Amendment

Amendment by Pub. L. 111–203 effective on the designated transfer date, see section 1100H of Pub. L. 11–203, set out as a note under section 552a of Title 5, Government Organization and Employees.

Amendment by Pub. L. 96–221 effective on expiration of two years and six months after Mar. 31, 1980, with all regulations, forms, and clauses required to be prescribed to be promulgated at least one year prior to such effective date, and allowing any creditor to comply with any amendments, in accordance with the regulations, forms, and clauses prescribed by the Board prior to such effective date, see section 625 of Pub. L. 96–221, set out as a note under section 1602 of this title.

¹ See References in Text note below.

§1642. Issuance of credit cards

No credit card shall be issued except in response to a request or application therefor. This prohibition does not apply to the issuance of a credit card in renewal of, or in substitution for, an accepted credit card.

(Pub. L. 90–321, title I, §132, as added Pub. L. 91–508, title V, §502(a), Oct. 26, 1970, 84 Stat. 1126.)

STATUTORY NOTES AND RELATED SUBSIDIARIES

EFFECTIVE DATE

Pub. L. 91–508, title V, §503(1), Oct. 26, 1970, 84 Stat. 1127, provided that: "Section 132 of such Act [this section] takes effect on date of enactment of this title [Oct. 26, 1970]."

§1643. Liability of holder of credit card

(a) Limits on liability

(1) A cardholder shall be liable for the unauthorized use of a credit card only if—

(A) the card is an accepted credit card;

(B) the liability is not in excess of $50;

(C) the card issuer gives adequate notice to the cardholder of the potential liability;

(D) the card issuer has provided the cardholder with a description of a means by which the card issuer may be notified of loss or theft of the card, which description may be provided on the face or reverse side of the statement required by section 1637(b) of this title or on a separate notice accompanying such statement;

(E) the unauthorized use occurs before the card issuer has been notified that an unauthorized use of the credit card has occurred or may occur as the result of loss, theft, or otherwise; and

(F) the card issuer has provided a method whereby the user of such card can be identified as the person authorized to use it.

(2) For purposes of this section, a card issuer has been notified when such steps as may be reasonably required in the ordinary course of business to provide the card issuer with the pertinent information have been taken, whether or not any particular officer, employee, or agent of the card issuer does in fact receive such information.

(b) Burden of proof

In any action by a card issuer to enforce liability for the use of a credit card, the burden of proof is upon the card issuer to show that the use was authorized or, if the use was unauthorized, then the burden of proof is upon the card issuer to show that the conditions of liability for the unauthorized use of a credit card, as set forth in subsection (a), have been met.

(c) Liability imposed by other laws or by agreement with issuer

Nothing in this section imposes liability upon a cardholder for the unauthorized use of a credit card in excess of his liability for such use under other applicable law or under any agreement with the card issuer.

(d) Exclusiveness of liability

Except as provided in this section, a cardholder incurs no liability from the unauthorized use of a credit card.

(Pub. L. 90–321, title I, §133, as added Pub. L. 91–508, title V, §502(a), Oct. 26, 1970, 84 Stat. 1126; amended Pub. L. 96–221, title VI, §617, Mar. 31, 1980, 94 Stat. 182.)

EDITORIAL NOTES

AMENDMENTS

1980—Subsec. (a). Pub. L. 96–221 revised existing provisions into pars. (1) and (2) and, as so revised, in par. (1) made changes in structure and phraseology and revised means of notice and verification, and in par. (2) made changes in phraseology.

STATUTORY NOTES AND RELATED SUBSIDIARIES

EFFECTIVE DATE OF 1980 AMENDMENT

Amendment by Pub. L. 96–221 effective on expiration of two years and six months after Mar. 31, 1980, with all regulations, forms, and clauses required to be prescribed to be promulgated at least one year prior to such effective date, and allowing any creditor to comply with any amendments, in accordance with the regulations, forms, and clauses prescribed by the Board prior to such effective date, see section 625 of Pub. L. 96–221, set out as a note under section 1602 of this title.

EFFECTIVE DATE

Pub. L. 91–508, title V, §503(2), Oct. 26, 1970, 84 Stat. 1127, provided that: "Section 133 of such Act [this section] takes effect upon the expiration of 90 days after such date of enactment [Oct. 26, 1970]."

§1644. Fraudulent use of credit cards; penalties

(a) Use, attempt or conspiracy to use card in transaction affecting interstate or foreign commerce

Whoever knowingly in a transaction affecting interstate or foreign commerce, uses or attempts or conspires to use any counterfeit, fictitious, altered, forged, lost, stolen, or fraudulently obtained credit card to obtain money, goods, services, or anything else of value which within any one-year period has a value aggregating $1,000 or more; or

(b) Transporting, attempting or conspiring to transport card in interstate commerce

Whoever, with unlawful or fraudulent intent, transports or attempts or conspires to transport in interstate or foreign commerce a counterfeit, fictitious, altered, forged, lost, stolen, or fraudulently obtained credit card knowing the same to be counterfeit, fictitious, altered, forged, lost, stolen, or fraudulently obtained; or

(c) Use of interstate commerce to sell or transport card

Whoever, with unlawful or fraudulent intent, uses any instrumentality of interstate or foreign commerce to sell or transport a counterfeit, fictitious, altered, forged, lost, stolen, or fraudulently obtained credit card knowing the same to be counterfeit, fictitious, altered, forged, lost, stolen, or fraudulently obtained; or

(d) Receipt, concealment, etc., of goods obtained by use of card

Whoever knowingly receives, conceals, uses, or transports money, goods, services, or anything else of value (except tickets for interstate or foreign transportation) which (1) within any one-year period has a value aggregating $1,000 or more, (2) has moved in or is part of, or which constitutes interstate or foreign commerce, and (3) has been obtained with a counterfeit, fictitious, altered, forged, lost, stolen, or fraudulently obtained credit card; or

(e) Receipt, concealment, etc., of tickets for interstate or foreign transportation obtained by use of card

Whoever knowingly receives, conceals, uses, sells, or transports in interstate or foreign commerce one or more tickets for interstate or foreign transportation, which (1) within any one-year period have a value aggregating $500 or more, and (2) have been purchased or obtained with one or more counterfeit, fictitious, altered, forged, lost, stolen, or fraudulently obtained credit cards; or

(f) Furnishing of money, etc., through use of card

Whoever in a transaction affecting interstate or foreign commerce furnishes money, property, services, or anything else of value, which within any one-year period has a value aggregating $1,000 or more, through the use of any counterfeit, fictitious, altered, forged, lost, stolen, or fraudulently obtained credit card knowing the same to be counterfeit, fictitious, altered, forged, lost, stolen, or fraudulently obtained—

shall be fined not more than $10,000 or imprisoned not more than ten years, or both.

(Pub. L. 90–321, title I, §134, as added Pub. L. 91–508, title V, §502(a), Oct. 26, 1970, 84 Stat. 1127; amended Pub. L. 93–495, title IV, §414, Oct. 28, 1974, 88 Stat. 1520.)

EDITORIAL NOTES

AMENDMENTS

1974—Pub. L. 93–495 generally reorganized provisions by designating former unlettered paragraph cls.) to (f), and as so designated, expanded prohibitions relating to fraudulent use of credit cards, decreased amount required for fraudulent use from a retail value aggregating $5,000, or more, to enumerated amounts for particular activities, and increased the punishment from a sentence of not more than five years to a sentence of not more than ten years.

STATUTORY NOTES AND RELATED SUBSIDIARIES

EFFECTIVE DATE OF 1974 AMENDMENT

Amendment by Pub. L. 93–495 effective Oct. 28, 1974, see section 416 of Pub. L. 93–495, set out as an Effective Date note under section 1665a of this title.

EFFECTIVE DATE

Pub. L. 91–508, title V, §503(3), Oct. 26, 1970, 84 Stat. 1127, provided that: "Section 134 of such Act [this section] applies to offenses committed on or after such date of enactment [Oct. 26, 1970]."

§1645. Business credit cards; limits on liability of employees

The exemption provided by section 1603(1) of this title does not apply to the provisions of sections 1642, 1643, and 1644 of this title, except that a card issuer and a business or other organization which provides credit cards issued by the same card issuer to ten or more of its employees may by contract agree as to liability of the business or other organization with respect to unauthorized use of such credit cards without regard to the provisions of section 1643 of this title, but in no case may such business or other organization or card issuer impose liability upon any employee with respect to unauthorized use of such a credit card except in accordance with and subject to the limitations of section 1643 of this title.

(Pub. L. 90–321, title I, §135, as added Pub. L. 93–495, title IV, §410(a), Oct. 28, 1974, 88 Stat. 1519.)

STATUTORY NOTES AND RELATED SUBSIDIARIES

EFFECTIVE DATE

Section effective Oct. 28, 1974, see section 416 of Pub. L. 93–495, set out as a note under section 1665a of this title.

§1646. Dissemination of annual percentage rates; implementation, etc.

(a) Annual percentage rates

The Bureau shall collect, publish, and disseminate to the public, on a demonstration basis in a number of standard metropolitan statistical areas to be determined by the Bureau, the annual percentage rates charged for representative types of nonsale credit by creditors in such areas. For the purpose of this section, the Bureau is authorized to require creditors in such areas to furnish information necessary for the Bureau to collect, publish, and disseminate such information.

(b) Credit card price and availability information

(1) Collection required

The Bureau shall collect, on a semiannual basis, credit card price and availability information, including the information required to be disclosed under section 1637(c) of this title, from a broad sample of financial institutions which offer credit card services.

(2) Sample requirements

The broad sample of financial institutions required under paragraph (1) shall include—

(A) the 25 largest issuers of credit cards; and

(B) not less than 125 additional financial institutions selected by the Bureau in a manner that ensures—

(i) an equitable geographical distribution within the sample; and

(ii) the representation of a wide spectrum of institutions within the sample.

(3) Report of information from sample

Each financial institution in the broad sample established pursuant to paragraph (2) shall report the information the Bureau in accordance with such regulations or orders as the Bureau may prescribe.

(4) Public availability of collected information; report to Congress

The Bureau shall—

(A) make the information collected pursuant to this subsection available to the public upon request; and

(B) report such information semiannually to Congress.

(c) Implementation

The Bureau is authorized to enter into contracts or other arrangements with appropriate persons, organizations, or State agencies to carry out its functions under subsections (a) and (b) and to furnish financial assistance in support thereof.

(Pub. L. 90–321, title I, §136, as added Pub. L. 96–221, title VI, §618(a), Mar. 31, 1980, 94 Stat. 183; amended Pub. L. 100–583, §5, Nov. 3, 1988, 102 Stat. 2967; Pub. L. 111–203, title X, §1100A(2), July 21, 2010, 124 Stat. 2107.)

Editorial Notes

Amendments

2010—Pub. L. 111–203 substituted "Bureau" for "Board" wherever appearing.
1988—Subsecs. (b), (c). Pub. L. 100–583 added subsec. (b), redesignated former subsec. (b) as (c), and substituted "subsections (a) and (b)" for "subsection (a)".

Statutory Notes and Related Subsidiaries

Effective Date of 2010 Amendment

Amendment by Pub. L. 111–203 effective on the designated transfer date, see section 1100H of Pub. L. 111–203, set out as a note under section 552a of Title 5, Government Organization and Employees.

Effective Date

Section effective on expiration of two years and six months after Mar. 31, 1980, with all regulations, forms, and clauses required to be prescribed to be promulgated at least one year prior to such effective date, and allowing any creditor to comply with any amendments, in accordance with the regulations, forms, and clauses prescribed by the Board prior to such effective date, see section 625 of Pub. L. 96–221, set out as an Effective Date of 1980 Amendment note under section 1602 of this title.

§1647. Home equity plans

(a) Index requirement

In the case of extensions of credit under an open end consumer credit plan which are subject to a variable rate and are secured by a consumer's principal dwelling, the index or other rate of interest to which changes in the annual percentage rate are related shall be based on an index or rate of interest which is publicly available and is not under the control of the creditor.

(b) Grounds for acceleration of outstanding balance

A creditor may not unilaterally terminate any account under an open end consumer credit plan under which extensions of credit are secured by a consumer's principal dwelling and require the immediate repayment of any outstanding balance at such time, except in the case of—

(1) fraud or material misrepresentation on the part of the consumer in connection with the account;
(2) failure by the consumer to meet the repayment terms of the agreement for any outstanding balance; or
(3) any other action or failure to act by the consumer which adversely affects the creditor's security for the account or any right of the creditor in such security.

This subsection does not apply to reverse mortgage transactions.

(c) Change in terms

(1) In general

No open end consumer credit plan under which extensions of credit are secured by a consumer's principal dwelling may contain a provision which permits a creditor to change unilaterally any term required to be disclosed under section 1637a(a) of this title or any other term, except a change in insignificant terms such as the address of the creditor for billing purposes.

(2) Certain changes not precluded

Notwithstanding the provisions of subsection ^{1} (1), a creditor may make any of the following changes:
(A) Change the index and margin applicable to extensions of credit under such plan if the index used by the creditor is no longer available and the substitute index and margin would result in a substantially similar interest rate.

(B) Prohibit additional extensions of credit or reduce the credit limit applicable to an account under the plan during any period in which the value of the consumer's principal dwelling which secures any outstanding balance is significantly less than the original appraisal value of the dwelling.

(C) Prohibit additional extensions of credit or reduce the credit limit applicable to the account during any period in which the creditor has reason to believe that the consumer will be unable to comply with the repayment requirements of the account due to a material change in the consumer's financial circumstances.

(D) Prohibit additional extensions of credit or reduce the credit limit applicable to the account during any period in which the consumer is in default with respect to any material obligation of the consumer under the agreement.

(E) Prohibit additional extensions of credit or reduce the credit limit applicable to the account during any period in which—

(i) the creditor is precluded by government action from imposing the annual percentage rate provided for in the account agreement; or

(ii) any government action is in effect which adversely affects the priority of the creditor's security interest in the account to the extent that the value of the creditor's secured interest in the property is less than 120 percent of the amount of the credit limit applicable to the account.

(F) Any change that will benefit the consumer.

(3) Material obligations

Upon the request of the consumer and at the time an agreement is entered into by a consumer to open an account under an open end consumer credit plan under which extensions of credit are secured by the consumer's principal dwelling, the consumer shall be given a list of the categories of contract obligations which are deemed by the creditor to be material obligations of the consumer under the agreement for purposes of paragraph (2)(D).

(4) Consumer benefit

(A) In general

For purposes of paragraph (2)(F), a change shall be deemed to benefit the consumer if the change is unequivocally beneficial to the borrower and the change is beneficial through the entire term of the agreement.

(B) Bureau categorization

The Bureau may, by regulation, determine categories of changes that benefit the consumer.

(d) Terms changed after application

If any term or condition described in section 1637a(a) of this title which is disclosed to a consumer in connection with an application to open an account under an open end consumer credit plan described in such section (other than a variable feature of the plan) changes before the account is opened, and if, as a result of such change, the consumer elects not to enter into the plan agreement, the creditor shall refund all fees paid by the consumer in connection with such application.

(e) Additional requirements relating to refunds and imposition of nonrefundable fees

(1) In general

No nonrefundable fee may be imposed by a creditor or any other person in connection with any application by a consumer to establish an account under any open end consumer credit plan which provides for extensions of credit which are secured by a consumer's principal dwelling before the end of the 3-day period beginning on the date such consumer receives the disclosure required under section 1637a(a) of this title and the pamphlet required under section 1637a(e) of this title with respect to such application.

(2) Constructive receipt

For purposes of determining when a nonrefundable fee may be imposed in accordance with this subsection if the disclosures and pamphlet referred to in paragraph (1) are mailed to the consumer, the date of the receipt of the disclosures by such consumer shall be deemed to be 3 business days after the date of mailing by the creditor.

(Pub. L. 90–321, title I, §137, as added Pub. L. 100–709, §3, Nov. 23, 1988, 102 Stat. 4731; amended Pub. L. 103–325, title I, §154(c), Sept. 23, 1994, 108 Stat. 2197; Pub. L. 111–203, title X, §1100A(2), July 21, 2010, 124 Stat. 2107

EDITORIAL NOTES

AMENDMENTS

2010—Subsec. (c)(4)(B). Pub. L. 111–203 substituted "Bureau" for "Board" in heading and text.
1994—Subsec. (b). Pub. L. 103–325 inserted at end "This subsection does not apply to reverse mortgage transactions."

STATUTORY NOTES AND RELATED SUBSIDIARIES

EFFECTIVE DATE OF 2010 AMENDMENT

Amendment by Pub. L. 111–203 effective on the designated transfer date, see section 1100H of Pub. L. 111–203, set out as a note under section 552a of Title 5, Government Organization and Employees.

EFFECTIVE DATE

For effective date of section, see Regulations; Effective Date note below.

REGULATIONS; EFFECTIVE DATE

For provisions relating to promulgation of regulations to implement amendment by Pub. L. 100–709 [enacting this section], and effective date of such amendment in connection with those regulations, see section 7 of Pub. L. 100–709, set out as a note under section 1637a of this title.

---

¹ So in original. Probably should be "paragraph".

§1648. Reverse mortgages

(a) In general

In addition to the disclosures required under this subchapter, for each reverse mortgage, the creditor shall, not less than 3 days prior to consummation of the transaction, disclose to the consumer in conspicuous type a good faith estimate of the projected total cost of the mortgage to the consumer expressed as a table of annual interest rates. Each annual interest rate shall be based on a projected total future credit extension balance under a projected appreciation rate for the dwelling and a term for the mortgage. The disclosure shall include—

(1) statements of the annual interest rates for not less than 3 projected appreciation rates and not less than 3 credit transaction periods, as determined by the Bureau, including—

(A) a short-term reverse mortgage;

(B) a term equaling the actuarial life expectancy of the consumer; and

(C) such longer term as the Bureau deems appropriate; and

(2) a statement that the consumer is not obligated to complete the reverse mortgage transaction merely because the consumer has received the disclosure required under this section or has signed an application for the reverse mortgage.

(b) Projected total cost

In determining the projected total cost of the mortgage to be disclosed to the consumer under subsection (a), the creditor shall take into account—

(1) any shared appreciation or equity that the lender will, by contract, be entitled to receive;

(2) all costs and charges to the consumer, including the costs of any associated annuity that the consumer elects or is required to purchase as part of the reverse mortgage transaction;

(3) all payments to and for the benefit of the consumer, including, in the case in which an associated annuity is purchased (whether or not required by the lender as a condition of making the reverse mortgage), the annuity payments received by the consumer and financed from the proceeds of the loan, instead of the proceeds used to finance the annuity; and

(4) any limitation on the liability of the consumer under reverse mortgage transactions (such as nonrecourse limits and equity conservation agreements).

(Pub. L. 90–321, title I, §138, as added Pub. L. 103–325, title I, §154(b), Sept. 23, 1994, 108 Stat. 2196; amended Pub. L. 111–203, title X, §1100A(2), July 21, 2010, 124 Stat. 2107.)

EDITORIAL NOTES

AMENDMENTS

2010—Subsec. (a)(1). Pub. L. 111–203 substituted "Bureau" for "Board" in two places.

STATUTORY NOTES AND RELATED SUBSIDIARIES

EFFECTIVE DATE OF 2010 AMENDMENT

Amendment by Pub. L. 111–203 effective on the designated transfer date, see section 1100H of Pub. L. 1–203, set out as a note under section 552a of Title 5, Government Organization and Employees.

§1649. Certain limitations on liability

(a) Limitations on liability

For any closed end consumer credit transaction that is secured by real property or a dwelling, that is subject to this subchapter, and that is consummated before September 30, 1995, a creditor or any assignee of a creditor shall have no civil, administrative, or criminal liability under this subchapter for, and a consumer shall have no extended rescission rights under section 1635(f) of this title with respect to—

    (1) the creditor's treatment, for disclosure purposes, of—

        (A) taxes described in section 1605(d)(3) of this title;

        (B) fees described in section 1605(e)(2) and (5) of this title;

        (C) fees and amounts referred to in the 3rd sentence of section 1605(a) of this title; or

        (D) borrower-paid mortgage broker fees referred to in section 1605(a)(6) of this title;

    (2) the form of written notice used by the creditor to inform the obligor of the rights of the obligor under section 1635 of this title if the creditor provided the obligor with a properly dated form of written notice published and adopted by the Bureau or a comparable written notice, and otherwise complied with all the requirements of this section regarding notice; or

    (3) any disclosure relating to the finance charge imposed with respect to the transaction if the amount or percentage actually disclosed—

        (A) may be treated as accurate for purposes of this subchapter if the amount disclosed as the finance charge does not vary from the actual finance charge by more than $200;

        (B) may, under section 1605(f)(2) of this title, be treated as accurate for purposes of section 1635 of this title; or

        (C) is greater than the amount or percentage required to be disclosed under this subchapter.

(b) Exceptions

Subsection (a) shall not apply to—

    (1) any individual action or counterclaim brought under this subchapter which was filed before June 1, 1995;

    (2) any class action brought under this subchapter for which a final order certifying a class was entered before January 1, 1995;

    (3) the named individual plaintiffs in any class action brought under this subchapter which was filed before June 1, 1995; or

    (4) any consumer credit transaction with respect to which a timely notice of rescission was sent to the creditor before June 1, 1995.

(Pub. L. 90–321, title I, §139, as added Pub. L. 104–29, §4(a), Sept. 30, 1995, 109 Stat. 273; amended Pub. L. 104–208, div. A, title II, §2107(a), Sept. 30, 1996, 110 Stat. 3009–402; Pub. L. 111–203, title X, §1100A(2), July 21, 2010, 124 Stat. 2107.)

EDITORIAL NOTES

AMENDMENTS

2010—Subsec. (a)(2). Pub. L. 111–203 substituted "Bureau" for "Board".

1996—Subsec. (a). Pub. L. 104–208 substituted "For any closed end consumer credit transaction that is secured by real property or a dwelling, that is subject to this subchapter, and" for "For any consumer credit transaction subject to this subchapter".

STATUTORY NOTES AND RELATED SUBSIDIARIES

EFFECTIVE DATE OF 2010 AMENDMENT

Amendment by Pub. L. 111–203 effective on the designated transfer date, see section 1100H of Pub. L. 111–203, set out as a note under section 552a of Title 5, Government Organization and Employees.

EFFECTIVE DATE OF 1996 AMENDMENT

Pub. L. 104–208, div. A, title II, §2107(b), Sept. 30, 1996, 110 Stat. 3009–402, provided that: "The amendment made by subsection (a) [amending this section] shall be effective as of September 30, 199

§1650. Preventing unfair and deceptive private educational lending practices and eliminating conflicts of interest

(a) Definitions

As used in this section—

(1) the term "cosigner"—

(A) means any individual who is liable for the obligation of another without compensation, regardless of how designated in the contract or instrument with respect to that obligation, other than an obligation under a private education loan extended to consolidate a consumer's pre-existing private education loans;

(B) includes any person the signature of which is requested as condition to grant credit or to forbear on collection; and

(C) does not include a spouse of an individual described in subparagraph (A), the signature of whom is needed to perfect the security interest in a loan.

(2) the term "covered educational institution"—

(A) means any educational institution that offers a postsecondary educational degree, certificate, or program of study (including any institution of higher education); and

(B) includes an agent, officer, or employee of the educational institution;

(3) the term "gift"—

(A)(i) means any gratuity, favor, discount, entertainment, hospitality, loan, or other item having more than a de minimis monetary value, including services, transportation, lodging, or meals, whether provided in kind, by purchase of a ticket, payment in advance, or reimbursement after the expense has been incurred; and

(ii) includes an item described in clause (i) provided to a family member of an officer, employee, or agent of a covered educational institution, or to any other individual based on that individual's relationship with the officer, employee, or agent, if—

(I) the item is provided with the knowledge and acquiescence of the officer, employee, or agent; and

(II) the officer, employee, or agent has reason to believe the item was provided because of the official position of the officer, employee, or agent; and

(B) does not include—

(i) standard informational material related to a loan, default aversion, default prevention, or financial literacy;

(ii) food, refreshments, training, or informational material furnished to an officer, employee, or agent of a covered educational institution, as an integral part of a training session or through participation in an advisory council that is designed to improve the service of the private educational lender to the covered educational institution, if such training or participation contributes to the professional development of the officer, employee, or agent of the covered educational institution;

(iii) favorable terms, conditions, and borrower benefits on a private education loan provided to a student employed by the covered educational institution, if such terms, conditions, or benefits are not provided because of the student's employment with the covered educational institution;

(iv) the provision of financial literacy counseling or services, including counseling or services provided in coordination with a covered educational institution, to the extent that such counseling or services are not undertaken to secure—

(I) applications for private education loans or private education loan volume;

(II) applications or loan volume for any loan made, insured, or guaranteed under title IV of the Higher Education Act of 1965 (20 U.S.C. 1070 et seq.); or

(III) the purchase of a product or service of a specific private educational lender;

(v) philanthropic contributions to a covered educational institution from a private educational lender that are unrelated to private education loans and are not made in exchange for any advantage related to private education loans; or

(vi) State education grants, scholarships, or financial aid funds administered by or on behalf of a State;

(4) the term "institution of higher education" has the same meaning as in section 102 of the Higher Education Act of 1965 (20 U.S.C. 1002);

(5) the term "postsecondary educational expenses" means any of the expenses that are included as part of the cost of attendance of a student, as defined under section 472 of the Higher Education Act of 1965 (20 U.S.C. 1087ll);

(6) the term "preferred lender arrangement" has the same meaning as in section 151 of the Higher Education Act of 1965 [20 U.S.C. 1019];

(7) the term "private educational lender" means—

(A) a financial institution, as defined in section 1813 of title 12 that solicits, makes, or extends private education loans;

(B) a Federal credit union, as defined in section 1752 of title 12 that solicits, makes, or extends private education loans; and

(C) any other person engaged in the business of soliciting, making, or extending private education loans;

(8) the term "private education loan"—

(A) means a loan provided by a private educational lender that—

(i) is not made, insured, or guaranteed under of [1] title IV of the Higher Education Act of 1965 (20 U.S.C. 1070 et seq.); and

(ii) is issued expressly for postsecondary educational expenses to a borrower, regardless of whether the loan is provided through the educational institution that the subject student attends or directly to the borrower from the private educational lender; and

(B) does not include an extension of credit under an open end consumer credit plan, a reverse mortgage transaction, a residential mortgage transaction, or any other loan that is secured by real property or a dwelling; and

(9) the term "revenue sharing" means an arrangement between a covered educational institution and a private educational lender under which—

(A) a private educational lender provides or issues private education loans with respect to students attending the covered educational institution;

(B) the covered educational institution recommends to students or others the private educational lender or the private education loans of the private educational lender; and

(C) the private educational lender pays a fee or provides other material benefits, including profit sharing, to the covered educational institution in connection with the private education loans provided to students attending the covered educational institution or a borrower acting on behalf of a student.

(b) Prohibition on certain gifts and arrangements

A private educational lender may not, directly or indirectly—

(1) offer or provide any gift to a covered educational institution in exchange for any advantage or consideration provided to such private educational lender related to its private education loan activities; or

(2) engage in revenue sharing with a covered educational institution.

(c) Prohibition on co-branding

A private educational lender may not use the name, emblem, mascot, or logo of the covered educational institution, or other words, pictures, or symbols readily identified with the covered educational institution, in the marketing of private education loans in any way that implies that the covered educational institution endorses the private education loans offered by the private educational lender.

(d) Advisory Board compensation

Any person who is employed in the financial aid office of a covered educational institution, or who otherwise has responsibilities with respect to private education loans or other financial aid of the institution, and who serves on an advisory board, commission, or group established by a private educational lender or group of such lenders shall be prohibited from receiving anything of value from the private educational lender or group of lenders. Nothing in this subsection prohibits the reimbursement of reasonable expenses incurred by an employee of a covered educational institution as part of their service on an advisory board, commission, or group described in this subsection.

(e) Prohibition on prepayment or repayment fees or penalty

It shall be unlawful for any private educational lender to impose a fee or penalty on a borrower for early repayment or prepayment of any private education loan.

(f) Credit card protections for college students

(1) Disclosure required

An institution of higher education shall publicly disclose any contract or other agreement made with a card issuer or creditor for the purpose of marketing a credit card.

(2) Inducements prohibited

No card issuer or creditor may offer to a student at an institution of higher education any tangible item to induce such student to apply for or participate in an open end consumer credit plan offered by such card issuer or creditor, such offer is made—

(A) on the campus of an institution of higher education;

(B) near the campus of an institution of higher education, as determined by rule of the Bureau; or

(C) at an event sponsored by or related to an institution of higher education.

(3) Sense of the Congress

It is the sense of the Congress that each institution of higher education should consider adopting the following policies relating to credit cards:

(A) That any card issuer that markets a credit card on the campus of such institution notify the institution of the location at which such marketing will take place.

(B) That the number of locations on the campus of such institution at which the marketing of credit cards takes place be limited.

(C) That credit card and debt education and counseling sessions be offered as a regular part of any orientation program for new students of such institution.

(g) Additional protections relating to borrower or cosigner of a private education loan

(1) Prohibition on automatic default in case of death or bankruptcy of non-student obligor

With respect to a private education loan involving a student obligor and 1 or more cosigners, the creditor shall not declare a default or accelerate the debt against the student obligor on the sole basis of a bankruptcy or death of a cosigner.

(2) Cosigner release in case of death of borrower

(A) Release of cosigner

The holder of a private education loan, when notified of the death of a student obligor, shall release within a reasonable timeframe any cosigner from the obligations of the cosigner under the private education loan.

(B) Notification of release

A holder or servicer of a private education loan, as applicable, shall within a reasonable time-frame notify any cosigners for the private education loan if a cosigner is released from the obligations of the cosigner for the private education loan under this paragraph.

(C) Designation of individual to act on behalf of the borrower

Any lender that extends a private education loan shall provide the student obligor an option to designate an individual to have the legal authority to act on behalf of the student obligor with respect to the private education loan in the event of the death of the student obligor.

(Pub. L. 90–321, title I, §140, as added Pub. L. 110–315, title X, §1011(a), Aug. 14, 2008, 122 Stat. 3479; amended Pub. L. 111–24, title III, §304, May 22, 2009, 123 Stat. 1749; Pub. L. 111–203, title X, §1100A(2), July 21, 2010, 124 Stat. 2107; Pub. L. 115–174, title VI, §601(a), May 24, 2018, 132 Stat. 1365.)

EDITORIAL NOTES

REFERENCES IN TEXT

The Higher Education Act of 1965, referred to in subsec. (a)(3)(B)(iv)(II), (8)(A)(i), is Pub. L. 89–329, Nov. 8, 1965, 79 Stat. 1219. Title IV of the Act is classified generally to subchapter IV (§1070 et seq.) of chapter 28 of Title 20, Education. For complete classification of this Act to the Code, see Short Title note set out under section 1001 of Title 20 and Tables.

AMENDMENTS

2018—Subsec. (a). Pub. L. 115–174, §601(a)(1), added par. (1) and redesignated former pars. (1) to (8) as (2) to (9), respectively.

Subsec. (g). Pub. L. 115–174, §601(a)(2), added subsec. (g).

2010—Subsec. (f)(2)(B). Pub. L. 111–203 substituted "Bureau" for "Board".

2009—Subsec. (f). Pub. L. 111–24 added subsec. (f).

STATUTORY NOTES AND RELATED SUBSIDIARIES

EFFECTIVE DATE OF 2018 AMENDMENT

Pub. L. 115–174, title VI, §601(b), May 24, 2018, 132 Stat. 1365, provided that: "The amendments made by subsection (a) [amending this section] shall only apply to private education loan agreements entered into on or after the date that is 180 days after the date of enactment of this Act [May 24, 2018]."

EFFECTIVE DATE OF 2010 AMENDMENT

Amendment by Pub. L. 111–203 effective on the designated transfer date, see section 1100H of Pub. L. 1–203, set out as a note under section 552a of Title 5, Government Organization and Employees.

EFFECTIVE DATE OF 2009 AMENDMENT

Amendment by Pub. L. 111–24 effective 9 months after May 22, 2009, except as otherwise specifically provided, see section 3 of Pub. L. 111–24, set out as a note under section 1602 of this title.

EFFECTIVE DATE

Subsec. (c) of this section effective on the earlier of the date on which regulations issued under section 02 of Pub. L. 110–315 (set out as a Regulations note under section 1638 of this title) become effective or 18 months after Aug. 14, 2008, see section 1003(b) of Pub. L. 110–315, set out as an Effective Date of 2008 Amendment note under section 1638 of this title. Such regulations were issued effective Sept. 14, 2009, with compliance optional until Feb. 14, 2010.

¹ So in original. The word "of" probably should not appear.

§1651. Procedure for timely settlement of estates of decedent obligors

The Bureau, in consultation with the Bureau ¹ and each other agency referred to in section 1607(a) of this title, shall prescribe regulations to require any creditor, with respect to any credit card account under an open end consumer credit plan, to establish procedures to ensure that any administrator of an estate of any deceased obligor with respect to such account can resolve outstanding credit balances in a timely manner.

(Pub. L. 90–321, title I, §140A, as added Pub. L. 111–24, title V, §504(a), May 22, 2009, 123 Stat. 1756; amended Pub. L. 111–203, title X, §1100A(2), (3), July 21, 2010, 124 Stat. 2107.)

EDITORIAL NOTES

AMENDMENTS

2010—Pub. L. 111–203, §1100A(3), substituted "the Bureau" for "the Federal Trade Commission".
Pub. L. 111–203, §1100A(2), substituted "The Bureau" for "The Board".

STATUTORY NOTES AND RELATED SUBSIDIARIES

EFFECTIVE DATE OF 2010 AMENDMENT

Amendment by Pub. L. 111–203 effective on the designated transfer date, see section 1100H of Pub. L. 111–203, set out as a note under section 552a of Title 5, Government Organization and Employees.

EFFECTIVE DATE

Section effective 9 months after May 22, 2009, except as otherwise specifically provided, see section 3 of Pub. L. 111–24, set out as an Effective Date of 2009 Amendment note under section 1602 of this title.

¹ So in original.

PART C—CREDIT ADVERTISING AND LIMITS ON CREDIT CARD FEES

§1661. Catalogs and multiple-page advertisements

For the purposes of this part, a catalog or other multiple-page advertisement shall be considered a single advertisement if it clearly and conspicuously displays a credit terms table on which the information required to be stated under this part is clearly set forth.

(Pub. L. 90–321, title I, §141, May 29, 1968, 82 Stat. 158.)

STATUTORY NOTES AND RELATED SUBSIDIARIES

EFFECTIVE DATE

Pub. L. 90–321, title V, §504(b), May 29, 1968, 82 Stat. 167, provided that chapter 3 of title I, which enact sections 1661 to 1665 of this title, is effective July 1, 1969.

§1662. Advertising of downpayments and installments

No advertisement to aid, promote, or assist directly or indirectly any extension of consumer credit may state
(1) that a specific periodic consumer credit amount or installment amount can be arranged, unless the creditor usually and customarily arranges credit payments or installments for that period and in that amount.

(2) that a specified downpayment is required in connection with any extension of consumer credit, unless the creditor usually and customarily arranges downpayments in that amount.

(Pub. L. 90–321, title I, §142, May 29, 1968, 82 Stat. 158.)

§1663. Advertising of open end credit plans

No advertisement to aid, promote, or assist directly or indirectly the extension of consumer credit under an open end credit plan may set forth any of the specific terms of that plan unless it also clearly and conspicuously sets forth all of the following items:

(1) Any minimum or fixed amount which could be imposed.

(2) In any case in which periodic rates may be used to compute the finance charge, the periodic rates expressed as annual percentage rates.

(3) Any other term that the Bureau may by regulation require to be disclosed.

(Pub. L. 90–321, title I, §143, May 29, 1968, 82 Stat. 158; Pub. L. 96–221, title VI, §§613(f), 619(a), Mar. 31, 1980, 94 Stat. 177, 183; Pub. L. 111–203, title X, §1100A(2), July 21, 2010, 124 Stat. 2107.)

EDITORIAL NOTES

AMENDMENTS

2010—Par. (3). Pub. L. 111–203 substituted "Bureau" for "Board".

1980—Pub. L. 96–221 in existing introductory text struck out applicability of rate determined under section 1637(a)(5) of this title, and amended section generally substituting items setting forth minimum or fixed amount, etc., set out in pars. (1) to (3), for items time period, etc., set out in pars. (1) to (5).

STATUTORY NOTES AND RELATED SUBSIDIARIES

EFFECTIVE DATE OF 2010 AMENDMENT

Amendment by Pub. L. 111–203 effective on the designated transfer date, see section 1100H of Pub. L. 111–203, set out as a note under section 552a of Title 5, Government Organization and Employees.

EFFECTIVE DATE OF 1980 AMENDMENT

Amendment by Pub. L. 96–221 effective on expiration of two years and six months after Mar. 31, 1980, with all regulations, forms, and clauses required to be prescribed to be promulgated at least one year prior to such effective date, and allowing any creditor to comply with any amendments, in accordance with the regulations, forms, and clauses prescribed by the Board prior to such effective date, see section 625 of Pub. L. 96–221, set out as a note under section 1602 of this title.

§1664. Advertising of credit other than open end plans

(a) Exclusion of open end credit plans

Except as provided in subsection (b), this section applies to any advertisement to aid, promote, or assist directly or indirectly any consumer credit sale, loan, or other extension of credit subject to the provisions of this subchapter, other than an open end credit plan.

(b) Advertisements of residential real estate

The provisions of this section do not apply to advertisements of residential real estate except to the extent that the Bureau may by regulation require.

(c) Rate of finance charge expressed as annual percentage rate

If any advertisement to which this section applies states the rate of a finance charge, the advertisement shall state the rate of that charge expressed as an annual percentage rate.

(d) Requisite disclosures in advertisement

If any advertisement to which this section applies states the amount of the downpayment, if any, the dollar amount of any finance charge, or the number of installments or the period of installment payment, the dollar amount of any finance charge, or the number of installments or the period of payment, then the advertisement shall state all of the following items:

(1) The downpayment, if any.

(2) The terms of repayment.

(3) The rate of the finance charge expressed as an annual percentage rate.

(e) Credit transaction secured by principal dwelling of consumer

Each advertisement to which this section applies that relates to a consumer credit transaction that is secured by the principal dwelling of a consumer in which the extension of credit may exceed the fair market value of the dwelling, and which advertisement is disseminated in paper form to the public or through the Internet, as opposed to by radio or television, shall clearly and conspicuously state that—

(1) the interest on the portion of the credit extension that is greater than the fair market value of the dwelling is not tax deductible for Federal income tax purposes; and

(2) the consumer should consult a tax adviser for further information regarding the deductibility of interest and charges.

(Pub. L. 90–321, title I, §144, May 29, 1968, 82 Stat. 158; Pub. L. 96–221, title VI, §619(b), Mar. 31, 1980, 94 Stat. 183; Pub. L. 109–8, title XIII, §1302(b)(2), Apr. 20, 2005, 119 Stat. 209; Pub. L. 111–203, title X, §1100A(2), July 21, 2010, 124 Stat. 2107.)

EDITORIAL NOTES

AMENDMENTS

2010—Subsec. (b). Pub. L. 111–203 substituted "Bureau" for "Board".

2005—Subsec. (e). Pub. L. 109–8 added subsec. (e).

1980—Subsec. (d). Pub. L. 97–221 substituted items setting forth downpayment, etc., set out in pars. (1) to (3), for items setting forth cash price or amount of loan, etc., set out in pars. (1) to (4).

STATUTORY NOTES AND RELATED SUBSIDIARIES

EFFECTIVE DATE OF 2010 AMENDMENT

Amendment by Pub. L. 111–203 effective on the designated transfer date, see section 1100H of Pub. L. 111–203, set out as a note under section 552a of Title 5, Government Organization and Employees.

EFFECTIVE DATE OF 2005 AMENDMENT

Amendment by Pub. L. 109–8 effective 180 days after Apr. 20, 2005, and not applicable with respect to cases commenced under Title 11, Bankruptcy, before such effective date, except as otherwise provided, see section 1501 of Pub. L. 109–8, set out as a note under section 101 of Title 11.

EFFECTIVE DATE OF 1980 AMENDMENT

Amendment by Pub. L. 96–221 effective on expiration of two years and six months after Mar. 31, 1980, with all regulations, forms, and clauses required to be prescribed to be promulgated at least one year prior to such effective date, and allowing any creditor to comply with any amendments, in accordance with the regulations, forms, and clauses prescribed by the Board prior to such effective date, see section 625 of Pub. L. 96–221, set out as a note under section 1602 of this title.

§1665. Nonliability of advertising media

There is no liability under this part on the part of any owner or personnel, as such, of any medium in which an advertisement appears or through which it is disseminated.

(Pub. L. 90–321, title I, §145, May 29, 1968, 82 Stat. 159.)

§1665a. Use of annual percentage rate in oral disclosures; exceptions

In responding orally to any inquiry about the cost of credit, a creditor, regardless of the method used to compute finance charges, shall state rates only in terms of the annual percentage rate, except that in the case of an open end credit plan, the periodic rate also may be stated and, in the case of an other than open end credit plan where a major component of the finance charge consists of interest computed at a simple annual rate, the simple annual rate also may be stated. The Bureau may, by regulation, modify the requirements of this section or provide an exception from this section for a transaction or class of transactions for which the creditor cannot determine in advance the applicable annual percentage rate.

(Pub. L. 90–321, title I, §146, as added Pub. L. 93–495, title IV, §401(a), Oct. 28, 1974, 88 Stat. 1517; amended Pub. L. 96–221, title VI, §623(a), Mar. 31, 1980, 94 Stat. 185; Pub. L. 111–203, title X, §1100A(2), July 21, 2010, 124 Stat. 2107.)

AMENDMENTS

2010—Pub. L. 111–203 substituted "Bureau" for "Board".

1980—Pub. L. 96–221 substituted provisions relating to use of annual percentage rate in oral disclosures by creditors, for provisions setting forth requirements for advertisements concerning consumer credit repayable in more than four installments.

EFFECTIVE DATE OF 2010 AMENDMENT

Amendment by Pub. L. 111–203 effective on the designated transfer date, see section 1100H of Pub. L. 111–203, set out as a note under section 552a of Title 5, Government Organization and Employees.

EFFECTIVE DATE OF 1980 AMENDMENT

Amendment by Pub. L. 96–221 effective on expiration of two years and six months after Mar. 31, 1980, with all regulations, forms, and clauses required to be prescribed to be promulgated at least one year prior to such effective date, and allowing any creditor to comply with any amendments, in accordance with the regulations, forms, and clauses prescribed by the Board prior to such effective date, see section 625 of Pub. L. 96–221, set out as a note under section 1602 of this title.

EFFECTIVE DATE

Pub. L. 93–495, title IV, §416, Oct. 28, 1974, 88 Stat. 1521, provided that: "This title [enacting this section and sections 1614 and 1645 of this title, amending sections 1603, 1607, 1635, 1637, 1640, and 1644 of this title, and enacting provision set out as a note under section 1640 of this title] takes effect upon the date of its enactment [Oct. 28, 1974], except that sections 409 [amending section 1631 of this title] and 411 [amending section 1637 of this title] take effect upon the expiration of one year after the date of its enactment [Oct. 28, 1974]."

§1665b. Advertising of open end consumer credit plans secured by consumer's principal dwelling

(a) In general

If any advertisement to aid, promote, or assist, directly or indirectly, the extension of consumer credit through an open end consumer credit plan under which extensions of credit are secured by the consumer's principal dwelling states, affirmatively or negatively, any of the specific terms of the plan, including any periodic payment amount required under such plan, such advertisement shall also clearly and conspicuously set forth the following information, in such form and manner as the Bureau may require:

(1) Loan fees and opening cost estimates

Any loan fee the amount of which is determined as a percentage of the credit limit applicable to an account under the plan and an estimate of the aggregate amount of other fees for opening the account, based on the creditor's experience with the plan and stated as a single amount or as a reasonable range.

(2) Periodic rates

In any case in which periodic rates may be used to compute the finance charge, the periodic rates expressed as an annual percentage rate.

(3) Highest annual percentage rate

The highest annual percentage rate which may be imposed under the plan.

(4) Other information

Any other information the Bureau may by regulation require.

(b) Tax deductibility

(1) In general

If any advertisement described in subsection (a) contains a statement that any interest expense incurred with respect to the plan is or may be tax deductible, the advertisement shall not be misleading with respect to such deductibility.

(2) Credit in excess of fair market value

117

Each advertisement described in subsection (a) that relates to an extension of credit that may exceed the fair market value of the dwelling, and which advertisement is disseminated in paper form to the public or through the Internet, as opposed to by radio or television, shall include a clear and conspicuous statement that—

(A) the interest on the portion of the credit extension that is greater than the fair market value of the dwelling is not tax deductible for Federal income tax purposes; and

(B) the consumer should consult a tax adviser for further information regarding the deductibility of interest and charges.

(c) Certain terms prohibited

No advertisement described in subsection (a) with respect to any home equity account may refer to such loan as "free money" or use other terms determined by the Bureau by regulation to be misleading.

(d) Discounted initial rate

(1) In general

If any advertisement described in subsection (a) includes an initial annual percentage rate that is not determined by the index or formula used to make later interest rate adjustments, the advertisement shall also state with equal prominence the current annual percentage rate that would have been applied using the index or formula if such initial rate had not been offered.

(2) Quoted rate must be reasonably current

The annual percentage rate required to be disclosed under the paragraph (1) rate must be current as of a reasonable time given the media involved.

(3) Period during which initial rate is in effect

Any advertisement to which paragraph (1) applies shall also state the period of time during which the initial annual percentage rate referred to in such paragraph will be in effect.

(e) Balloon payment

If any advertisement described in subsection (a) contains a statement regarding the minimum monthly payment under the plan, the advertisement shall also disclose, if applicable, the fact that the plan includes a balloon payment.

(f) "Balloon payment" defined

For purposes of this section and section 1637a of this title, the term "balloon payment" means, with respect to any open end consumer credit plan under which extensions of credit are secured by the consumer's principal dwelling, any repayment option under which—

(1) the account holder is required to repay the entire amount of any outstanding balance as of a specified date or at the end of a specified period of time, as determined in accordance with the terms of the agreement pursuant to which such credit is extended; and

(2) the aggregate amount of the minimum periodic payments required would not fully amortize such outstanding balance by such date or at the end of such period.

(Pub. L. 90–321, title I, §147, as added Pub. L. 100–709, §2(c), Nov. 23, 1988, 102 Stat. 4730; amended Pub. L. 109–8, title XIII, §1302(a)(2), Apr. 20, 2005, 119 Stat. 208; Pub. L. 111–203, title X, §1100A(2), July 21, 2010, 124 Stat. 2107.)

EDITORIAL NOTES

AMENDMENTS

2010—Subsecs. (a), (c). Pub. L. 111–203 substituted "Bureau" for "Board" wherever appearing.

2005—Subsec. (b). Pub. L. 109–8 designated existing provisions as par. (1), inserted par. heading, and added par. (2).

STATUTORY NOTES AND RELATED SUBSIDIARIES

EFFECTIVE DATE OF 2010 AMENDMENT

Amendment by Pub. L. 111–203 effective on the designated transfer date, see section 1100H of Pub. L. 111–203, set out as a note under section 552a of Title 5, Government Organization and Employees.

EFFECTIVE DATE OF 2005 AMENDMENT

Amendment by Pub. L. 109–8 effective 180 days after Apr. 20, 2005, and not applicable with respect to cases commenced under Title 11, Bankruptcy, before such effective date, except as otherwise provided, see section 1501 of Pub. L. 109–8, set out as a note under section 101 of Title 11.

EFFECTIVE DATE

For effective date of section, see Regulations; Effective Date note below.

REGULATIONS; EFFECTIVE DATE

For provisions relating to promulgation of regulations to implement amendment by Pub. L. 100–709 [enacting this section], and effective date of such amendment in connection with those regulations, see section 7 of Pub. L. 100–709, set out as a note under section 1637a of this title.

§1665c. Interest rate reduction on open end consumer credit plans

(a) In general

If a creditor increases the annual percentage rate applicable to a credit card account under an open end consumer credit plan, based on factors including the credit risk of the obligor, market conditions, or other factors, the creditor shall consider changes in such factors in subsequently determining whether to reduce the annual percentage rate for such obligor.

(b) Requirements

With respect to any credit card account under an open end consumer credit plan, the creditor shall—
(1) maintain reasonable methodologies for assessing the factors described in subsection (a);
(2) not less frequently than once every 6 months, review accounts as to which the annual percentage rate has been increased since January 1, 2009, to assess whether such factors have changed (including whether any risk has declined);
(3) reduce the annual percentage rate previously increased when a reduction is indicated by the review; and
(4) in the event of an increase in the annual percentage rate, provide in the written notice required under section 1637(i) of this title a statement of the reasons for the increase.

(c) Rule of construction

This section shall not be construed to require a reduction in any specific amount.

(d) Rulemaking

The Bureau [1] shall issue final rules not later than 9 months after May 22, 2009, to implement the requirements of and evaluate compliance with this section, and subsections (a), (b), and (c) shall become effective 15 months after May 22, 2009.

(Pub. L. 90–321, title I, §148, as added Pub. L. 111–24, title I, §101(c), May 22, 2009, 123 Stat. 1737; amended Pub. L. 111–203, title X, §1100A(2), July 21, 2010, 124 Stat. 2107.)

EDITORIAL NOTES

AMENDMENTS

2010—Subsec. (d). Pub. L. 111–203 substituted "Bureau" for "Board".

STATUTORY NOTES AND RELATED SUBSIDIARIES

EFFECTIVE DATE OF 2010 AMENDMENT

Amendment by Pub. L. 111–203 effective on the designated transfer date, see section 1100H of Pub. L. 11–203, set out as a note under section 552a of Title 5, Government Organization and Employees.

EFFECTIVE DATE

Section effective 9 months after May 22, 2009, except as otherwise specifically provided, see section 3 f Pub. L. 111–24, set out as an Effective Date of 2009 Amendment note under section 1602 of this title.

[1] So in original. Probably should be "Board".

665d. Reasonable penalty fees on open end consumer credit plans

In general

he amount of any penalty fee or charge that a card issuer may impose with respect to a credit card account under open end consumer credit plan in connection with any omission with respect to, or violation of, the cardholder agreement, including any late payment fee, over-the-limit fee, or any other penalty fee or charge, shall be reasonable and proportional to such omission or violation.

(b) Rulemaking required

The Bureau, in consultation with the Comptroller of the Currency, the Board of Directors of the Federal Deposit Insurance Corporation, the Director of the Office of Thrift Supervision, and the National Credit Union Administration Board, shall issue final rules not later than 9 months after May 22, 2009, to establish standards for assessing whether the amount of any penalty fee or charge described under subsection (a) is reasonable and proportional to the omission or violation to which the fee or charge relates. Subsection (a) shall become effective 15 months after May 22, 2009.

(c) Considerations

In issuing rules required by this section, the Bureau shall consider—
(1) the cost incurred by the creditor from such omission or violation;
(2) the deterrence of such omission or violation by the cardholder;
(3) the conduct of the cardholder; and
(4) such other factors as the Bureau may deem necessary or appropriate.

(d) Differentiation permitted

In issuing rules required by this subsection, the Bureau may establish different standards for different types of fees and charges, as appropriate.

(e) Safe harbor rule authorized

The Bureau, in consultation with the Comptroller of the Currency, the Board of Directors of the Federal Deposit Insurance Corporation, the Director of the Office of Thrift Supervision, and the National Credit Union Administration Board, may issue rules to provide an amount for any penalty fee or charge described under subsection (a) that is presumed to be reasonable and proportional to the omission or violation to which the fee or charge relates.

(Pub. L. 90–321, title I, §149, as added Pub. L. 111–24, title I, §102(b)(1), May 22, 2009, 123 Stat. 1740; amended Pub. L. 111–203, title X, §1100A(2), July 21, 2010, 124 Stat. 2107.)

EDITORIAL NOTES

AMENDMENTS

2010—Subsecs. (b) to (e). Pub. L. 111–203, §1100A(2), which directed amendment of this section by substituting "Bureau" for "Board" wherever appearing, was executed by making the substitution for "Board" the first time appearing in subsecs. (b) and (e), and wherever appearing in subsecs. (c) and (d), to reflect the probable intent of Congress.

STATUTORY NOTES AND RELATED SUBSIDIARIES

EFFECTIVE DATE OF 2010 AMENDMENT

Amendment by Pub. L. 111–203 effective on the designated transfer date, see section 1100H of Pub. L. 111–203, set out as a note under section 552a of Title 5, Government Organization and Employees.

EFFECTIVE DATE

Section effective 9 months after May 22, 2009, except as otherwise specifically provided, see section of Pub. L. 111–24, set out as an Effective Date of 2009 Amendment note under section 1602 of this title.

§1665e. Consideration of ability to repay

A card issuer may not open any credit card account for any consumer under an open end consumer credit plan, or increase any credit limit applicable to such account, unless the card issuer considers the ability of the consumer to make the required payments under the terms of such account.

(Pub. L. 90–321, title I, §150, as added Pub. L. 111–24, title I, §109(a), May 22, 2009, 123 Stat. 1743.)

STATUTORY NOTES AND RELATED SUBSIDIARIES

EFFECTIVE DATE

Section effective 9 months after May 22, 2009, except as otherwise specifically provided, see sectio of Pub. L. 111–24, set out as an Effective Date of 2009 Amendment note under section 1602 of this title.

§1666. Correction of billing errors

(a) Written notice by obligor to creditor; time for and contents of notice; procedure upon receipt of notice by creditor

If a creditor, within sixty days after having transmitted to an obligor a statement of the obligor's account in connection with an extension of consumer credit, receives at the address disclosed under section 1637(b)(10) of this title a written notice (other than notice on a payment stub or other payment medium supplied by the creditor if the creditor so stipulates with the disclosure required under section 1637(a)(7) of this title) from the obligor in which the obligor—

(1) sets forth or otherwise enables the creditor to identify the name and account number (if any) of the obligor,

(2) indicates the obligor's belief that the statement contains a billing error and the amount of such billing error, and

(3) sets forth the reasons for the obligor's belief (to the extent applicable) that the statement contains a billing error,

the creditor shall, unless the obligor has, after giving such written notice and before the expiration of the time limits herein specified, agreed that the statement was correct—

(A) not later than thirty days after the receipt of the notice, send a written acknowledgment thereof to the obligor, unless the action required in subparagraph (B) is taken within such thirty-day period, and

(B) not later than two complete billing cycles of the creditor (in no event later than ninety days) after the receipt of the notice and prior to taking any action to collect the amount, or any part thereof, indicated by the obligor under paragraph (2) either—

(i) make appropriate corrections in the account of the obligor, including the crediting of any finance charges on amounts erroneously billed, and transmit to the obligor a notification of such corrections and the creditor's explanation of any change in the amount indicated by the obligor under paragraph (2) and, if any such change is made and the obligor so requests, copies of documentary evidence of the obligor's indebtedness; or

(ii) send a written explanation or clarification to the obligor, after having conducted an investigation, setting forth to the extent applicable the reasons why the creditor believes the account of the obligor was correctly shown in the statement and, upon request of the obligor, provide copies of documentary evidence of the obligor's indebtedness. In the case of a billing error where the obligor alleges that the creditor's billing statement reflects goods not delivered to the obligor or his designee in accordance with the agreement made at the time of the transaction, a creditor may not construe such amount to be correctly shown unless he determines that such goods were actually delivered, mailed, or otherwise sent to the obligor and provides the obligor with a statement of such determination.

After complying with the provisions of this subsection with respect to an alleged billing error, a creditor has no further responsibility under this section if the obligor continues to make substantially the same allegation with respect to such error.

(b) Billing error

For the purpose of this section, a "billing error" consists of any of the following:

(1) A reflection on a statement of an extension of credit which was not made to the obligor or, if made, was not in the amount reflected on such statement.

(2) A reflection on a statement of an extension of credit for which the obligor requests additional clarification including documentary evidence thereof.

(3) A reflection on a statement of goods or services not accepted by the obligor or his designee or not delivered to the obligor or his designee in accordance with the agreement made at the time of a transaction.

(4) The creditor's failure to reflect properly on a statement a payment made by the obligor or a credit issued to the obligor.

(5) A computation error or similar error of an accounting nature of the creditor on a statement.

(6) Failure to transmit the statement required under section 1637(b) of this title to the last address of the obligor which has been disclosed to the creditor, unless that address was furnished less than twenty days before the end of the billing cycle for which the statement is required.

(7) Any other error described in regulations of the Bureau.

(c) Action by creditor to collect amount or any part thereof regarded by obligor to be a billing error

For the purposes of this section, "action to collect the amount, or any part thereof, indicated by an obligor under paragraph (2)" does not include the sending of statements of account, which may include finance charges on amounts in dispute, to the obligor following written notice from the obligor as specified under subsection (a), if—

(1) the obligor's account is not restricted or closed because of the failure of the obligor to pay the amount indicated under paragraph (2) of subsection (a), and

(2) the creditor indicates the payment of such amount is not required pending the creditor's compliance with this section.

Nothing in this section shall be construed to prohibit any action by a creditor to collect any amount which has not been indicated by the obligor to contain a billing error.

(d) Restricting or closing by creditor of account regarded by obligor to contain a billing error

Pursuant to regulations of the Bureau, a creditor operating an open end consumer credit plan may not, prior to the sending of the written explanation or clarification required under paragraph (B)(ii), restrict or close an account with respect to which the obligor has indicated pursuant to subsection (a) that he believes such account to contain a billing error solely because of the obligor's failure to pay the amount indicated to be in error. Nothing in this subsection shall be deemed to prohibit a creditor from applying against the credit limit on the obligor's account the amount indicated to be in error.

(e) Effect of noncompliance with requirements by creditor

Any creditor who fails to comply with the requirements of this section or section 1666a of this title forfeits any right to collect from the obligor the amount indicated by the obligor under paragraph (2) of subsection (a) of this section, and any finance charges thereon, except that the amount required to be forfeited under this subsection may not exceed $50.

(Pub. L. 90–321, title I, §161, as added Pub. L. 93–495, title III, §306, Oct. 28, 1974, 88 Stat. 1512; amended Pub. L. 96–221, title VI §§613(g), 620, Mar. 31, 1980, 94 Stat. 177, 184; Pub. L. 111–203, title X, §§1087, 1100A(2), July 21, 2010, 124 Stat. 2086, 2107.)

EDITORIAL NOTES

CODIFICATION

Pub L. 111–203, §1100A(2), which directed the substitution of "Bureau" for "Board" wherever appearing in title I of Pub. L. 90–321, was executed to this section, which is section 161 of title I of Pub. L. 90–321. Section 1087 of Pub. L. 111–203, which directed the making of an identical amendment in title III of Pub. L. 93–495, which added this section to title I of Pub. L. 90–321, has not been executed.

AMENDMENTS

2010—Subsecs. (b)(7), (d). Pub. L. 111–203, §1100A(2), substituted "Bureau" for "Board". See Codification note above.

1980—Subsec. (a). Pub. L. 96–221, §613(g), substituted "(b)(10)" for "(b)(11)" and "(a)(7)" for "(a)(8)".

Subsec. (b)(6), (7). Pub. L. 96–221, §620(a), added par. (6) and redesignated former par. (6) as (7).

Subsec. (c). Pub. L. 96–221, §620(b), inserted provisions respecting finance charges on amounts in dispute.

STATUTORY NOTES AND RELATED SUBSIDIARIES

EFFECTIVE DATE OF 2010 AMENDMENT

Amendment by Pub. L. 111–203 effective on the designated transfer date, see section 1100H of Pub. L. 111–203, set out as a note under section 552a of Title 5, Government Organization and Employees.

EFFECTIVE DATE OF 1980 AMENDMENT

Amendment by Pub. L. 96–221 effective on expiration of two years and six months after Mar. 31, 1980, with all regulations, forms, and clauses required to be prescribed to be promulgated at least one year prior to such effective date, and allowing any creditor to comply with any amendments, in accordance with the regulations, forms, and clauses prescribed by the Board prior to such effective date, see section 625 of Pub. L. 96–221, set out as a note under section 1602 of this title.

EFFECTIVE DATE

Pub. L. 93–495, title III, §308, Oct. 28, 1974, 88 Stat. 1517, provided that: "This title [enacting this section and sections 1666a to 1666j of this title, amending sections 1601, 1602, 1610, 1631, 1632, and 1637 of this title, and enacting provision set out as a note under section 1601 of this title] takes effect upon the expiration of one year after the date of its enactment [Oct. 28, 1974]."

SHORT TITLE

Title III of Pub. L. 93–495, which is classified principally to this part, is known as the "Fair Credit Billing Act". For complete classification of Title III to the Code, see Short Title of 1974 Amendment note set out under section 1601 of this title and Tables.

§1666a. Regulation of credit reports

(a) Reports by creditor on obligor's failure to pay amount regarded as billing error

After receiving a notice from an obligor as provided in section 1666(a) of this title, a creditor or his agent may not directly or indirectly threaten to report to any person adversely on the obligor's credit rating or credit standing because of the obligor's failure to pay the amount indicated by the obligor under section 1666(a)(2) of this title, and such amount may not be reported as delinquent to any third party until the creditor has met the requirements of section 1666 of this title and has allowed the obligor the same number of days (not less than ten) thereafter to make payment as is provided under the credit agreement with the obligor for the payment of undisputed amounts.

(b) Reports by creditor on delinquent amounts in dispute; notification of obligor of parties notified of delinquency

If a creditor receives a further written notice from an obligor that an amount is still in dispute within the time allowed for payment under subsection (a) of this section, a creditor may not report to any third party that the amount of the obligor is delinquent because the obligor has failed to pay an amount which he has indicated under section 1666(a)(2) of this title, unless the creditor also reports that the amount is in dispute and, at the same time, notifies the obligor of the name and address of each party to whom the creditor is reporting information concerning the delinquency.

(c) Reports by creditor of subsequent resolution of delinquent amounts

A creditor shall report any subsequent resolution of any delinquencies reported pursuant to subsection (b) to the parties to whom such delinquencies were initially reported.

(Pub. L. 90–321, title I, §162, as added Pub. L. 93–495, title III, §306, Oct. 28, 1974, 88 Stat. 1513.)

§1666b. Timing of payments

(a) Time to make payments

A creditor may not treat a payment on a credit card account under an open end consumer credit plan as late for any purpose, unless the creditor has adopted reasonable procedures designed to ensure that each periodic statement including the information required by section 1637(b) of this title is mailed or delivered to the consumer not later than 21 days before the payment due date.

(b) Grace period

If an open end consumer credit plan provides a time period within which an obligor may repay any portion of the credit extended without incurring an additional finance charge, such additional finance charge may not be imposed with respect to such portion of the credit extended for the billing cycle of which such period is a part, unless a statement which includes the amount upon which the finance charge for the period is based was mailed or delivered to the consumer not later than 21 days before the date specified in the statement by which payment must be made in order to avoid imposition of that finance charge.

(Pub. L. 90–321, title I, §163, as added Pub. L. 93–495, title III, §306, Oct. 28, 1974, 88 Stat. 1514; amended Pub. L. 111–24, title I, §106(b)(1), May 22, 2009, 123 Stat. 1742; Pub. L. 111–93, §2, Nov. 6, 2009, 123 Stat. 2998.)

EDITORIAL NOTES

AMENDMENTS

2009—Pub. L. 111–24 amended section generally, adding provisions relating to late payments and delivery of periodic statements, substituting provisions requiring a 21-day statement delivery period for provisions requiring a 14-day period before the imposition of additional finance charges, and striking provisions relating to excusable cause for creditor's failure to make timely mailing or delivery of periodic statements.

Subsec. (a). Pub. L. 111–93 inserted "a credit card account under" after "payment on".

STATUTORY NOTES AND RELATED SUBSIDIARIES

EFFECTIVE DATE

Pub. L. 111–24, title I, §106(b)(2), May 22, 2009, 123 Stat. 1742, provided that: "Notwithstanding section 3, the Effective Date of 2009 Amendment note set out under section 1602 of this title], section 163 of the Truth in Lending Act [15 U.S.C. 1666b], as amended by this subsection, shall become effective 90 days after the date of enactment of this Act [May 22, 2009]."

§1666c. Prompt and fair crediting of payments

(a) In general

Payments received from an obligor under an open end consumer credit plan by the creditor shall be posted promptly to the obligor's account as specified in regulations of the Bureau. Such regulations shall prevent a finance charge from being imposed on any obligor if the creditor has received the obligor's payment in readily identifiable form, by 5:00 p.m. on the date on which such payment is due, in the amount, manner, and location indicated by the creditor to avoid the imposition thereof.

(b) Application of payments

(1) In general

Upon receipt of a payment from a cardholder, the card issuer shall apply amounts in excess of the minimum payment amount first to the card balance bearing the highest rate of interest, and then to each successive balance bearing the next highest rate of interest, until the payment is exhausted.

(2) Clarification relating to certain deferred interest arrangements

A creditor shall allocate the entire amount paid by the consumer in excess of the minimum payment amount to a balance on which interest is deferred during the last 2 billing cycles immediately preceding the expiration of the period during which interest is deferred.

(c) Changes by card issuer

If a card issuer makes a material change in the mailing address, office, or procedures for handling cardholder payments, and such change causes a material delay in the crediting of a cardholder payment made during the 60-day period following the date on which such change took effect, the card issuer may not impose any late fee or finance charge for a late payment on the credit card account to which such payment was credited.

(Pub. L. 90–321, title I, §164, as added Pub. L. 93–495, title III, §306, Oct. 28, 1974, 88 Stat. 1514; amended Pub. L. 111–24, title I, §104, May 22, 2009, 123 Stat. 1741; Pub. L. 111–203, title X, §§1087, 1100A(2), July 21, 2010, 124 Stat. 2086, 2107.)

EDITORIAL NOTES

CODIFICATION

Pub L. 111–203, §1100A(2), which directed the substitution of "Bureau" for "Board" wherever appearing in title I of Pub. L. 90–321, was executed to this section, which is section 164 of title I of Pub. L. 90–321. Section 1087 of Pub. L. 111–203, which directed the making of an identical amendment in title III of Pub. L. 93–495, which added this section to title I of Pub. L. 90–321, has not been executed.

AMENDMENTS

2010—Subsec. (a). Pub. L. 111–203, §1100A(2), substituted "Bureau" for "Board". See Codification note above.

2009—Pub. L. 111–24, §104(1), substituted "Prompt and fair crediting of payments" for "Prompt crediting of payments" in section catchline, designated existing provisions as subsec. (a), and inserted subsec. (a) heading.

Subsec. (a). Pub. L. 111–24, §104(2), (3), inserted ", by 5:00 p.m. on the date on which such payment is due," after "in readily identifiable form" and substituted "manner, and location" for "manner, location, and time".

Subsecs. (b), (c). Pub. L. 111–24, §104(4), added subsecs. (b) and (c).

STATUTORY NOTES AND RELATED SUBSIDIARIES

EFFECTIVE DATE OF 2010 AMENDMENT

Amendment by Pub. L. 111–203 effective on the designated transfer date, see section 1100H of Pub. L. 111–203, set out as a note under section 552a of Title 5, Government Organization and Employees.

EFFECTIVE DATE OF 2009 AMENDMENT

Amendment by Pub. L. 111–24 effective 9 months after May 22, 2009, except as otherwise specifically provided, see section 3 of Pub. L. 111–24, set out as a note under section 1602 of this title.

§1666d. Treatment of credit balances

Whenever a credit balance in excess of $1 is created in connection with a consumer credit transaction through (transmittal of funds to a creditor in excess of the total balance due on an account, (2) rebates of unearned finance charges or insurance premiums, or (3) amounts otherwise owed to or held for the benefit of an obligor, the creditor shall—

    (A) credit the amount of the credit balance to the consumer's account;

    (B) refund any part of the amount of the remaining credit balance, upon request of the consumer; and

    (C) make a good faith effort to refund to the consumer by cash, check, or money order any part of the amount of the credit balance remaining in the account for more than six months, except that no further action is required in any case in which the consumer's current location is not known by the creditor and cannot be traced through the consumer's last known address or telephone number.

(Pub. L. 90–321, title I, §165, as added Pub. L. 93–495, title III, §306, Oct. 28, 1974, 88 Stat. 1514; amended Pub. L. 96–221, title VI, §621(a), Mar. 31, 1980, 94 Stat. 184.)

EDITORIAL NOTES

AMENDMENTS

1980—Pub. L. 96–221 substituted provisions relating to duties of creditor whenever a credit balance in excess of $1 is created in connection with a consumer credit transaction, for provisions relating to duties of creditor whenever an obligor transmits funds to creditor in excess of the total balance due on an open end consumer credit account.

STATUTORY NOTES AND RELATED SUBSIDIARIES

EFFECTIVE DATE OF 1980 AMENDMENT

Amendment by Pub. L. 96–221 effective on expiration of two years and six months after Mar. 31, 1980, with all regulations, forms, and clauses required to be prescribed to be promulgated at least one year prior to such effective date, and allowing any creditor to comply with any amendments, in accordance with the regulations, forms, and clauses prescribed by the Board prior to such effective date, see section 625 of Pub. L. 96–221, set out as a note under section 1602 of this title.

§1666e. Notification of credit card issuer by seller of return of goods, etc., by obligor; credit for account of obligor

With respect to any sales transaction where a credit card has been used to obtain credit, where the seller is a person other than the card issuer, and where the seller accepts or allows a return of the goods or forgiveness of a debit for services which were the subject of such sale, the seller shall promptly transmit to the credit card issuer, a credit statement with respect thereto and the credit card issuer shall credit the account of the obligor for the amount of the transaction.

(Pub. L. 90–321, title I, §166, as added Pub. L. 93–495, title III, §306, Oct. 28, 1974, 88 Stat. 1514.)

§1666f. Inducements to cardholders by sellers of cash discounts for payments by cash, check or similar means; finance charge for sales transactions involving cash discounts

a) Cash discounts

With respect to credit [1] card which may be used for extensions of credit in sales transactions in which the seller is a person other than the card issuer, the card issuer may not, by contract or otherwise, prohibit any such seller from offering a discount to a cardholder to induce the cardholder to pay by cash, check, or similar means rather than use a credit card.

b) Finance charge

With respect to any sales transaction, any discount from the regular price offered by the seller for the purpose of inducing payment by cash, checks, or other means not involving the use of an open-end credit plan or a credit card shall not constitute a finance charge as determined under section 1605 of this title if such discount is offered to all prospective buyers and its availability is disclosed clearly and conspicuously.

(Pub. L. 90–321, title I, §167, as added Pub. L. 93–495, title III, §306, Oct. 28, 1974, 88 Stat. 1515; amended Pub. L. 94–222, §3(c)(1), Feb. 27, 1976, 90 Stat. 197; Pub. L. 97–25, title I, §101, July 27, 1981, 95 Stat. 144.)

AMENDMENTS

1981—Subsec. (b). Pub. L. 97–25 substituted "With respect to any sales transaction, any discount from the regular price offered by the seller for the purpose of inducing payment by cash, checks, or other means not involving the use of an open-end credit plan or a credit card shall not constitute a finance charge as determined under section 1605 of this title if such discount is offered to all prospective buyers and its availability is disclosed clearly and conspicuously" for "With respect to any sales transaction, any discount not in excess of 5 per centum offered by the seller for the purpose of inducing payment by cash, check, or other means not involving the use of a credit card shall not constitute a finance charge as determined under section 1605 of this title, if such discount is offered to all prospective buyers and its availability is disclosed to all prospective buyers clearly and conspicuously in accordance with regulations of the Board".

1976—Subsec. (a). Pub. L. 94–222 temporarily designated existing provisions as par. (1) and added par. (2). See Termination Date of 1976 Amendment note below.

STATUTORY NOTES AND RELATED SUBSIDIARIES

TERMINATION DATE OF 1976 AMENDMENT

Section 3(c)(2) of Pub. L. 94–222, as amended by Pub. L. 95–630, title XV, §1501, Nov. 10, 1978, 92 Stat. 3713; Pub. L. 97–25, title II, §201, July 27, 1981, 95 Stat. 44, provided that: "The amendments made by paragraph (1) [amending this section] shall cease to be effective on February 27, 1984."

NULLIFICATION OF BOARD RULES AND REGULATIONS UNDER SUBSECTION (B) OF THIS SECTION IN EFFECT ON JULY 26, 1981

Pub. L. 97–25, title I, §103, July 27, 1981, 95 Stat. 144, provided that: "Any rule or regulation of the Board of Governors of the Federal Reserve System pursuant to section 167(b) of the Truth in Lending Act [subsec. (b) of this section], as such section was in effect on the day before the date of enactment of this Act [July 27, 1981], is null and void."

---

[1] So in original. Probably should be preceded by "a".

§1666g. Tie-in services prohibited for issuance of credit card

Notwithstanding any agreement to the contrary, a card issuer may not require a seller, as a condition to participating in a credit card plan, to open an account with or procure any other service from the card issuer or its subsidiary or agent.

(Pub. L. 90–321, title I, §168, as added Pub. L. 93–495, title III, §306, Oct. 28, 1974, 88 Stat. 1515.)

§1666h. Offset of cardholder's indebtedness by issuer of credit card with funds deposited with issuer by cardholder; remedies of creditors under State law not affected

(a) Offset against consumer's funds

A card issuer may not take any action to offset a cardholder's indebtedness arising in connection with a consumer credit transaction under the relevant credit card plan against funds of the cardholder held on deposit with the card issuer unless—

(1) such action was previously authorized in writing by the cardholder in accordance with a credit plan whereby cardholder agrees periodically to pay debts incurred in his open end credit account by permitting the card issuer periodically to deduct all or a portion of such debt from the cardholder's deposit account, and

(2) such action with respect to any outstanding disputed amount not be taken by the card issuer upon request of the cardholder.

In the case of any credit card account in existence on the effective date of this section, the previous written authorization referred to in clause (1) shall not be required until the date (after such effective date) when such account is renewed, but in no case later than one year after such effective date. Such written authorization shall be deemed to exist if the card issuer has previously notified the cardholder that the use of his credit card account will subject any funds which the card issuer holds in deposit accounts of such cardholder to offset against any amounts due and payable on his credit card account which have not been paid in accordance with the terms of the agreement between the card issuer and the cardholder.

(b) Attachments and levies

This section does not alter or affect the right under State law of a card issuer to attach or otherwise levy upon funds of a cardholder held on deposit with the card issuer if that remedy is constitutionally available to creditors generally.

(Pub. L. 90–321, title I, §169, as added Pub. L. 93–495, title III, §306, Oct. 28, 1974, 88 Stat. 1515.)

EDITORIAL NOTES

REFERENCES IN TEXT

For effective date of this section, referred to in subsec. (a), see Effective Date note set out under section 1666 of this title.

§1666i. Assertion by cardholder against card issuer of claims and defenses arising out of credit card transaction; prerequisites; limitation on amount of claims or defenses

(a) Claims and defenses assertible

Subject to the limitation contained in subsection (b), a card issuer who has issued a credit card to a cardholder pursuant to an open end consumer credit plan shall be subject to all claims (other than tort claims) and defenses arising out of any transaction in which the credit card is used as a method of payment or extension of credit if (1) the obligor has made a good faith attempt to obtain satisfactory resolution of a disagreement or problem relative to the transaction from the person honoring the credit card; (2) the amount of the initial transaction exceeds $50; and (3) the place where the initial transaction occurred was in the same State as the mailing address previously provided by the cardholder or was within 100 miles from such address, except that the limitations set forth in clauses (2) and (3) with respect to an obligor's right to assert claims and defenses against a card issuer shall not be applicable to any transaction in which the person honoring the credit card (A) is the same person as the card issuer, (B) is controlled by the card issuer, (C) is under direct or indirect common control with the card issuer, (D) is a franchised dealer in the card issuer's products or services, or (E) has obtained the order for such transaction through a mail solicitation made by or participated in by the card issuer in which the cardholder is solicited to enter into such transaction by using the credit card issued by the card issuer.

(b) Amount of claims and defenses assertible

The amount of claims or defenses asserted by the cardholder may not exceed the amount of credit outstanding with respect to such transaction at the time the cardholder first notifies the card issuer or the person honoring the credit card of such claim or defense. For the purpose of determining the amount of credit outstanding in the preceding sentence, payments and credits to the cardholder's account are deemed to have been applied, in the order indicated, to the payment of: (1) late charges in the order of their entry to the account; (2) finance charges in order of their entry to the account; and (3) debits to the account other than those set forth above, in the order in which each debit entry to the account was made.

(Pub. L. 90–321, title I, §170, as added Pub. L. 93–495, title III, §306, Oct. 28, 1974, 88 Stat. 1515.)

§1666i–1. Limits on interest rate, fee, and finance charge increases applicable to outstanding balances

In general

In the case of any credit card account under an open end consumer credit plan, no creditor may increase any annual percentage rate, fee, or finance charge applicable to any outstanding balance, except as permitted under subsection

Exceptions

The prohibition under subsection (a) shall not apply to—

(1) an increase in an annual percentage rate upon the expiration of a specified period of time, provided that—

(A) prior to commencement of that period, the creditor disclosed to the consumer, in a clear and conspicuous manner, the length of the period and the annual percentage rate that would apply after expiration of the period;

(B) the increased annual percentage rate does not exceed the rate disclosed pursuant to subparagraph (A); and

(C) the increased annual percentage rate is not applied to transactions that occurred prior to commencement of the period;

(2) an increase in a variable annual percentage rate in accordance with a credit card agreement that provides for changes in the rate according to operation of an index that is not under the control of the creditor and is available to the general public;

(3) an increase due to the completion of a workout or temporary hardship arrangement by the obligor or the failure of the obligor to comply with the terms of a workout or temporary hardship arrangement, provided that—

(A) the annual percentage rate, fee, or finance charge applicable to a category of transactions following any such increase does not exceed the rate, fee, or finance charge that applied to that category of transactions prior to commencement of the arrangement; and

(B) the creditor has provided the obligor, prior to the commencement of such arrangement, with clear and conspicuous disclosure of the terms of the arrangement (including any increases due to such completion or failure); or

(4) an increase due solely to the fact that a minimum payment by the obligor has not been received by the creditor within 60 days after the due date for such payment, provided that the creditor shall—

(A) include, together with the notice of such increase required under section 1637(i) of this title, a clear and conspicuous written statement of the reason for the increase and that the increase will terminate not later than 6 months after the date on which it is imposed, if the creditor receives the required minimum payments on time from the obligor during that period; and

(B) terminate such increase not later than 6 months after the date on which it is imposed, if the creditor receives the required minimum payments on time during that period.

(c) Repayment of outstanding balance

(1) In general

The creditor shall not change the terms governing the repayment of any outstanding balance, except that the creditor may provide the obligor with one of the methods described in paragraph (2) of repaying any outstanding balance, or a method that is no less beneficial to the obligor than one of those methods.

(2) Methods

The methods described in this paragraph are—

(A) an amortization period of not less than 5 years, beginning on the effective date of the increase set forth in the notice required under section 1637(i) of this title; or

(B) a required minimum periodic payment that includes a percentage of the outstanding balance that is equal to not more than twice the percentage required before the effective date of the increase set forth in the notice required under section 1637(i) of this title.

(d) Outstanding balance defined

For purposes of this section, the term "outstanding balance" means the amount owed on a credit card account under an open end consumer credit plan as of the end of the 14th day after the date on which the creditor provides notice of an increase in the annual percentage rate, fee, or finance charge in accordance with section 1637(i) of this title.

(Pub. L. 90–321, title I, §171, as added Pub. L. 111–24, title I, §101(b)(2), May 22, 2009, 123 Stat. 1736.)

EDITORIAL NOTES

PRIOR PROVISIONS

A prior section 171 of Pub. L. 90–321 was renumbered section 173 and is classified to section 1666j of this title.

STATUTORY NOTES AND RELATED SUBSIDIARIES

EFFECTIVE DATE

Section effective 9 months after May 22, 2009, except as otherwise specifically provided, see section of Pub. L. 111–24, set out as an Effective Date of 2009 Amendment note under section 1602 of this title.

§1666i–2. Additional limits on interest rate increases

(a) Limitation on increases within first year

Except in the case of an increase described in paragraph (1), (2), (3), or (4) of section 1666i–1(b) of this title, no increase in any annual percentage rate, fee, or finance charge on any credit card account under an open end consumer credit plan shall be effective before the end of the 1-year period beginning on the date on which the acc is opened.

(b) Promotional rate minimum term

No increase in any annual percentage rate applicable to a credit card account under an open end consumer credit plan that is a promotional rate (as that term is defined by the Bureau) shall be effective before the end of the 6-month period beginning on the date on which the promotional rate takes effect, subject to such reasonable exceptions as the Bureau may establish, by rule.

(Pub. L. 90–321, title I, §172, as added Pub. L. 111–24, title I, §101(d), May 22, 2009, 123 Stat. 1738; amended Pub. L. 111–203, title X, §1100A(2), July 21, 2010, 124 Stat. 2107.)

EDITORIAL NOTES

AMENDMENTS

2010—Subsec. (b). Pub. L. 111–203 substituted "Bureau" for "Board" in two places.

STATUTORY NOTES AND RELATED SUBSIDIARIES

EFFECTIVE DATE OF 2010 AMENDMENT

Amendment by Pub. L. 111–203 effective on the designated transfer date, see section 1100H of Pub. L. 111–203, set out as a note under section 552a of Title 5, Government Organization and Employees.

EFFECTIVE DATE

Section effective 9 months after May 22, 2009, except as otherwise specifically provided, see section 3 of Pub. L. 111–24, set out as an Effective Date of 2009 Amendment note under section 1602 of this title.

§1666j. Applicability of State laws

(a) Consistency of provisions

This part does not annul, alter, or affect, or exempt any person subject to the provisions of this part from complying with, the laws of any State with respect to credit billing practices, except to the extent that those laws are inconsistent with any provision of this part, and then only to the extent of the inconsistency. The Bureau is authorized to determine whether such inconsistencies exist. The Bureau may not determine that any State law is inconsistent with any provision of this part if the Bureau determines that such law gives greater protection to the consumer.

(b) Exemptions by Bureau from credit billing requirements

The Bureau shall by regulation exempt from the requirements of this part any class of credit transactions within any State if it determines that under the law of that State that class of transactions is subject to requirements substantially similar to those imposed under this part or that such law gives greater protection to the consumer, and that there is adequate provision for enforcement.

(c) Finance charge or other charge for credit for sales transactions involving cash discounts

Notwithstanding any other provisions of this subchapter, any discount offered under section 1666f(b) of this title shall not be considered a finance charge or other charge for credit under the usury laws of any State or under the laws of any State relating to disclosure of information in connection with credit transactions, or relating to the types, amounts or rates of charges, or to any element or elements of charges permissible under such laws in connection with the extension or use of credit.

(Pub. L. 90–321, title I, §173, formerly §171, as added Pub. L. 93–495, title III, §306, Oct. 28, 1974, 88 Stat. 1516; amended Pub. L. 94–222, §3(d), Feb. 27, 1976, 90 Stat. 198; renumbered §173, Pub. L. 111–24, title I, §101(b)(1), May 22, 2009, 123 Stat. 1736; Pub. L. 111–203, title X, §§1087, 1100A(2), July 21, 2010, 124 Stat. 2086, 2107.)

EDITORIAL NOTES

CODIFICATION

Pub L. 111–203, §1100A(2), which directed the substitution of "Bureau" for "Board" wherever appearing in title I of Pub. L. 90–321, was executed to this section, which is section 173 of title I of Pub. L. 90–321. Section 1087 of Pub. L. 111–203, which directed the making of an identical amendment in title III of Pub. L. 93–495, which added this section to title I of Pub. L. 90–321, has not been executed.

AMENDMENTS

2010—Subsecs. (a), (b). Pub. L. 111–203, §1100A(2), substituted "Bureau" for "Board" wherever appearing. See Codification note above.

1976—Subsec. (c). Pub. L. 94–222 added subsec. (c).

STATUTORY NOTES AND RELATED SUBSIDIARIES

EFFECTIVE DATE OF 2010 AMENDMENT

Amendment by Pub. L. 111–203 effective on the designated transfer date, see section 1100H of Pub. L. 111–203, set out as a note under section 552a of Title 5, Government Organization and Employees.

PART E—CONSUMER LEASES

§1667. Definitions

For purposes of this part—

(1) The term "consumer lease" means a contract in the form of a lease or bailment for the use of personal property by a natural person for a period of time exceeding four months, and for a total contractual obligation not exceeding $50,000,[1] primarily for personal, family, or household purposes, whether or not the lessee has the option to purchase or otherwise become the owner of the property at the expiration of the lease, except that such term shall not include any credit sale as defined in section 1602(g) [2] of this title. Such term does not include a lease for agricultural, business, or commercial purposes, or to a government or governmental agency or instrumentality, or to an organization.

(2) The term "lessee" means a natural person who leases or is offered a consumer lease.

(3) The term "lessor" means a person who is regularly engaged in leasing, offering to lease, or arranging to lease under a consumer lease.

(4) The term "personal property" means any property which is not real property under the laws of the State where situated at the time offered or otherwise made available for lease.

(5) The terms "security" and "security interest" mean any interest in property which secures payment or performance of an obligation.

(Pub. L. 90–321, title I, §181, as added Pub. L. 94–240, §3, Mar. 23, 1976, 90 Stat. 257; amended Pub. L. 111–203, title X, §1100E(a)(2), July 21, 2010, 124 Stat. 2111.)

EDITORIAL NOTES

REFERENCES IN TEXT

Section 1602(g) of this title, referred to in par. (1), was redesignated section 1602(h) of this title by Pub. L. 111–203, title X, §1100A(1)(A), July 21, 2010, 124 Stat. 2107.

AMENDMENTS

2010—Par. (1). Pub. L. 111–203 substituted "$50,000" for "$25,000".

STATUTORY NOTES AND RELATED SUBSIDIARIES

EFFECTIVE DATE OF 2010 AMENDMENT

Amendment by Pub. L. 111–203 effective on the designated transfer date, see section 1100H of Pub. L. 111–203, set out as a note under section 552a of Title 5, Government Organization and Employees.

EFFECTIVE DATE

Pub. L. 94–240, §6, Mar. 23, 1976, 90 Stat. 261, provided that: "This Act [enacting this section and secti[on] 1667a to 1667e of this title, amending sections 1601 and 1640 of this title, and enacting provisions set out as note under section 1601 of this title] takes effect one year after the date of its enactment [Mar. 23, 1976].

ADJUSTMENTS FOR INFLATION

On and after Dec. 31, 2011, dollar amount described in par. (1) of this section to be adjusted annua[lly] by the annual percentage increase in the Consumer Price Index for Urban Wage Earners and Clerica[l] Workers, see section 1100E(b) of Pub. L. 111–203, set out as a note under section 1603 of this title.

§1667a. Consumer lease disclosures

Each lessor shall give a lessee prior to the consummation of the lease a dated written statement on which the lessor and lessee are identified setting out accurately and in a clear and conspicuous manner the following information with respect to that lease, as applicable:

(1) A brief description or identification of the leased property;

(2) The amount of any payment by the lessee required at the inception of the lease;

(3) The amount paid or payable by the lessee for official fees, registration, certificate of title, or license fees or taxes;

(4) The amount of other charges payable by the lessee not included in the periodic payments, a description of the charges and that the lessee shall be liable for the differential, if any, between the anticipated fair market value of the leased property and its appraised actual value at the termination of the lease, if the lessee has such liability;

(5) A statement of the amount or method of determining the amount of any liabilities the lease imposes upon the lessee at the end of the term and whether or not the lessee has the option to purchase the leased property and at what price and time;

(6) A statement identifying all express warranties and guarantees made by the manufacturer or lessor with respect to the leased property, and identifying the party responsible for maintaining or servicing the leased property together with a description of the responsibility;

(7) A brief description of insurance provided or paid for by the lessor or required of the lessee, including the types and amounts of the coverages and costs;

(8) A description of any security interest held or to be retained by the lessor in connection with the lease and a clear identification of the property to which the security interest relates;

(9) The number, amount, and due dates or periods of payments under the lease and the total amount of such periodic payments;

(10) Where the lease provides that the lessee shall be liable for the anticipated fair market value of the property on expiration of the lease, the fair market value of the property at the inception of the lease, the aggregate cost of the lease on expiration, and the differential between them; and

(11) A statement of the conditions under which the lessee or lessor may terminate the lease prior to the end of the term and the amount or method of determining any penalty or other charge for delinquency, default, late payments, or early termination.

The disclosures required under this section may be made in the lease contract to be signed by the lessee. The Bureau may provide by regulation that any portion of the information required to be disclosed under this section may be given in the form of estimates where the lessor is not in a position to know exact information.

(Pub. L. 90–321, title I, §182, as added Pub. L. 94–240, §3, Mar. 23, 1976, 90 Stat. 258; amended Pub. L. 111–203, title X, §1100A(2), (10)(B), July 21, 2010, 124 Stat. 2107, 2109.)

Editorial Notes

Amendments

2010—Pub. L. 111–203, §1100A(2), (10)(B), made similar amendments, resulting in the substitution of "The Bureau" for "The Board" in concluding provisions.

Statutory Notes and Related Subsidiaries

Effective Date of 2010 Amendment

Amendment by Pub. L. 111–203 effective on the designated transfer date, see section 1100H of Pub. L. 111–203, set out as a note under section 552a of Title 5, Government Organization and Employees.

§1667b. Lessee's liability on expiration or termination of lease

Estimated residual value of property as basis; presumptions; action by lessor for excess liability; mutually agreeable final adjustment

Where the lessee's liability on expiration of a consumer lease is based on the estimated residual value of the property such estimated residual value shall be a reasonable approximation of the anticipated actual fair market value of the property on lease expiration. There shall be a rebuttable presumption that the estimated residual value is unreasonable to the extent that the estimated residual value exceeds the actual residual value by more than three times the average payment allocable to a monthly period under the lease. In addition, where the lessee has such liability on expiration of a consumer lease there shall be a rebuttable presumption that the lessor's estimated residual value is not in good faith to the extent that the estimated residual value exceeds the actual residual value by more than three times the average payment allocable to a monthly period under the lease and such lessor shall not collect from the lessee the amount of such excess liability on expiration of a consumer lease unless the lessor brings a successful action with respect to such excess liability. In all actions, the lessor shall pay the lessee's reasonable attorney's fees. The presumptions stated in this section shall not apply to the extent the excess of estimated over actual residual value is due to physical damage to the property beyond reasonable wear and use, or to excessive use, and the lease may set standards for such wear and use if such standards are not unreasonable. Nothing in this subsection shall preclude the right of a willing lessee to make any mutually agreeable final adjustment with respect to such excess residual liability, provided such an agreement is reached after termination of the lease.

(b) Penalties and charges for delinquency, default, or early termination

Penalties or other charges for delinquency, default, or early termination may be specified in the lease but only at an amount which is reasonable in the light of the anticipated or actual harm caused by the delinquency, default, or early termination, the difficulties of proof of loss, and the inconvenience or nonfeasibility of otherwise obtaining an adequate remedy.

(c) Independent professional appraisal of residual value of property at termination of lease; finality

If a lease has a residual value provision at the termination of the lease, the lessee may obtain at his expense, a professional appraisal of the leased property by an independent third party agreed to by both parties. Such appraisal shall be final and binding on the parties.

(Pub. L. 90–321, title I, §183, as added Pub. L. 94–240, §3, Mar. 23, 1976, 90 Stat. 259.)

§1667c. Consumer lease advertising; liability of advertising media

(a) In general

If an advertisement for a consumer lease includes a statement of the amount of any payment or a statement that any or no initial payment is required, the advertisement shall clearly and conspicuously state, as applicable—

(1) the transaction advertised is a lease;

(2) the total amount of any initial payments required on or before consummation of the lease or delivery of the property, whichever is later;

(3) that a security deposit is required;

(4) the number, amount, and timing of scheduled payments; and

(5) with respect to a lease in which the liability of the consumer at the end of the lease term is based on the anticipated residual value of the property, that an extra charge may be imposed at the end of the lease term.

(b) Advertising medium not liable

No owner or employee of any entity that serves as a medium in which an advertisement appears or through which an advertisement is disseminated, shall be liable under this section.

(c) Radio advertisements

(1) In general

An advertisement by radio broadcast to aid, promote, or assist, directly or indirectly, any consumer lease shall be deemed to be in compliance with the requirements of subsection (a) if such advertisement clearly and conspicuous—

(A) states the information required by paragraphs (1) and (2) of subsection (a);

(B) states the number, amounts, due dates or periods of scheduled payments, and the total of such payments under the lease;

(C) includes—

(i) a referral to—

(I) a toll-free telephone number established in accordance with paragraph (2) that may be used by consumers to obtain the information required under subsection (a); or

(II) a written advertisement that—

(aa) appears in a publication in general circulation in the community served by the radio station on which such advertisement is broadcast during the period beginning 3 days before any such broadcast and end 10 days after such broadcast; and

(bb) includes the information required to be disclosed under subsection (a); and

(ii) the name and dates of any publication referred to in clause (i)(II); and

(D) includes any other information which the Bureau determines necessary to carry out this part.

(2) Establishment of toll-free number

(A) In general

In the case of a radio broadcast advertisement described in paragraph (1) that includes a referral to a toll-free telephone number, the lessor who offers the consumer lease shall—

(i) establish such a toll-free telephone number not later than the date on which the advertisement including the referral is broadcast;

(ii) maintain such telephone number for a period of not less than 10 days, beginning on the date of any such broadcast; and

(iii) provide the information required under subsection (a) with respect to the lease to any person who calls such number.

(B) Form of information

The information required to be provided under subparagraph (A)(iii) shall be provided verbally or, if requested by the consumer, in written form.

(3) No effect on other law

Nothing in this subsection shall affect the requirements of Federal law as such requirements apply to advertisement by any medium other than radio broadcast.

(Pub. L. 90–321, title I, §184, as added Pub. L. 94–240, §3, Mar. 23, 1976, 90 Stat. 259; amended Pub. L. 103–325, title III, §336(a), Sept. 23, 1994, 108 Stat. 2234; Pub. L. 104–208, div. A, title II, §2605(c), Sept. 30, 1996, 110 Stat. 3009–473; Pub. L. 111–203, title X, §1100A(2), (10)(A), July 21, 2010, 124 Stat. 2107, 2109.)

EDITORIAL NOTES

AMENDMENTS

2010—Subsec. (c)(1)(D). Pub. L. 111–203, §1100A(2), (10)(A), made similar amendments, resulting in the substitution of "the Bureau" for "the Board".

1996—Subsec. (a). Pub. L. 104–208, §2605(c)(1), (3), added subsec. (a) and struck out former subsec. (a) consisting of introductory provisions and 5 pars. relating to contents of lease agreements required if consumer lease advertisement stated amount of payment, number of required payments, or that any or no payments were required at lease inception.

Subsec. (b). Pub. L. 104–208, §2605(c)(3), added subsec. (b). Former subsec. (b) redesignated (c).

Subsec. (c). Pub. L. 104–208, §2605(c)(1), (2), redesignated subsec. (b) as (c) and struck out former subsec. (c) which read as follows: "There is no liability under this section on the part of any owner or personnel, as such, of any medium in which an advertisement appears or through which it is disseminated."

1994—Subsecs. (b), (c). Pub. L. 103–325 added subsec. (b) and redesignated former subsec. (b) as (c).

STATUTORY NOTES AND RELATED SUBSIDIARIES

EFFECTIVE DATE OF 2010 AMENDMENT

Amendment by Pub. L. 111–203 effective on the designated transfer date, see section 1100H of Pub. L. 111–203, set out as a note under section 552a of Title 5, Government Organization and Employees.

STUDY OF ADVERTISING RULES

Pub. L. 103–325, title III, §336(b), Sept. 23, 1994, 108 Stat. 2235, provided that not later than 365 days after Sept. 23, 1994, the Board of Governors of the Federal Reserve System shall submit a report to the Congress on credit advertising rules.

1667d. Civil liability of lessors

Grounds for maintenance of action

Any lessor who fails to comply with any requirement imposed under section 1667a or 1667b of this title with respect to any person is liable to such person as provided in section 1640 of this title.

Additional grounds for maintenance of action; "creditor" defined

Any lessor who fails to comply with any requirement imposed under section 1667c of this title with respect to any person who suffers actual damage from the violation is liable to such person as provided in section 1640 of this title. For the purposes of this section, the term "creditor" as used in sections 1640 and 1641 of this title shall include a lessor as defined in this part.

(c) Jurisdiction of courts; time limitation

Notwithstanding section 1640(e) of this title, any action under this section may be brought in any United States district court or in any other court of competent jurisdiction. Such actions alleging a failure to disclose or otherwise comply with the requirements of this part shall be brought within one year of the termination of the lease agreement.

(Pub. L. 90–321, title I, §185, as added Pub. L. 94–240, §3, Mar. 23, 1976, 90 Stat. 260; amended Pub. L. 96–221, title VI, §624, Mar. 31, 1980, 94 Stat. 185.)

EDITORIAL NOTES

AMENDMENTS

1980—Subsec. (b). Pub. L. 96–221 struck out applicability of section 1614 of this title to term "creditor".

STATUTORY NOTES AND RELATED SUBSIDIARIES

EFFECTIVE DATE OF 1980 AMENDMENT

Amendment by Pub. L. 96–221 effective on expiration of two years and six months after Mar. 31, 1980, with all regulations, forms, and clauses required to be prescribed to be promulgated at least one year prior to such effective date, and allowing any creditor to comply with any amendments, in accordance with the regulations, forms, and clauses prescribed by the Board prior to such effective date, see section 625 of Pub. L. 96–221, set out as a note under section 1602 of this title.

§1667e. Applicability of State laws; exemptions by Bureau from leasing requirements

(a) This part does not annul, alter, or affect, or exempt any person subject to the provisions of this part from complying with, the laws of any State with respect to consumer leases, except to the extent that those laws are inconsistent with any provision of this part, and then only to the extent of the inconsistency. The Bureau is authorized to determine whether such inconsistencies exist. The Bureau may not determine that any State law is inconsistent with any provision of this part if the Bureau determines that such law gives greater protection and benefit to the consumer.

(b) The Bureau shall by regulation exempt from the requirements of this part any class of lease transactions within any State if it determines that under the law of that State that class of transactions is subject to requirements substantially similar to those imposed under this part or that such law gives greater protection and benefit to the consumer, and that there is adequate provision for enforcement.

(Pub. L. 90–321, title I, §186, as added Pub. L. 94–240, §3, Mar. 23, 1976, 90 Stat. 260; amended Pub. L. 111–203, title X, §1100A(2), (10), July 21, 2010, 124 Stat. 2107, 2109.)

EDITORIAL NOTES

AMENDMENTS

2010—Pub. L. 111–203, §1100A(2), (10), substituted "Bureau" for "Board", "the Bureau" for "the Board", and "The Bureau" for "The Board" wherever appearing.

STATUTORY NOTES AND RELATED SUBSIDIARIES

EFFECTIVE DATE OF 2010 AMENDMENT

Amendment by Pub. L. 111–203 effective on the designated transfer date, see section 1100H of Pub. L 111–203, set out as a note under section 552a of Title 5, Government Organization and Employees.

§1667f. Regulations

(a) Regulations authorized

(1) In general

The Bureau shall prescribe regulations to update and clarify the requirements and definitions applicable to lea disclosures and contracts, and any other issues specifically related to consumer leasing, to the extent that the Bureau determines such action to be necessary—

(A) to carry out this part;

(B) to prevent any circumvention of this part; or

(C) to facilitate compliance with the requirements of the ¹ part.

(2) Classifications, adjustments

Any regulations prescribed under paragraph (1) may contain classifications and differentiations, and may provide for adjustments and exceptions for any class of transactions, as the Bureau considers appropriate.

(b) Model disclosure

(1) Publication

The Bureau shall establish and publish model disclosure forms to facilitate compliance with the disclosure requirements of this part and to aid the consumer in understanding the transaction to which the subject disclosure form relates.

(2) Use of automated equipment

In establishing model forms under this subsection, the Bureau shall consider the use by lessors of data processing or similar automated equipment.

(3) Use optional

A lessor may utilize a model disclosure form established by the Bureau under this subsection for purposes of compliance with this part, at the discretion of the lessor.

(4) Effect of use

Any lessor who properly uses the material aspects of any model disclosure form established by the Bureau under this subsection shall be deemed to be in compliance with the disclosure requirements to which the form relates.

(Pub. L. 90–321, title I, §187, as added Pub. L. 104–208, div. A, title II, §2605(b)(1), Sept. 30, 1996, 110 Stat. 3009–471; amended Pub. L. 111–203, title X, §1100A(2), (10), July 21, 2010, 124 Stat. 2107, 2109.)

"(A) competition among the various financial institutions and other firms engaged in the business of consumer leasing is greatest when there is informed use of leasing;

"(B) the informed use of leasing results from an awareness of the cost of leasing by consumers; and

"(C) there has been a continued trend toward leasing automobiles and other durable goods for consumer use as an alternative to installment credit sales and that leasing product advances have occurred such that lessors have been unable to provide consistent industry-wide disclosures to fully account for the competitive progress that has occurred.

"(2) PURPOSES.—The purposes of this section are—

"(A) to assure a simple, meaningful disclosure of leasing terms so that the consumer will be able to compare more readily the various leasing terms available to the consumer and avoid the uninformed use of leasing, and to protect the consumer against inaccurate and unfair leasing practices;

"(B) to provide for adequate cost disclosures that reflect the marketplace without impairing competition and the development of new leasing products; and

"(C) to provide the Board with the regulatory authority to assure a simplified, meaningful definition and disclosure of the terms of certain leases of personal property for personal, family, or household purposes so as to—

"(i) enable the lessee to compare more readily the various lease terms available to the lessee;

"(ii) enable comparison of lease terms with credit terms, as appropriate; and

"(iii) assure meaningful and accurate disclosures of lease terms in advertisements."

---

¹ So in original. Probably should be "this".

This edition is revised and current as of January 2024.

2024 | Applied Legal Publications

Made in the USA
Las Vegas, NV
19 April 2024

88872345R10081